The Climber's Guide to North America

The Climber's Guide to North America

Volume I
West Coast Rock Climbs

by

John Harlin III

illustrations by Adele Hammond

CHOCKSTONE PRESS

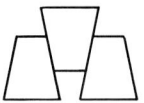

Denver, Colorado   1984

© 1984 John Harlin III. All rights reserved

Published by
Chockstone Press
526 Franklin Street
Denver, Colorado 80218

Distributed in Great Britain and Europe by
Cordee, Ltd
3a DeMontfort St.
Leicester
England
LE1 7HD

Printed in the United States of America

Library of Congress Cataloging in Publication Data
Harlin, John, 1956-
  West Coast Rock Climbs

  The Climber's Guide to North America; v. 1)
  Includes bibliographical references and index.
  1. Rock climbing—Pacific coast (North America)—Guide-books.
2. Pacific coast (North America)—Description and travel—Guide-books.
I. Hammond, Adele. II. Title. III. Series.
GV199.44.P14H37 1984 917 84-15598

ISBN 0-9609452-2-9 (West Coast Rock Climbs)
ISBN 0-9609452-5-3 (Climber's Guide to North America—full series)

ACKNOWLEDGEMENTS

A number of people have helped to make this book possible. The list below is of those who have made important contributions. If I have inadvertently forgotten someone, my most sincere appologies are hereby extended.

The following people have made an extra effort to help me with this book. The hours and sometimes days that they have put in have made this a far better book than it would have been without their help. Were I not so lazy, I would give them all the individualized acknowledgements they deserve.

> Don Brooks, Jim Campbell, Lee Cunningham, Greg Donaldson, Adele Hammond, Marilyn Harlin, Bruce Hildenbrand, John Howe, Paul G. Gagner, E.C. Joe, Steve Komito, Alan Lester, George Meyers, Robs John Muir, Bob McGown, Kevin McLane, Rob Newsom, Dex Perkins, Tom Rogers, Dick Shockley, Carl W. Smith, Jay Smith, Jeff Thomas, Joanne Urioste, Greg Vernon, and Brock Wagstaff.

These people have either supplied me with photographs or helped in various ways to make this a better book.

> Eric Barrett, Todd Bibler, RD Caughron, Bill Deisman: Tule River Ranger District, Wayne Eden—Beacon Rock State Park, David Ek, Catherine Freer, Wanda H. Gast—U.S. Department of Agriculture, Cheryl Hammond, Roger Johnson, Chris Jones, Matt Kerns, Barry Lazarus, Randy Leavitt, Doug Leen, Greg Lilley, Jim Nelson, Anders Ourom, Patrick Paul, Ken Phillips—Pinnacles National Monument, Prudence Pigott, Terry Pigott, Galen Rowell, Eric Sanford, Karl Schneider, Robert True—Oregon Parks and Recreation Division, Randy Vogel, and David Whitelaw.

In addition, topos found in the Yosemite Valley chapter were copied, with permission, from Yosemite Climbs, c 1982 by Chockstone Press.

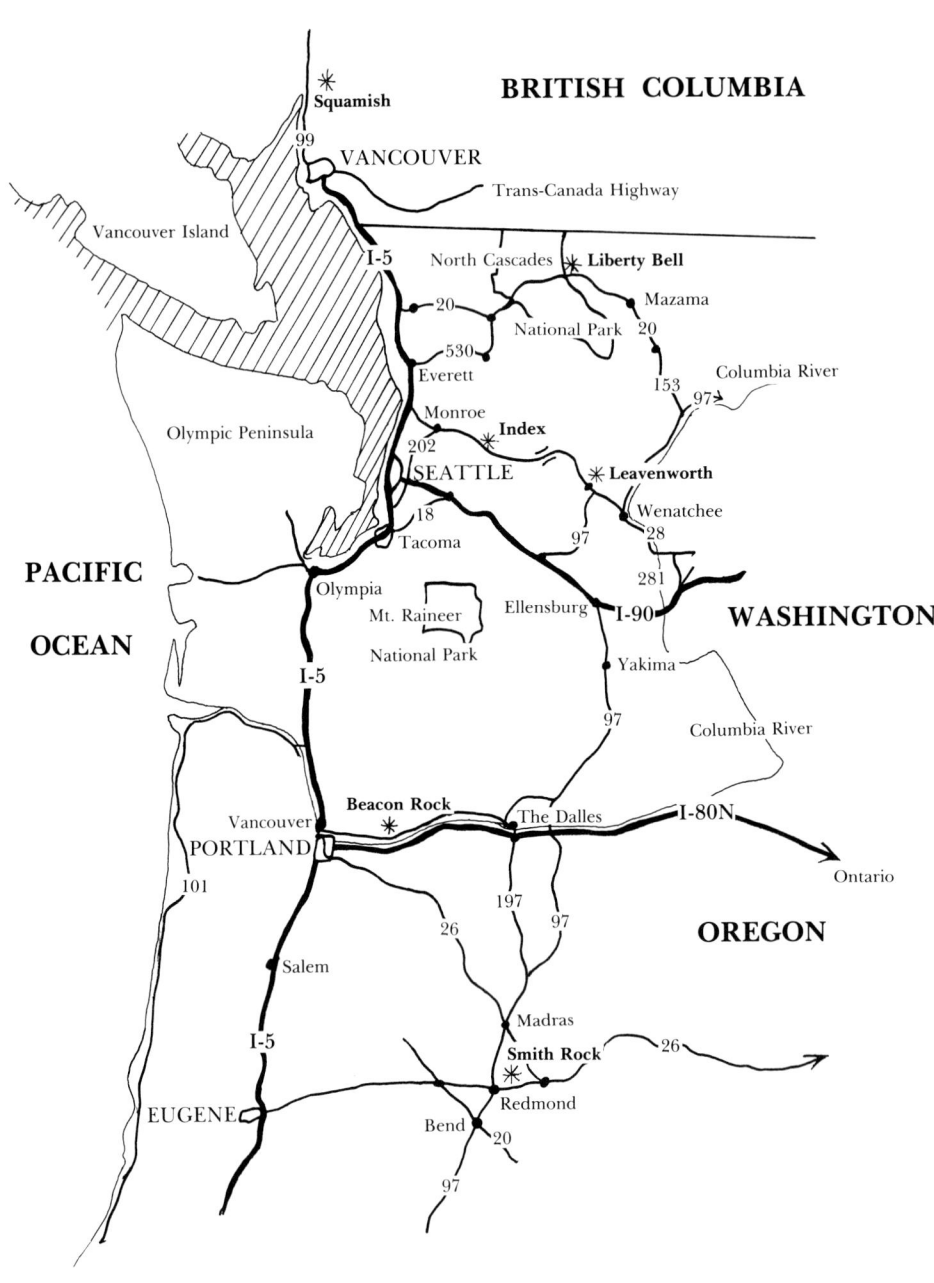

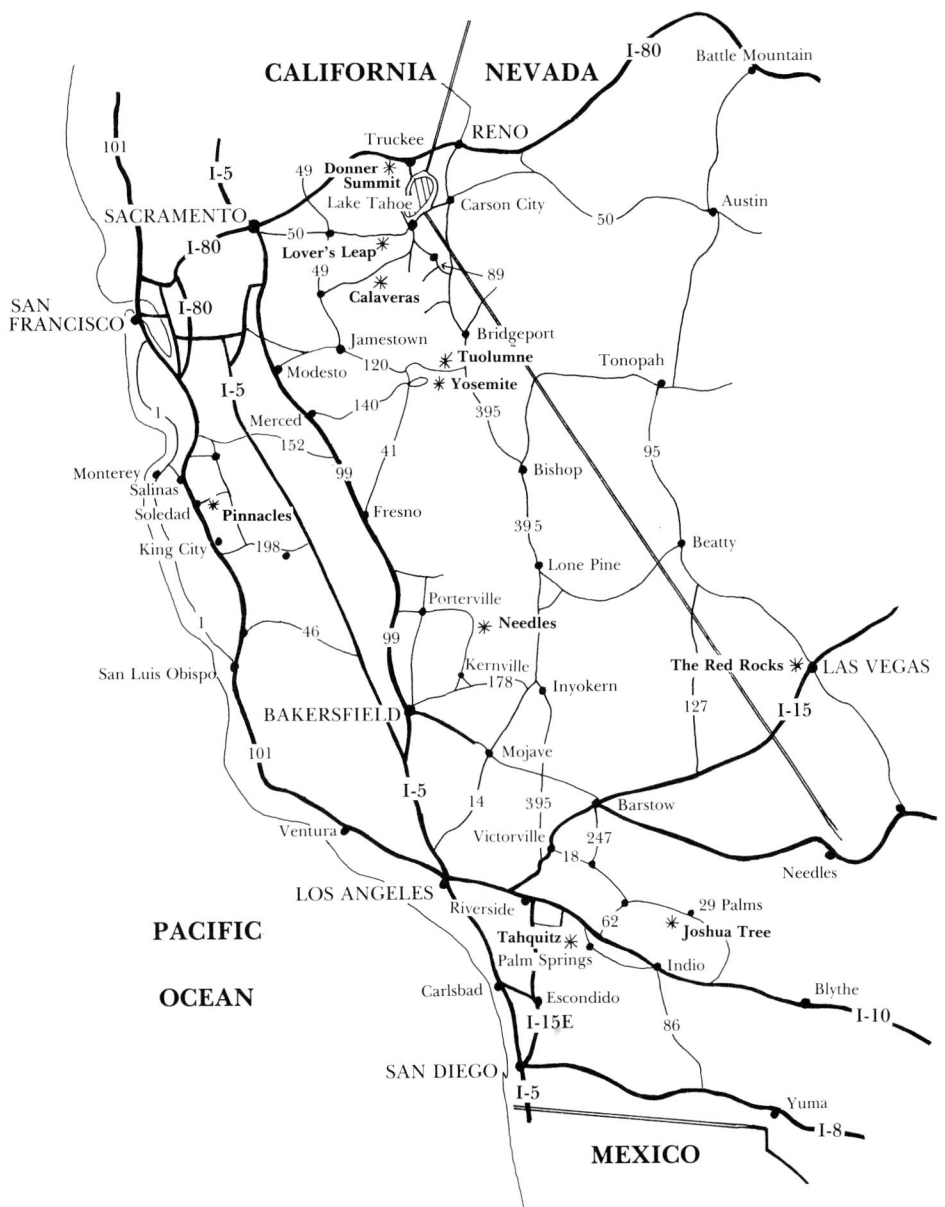

ENVIRONMENTAL IMPACT

While this guide may reduce the environmental impact on certain popular climbing areas, it will cause increased strain on others. To alleviate this stress, climbers are strongly urged to respect the individual character of each area that they visit.

Many people can be absorbed into a wilderness and still maintain a quality experience if one basic rule is followed: minimize your impact. Shouting, including belay signals, should be reduced or eliminated. Camping, if out of designated sites, should be kept as discreet as possible; and, above all, nothing should be left behind that leaves any indication that you have been there.

Littering is unthinkable in the outdoors. This includes not just scattered garbage, but also unburied excrement, new fire-rings, and dishes washed in lakes and streams.

People who are disrespectful of the environment should be tactfully educated about the consequences of their actions. In addition, we should pick up after those who defile our communal space. This demonstration of love for the environment is the best educational eye-opener. It also means that we don't have to endure that particular piece of litter more than once.

TABLE OF CONTENTS

Introduction
  The Climber's Guide to North America
    How to Use This Book 2
    Ratings 6
    Warnings and Safety Considerations 9
    American Climbing Style and Ethics 11
    Supplementary Information 13
  West Coast Rock Climbs
    Overview 15
    Brief History 19

The Red Rocks 29
Tahquitz/Suicide 47
Joshua Tree 67
Needles 95
Pinnacles 115
Yosemite Valley 135
Tuolumne Meadows 173
Calaveras Dome 197
Lover's Leap 209
Donner Summit 223
Smith Rock 233
Beacon Rock 251
Leavenworth 261
Liberty Bell 283
Index Town Walls 303
Squamish Chief 315
West Coast Bouldering 335
Index 351

INTRODUCTION

Levitation 29 photo: Jorge Urioste

THE CLIMBER'S GUIDE TO NORTH AMERICA

For many years, the imagination of most climbers could be caught by only a few famous cliffs and mountains. But as the sport grew in popularity, climbers began searching out unheralded areas—places where they could explore new territory and leave behind some of the increasing crowds. Soon, they discovered that North America holds a great diversity of climbing areas, each unique in its climbing experience.

This series of guides was conceived to provide an efficient sampling of many different North American climbing areas. Based primarily on photographs, the books also offer selected route descriptions, access maps, and background information for each covered area. *The Climber's Guide to North America* will allow travelling climbers to experience for themselves the special character of these places through several days of excellent climbing.

AREA SELECTION

The areas for this volume are chosen with the following criteria: the climbing must be accessible by moderate hiking from a car-camping basecamp, and it must be interesting enough to make it worth either a special trip or a brief stop for climbers on their way elsewhere. In addition, the popularity and quality of the area has generally gained it national or international attention.

Because some people deeply resent the popularization of their favorite haunts—fearing that publicity will spoil the original environment and atmosphere—climbers are urged to respect the individual character of the place they are visiting. It is especially important to minimize one's impact on the environment.

The many areas not included in this book will remain a bit mysterious and wild. Eventually, some of these may be opened to the public through guidebooks or magazine articles, but it is not for this book to do so prematurely.

SELECTION OF ROUTES

A sufficient number of routes have been included to provide a good sampling of the climbing in each area. Depending on the size of the area, this will vary from several days' to a couple of weeks' worth of climbing.

INTRODUCTION

Routes are included in the most popular difficulty range: from 5.6 to 5.11. Should 5.12 climbs become more popular, they will be included in future updates of this series.

While the routes included are intended to represent the better routes at an area, not all will be considered "classic." Sometimes, especially in the lower grades, lesser routes were included in the book in order to provide climbing at a particular level. Some classic routes may not be included because of layout considerations.

HOW TO USE THIS BOOK

Each chapter has the same format. Photographs and route information follow a written description of each area, including the nature of the climbing and environment. Below is a more detailed explanation of how to interpret each chapter.

HIGHLIGHTS This is a one paragraph overview of the characteristics of the area.

CLIMBING This section comments on the different cliffs, the type of rock, the nature of climbing (whether it be face, crack, slab, free, or aid), the approach hikes, and descents.

ENVIRONMENT The natural and social environment described in this paragraph gives a feeling for the area. The climbing experience can, of course, vary from wilderness, to that of a crowded climber's gymnasium. This section will also mention some alternate attractions that the area offers, including hikes, scenery, and river rafting.

CLIMBING HISTORY A brief overview of the local climbing history is presented in this section. Individual names have been omitted, however, because in such a brief treatment it is difficult to properly recognize those people who have contributed to the development of an area. The important names can often, though not always, be garnered from the first ascent list. Local guidebooks will sometimes help considerably in providing a more in-depth historical overview.

CAMPING A description of the availability and nature of camping (legal), showering, and laundry facilities is covered here. Free illegal or discretionary camping can often be found, but such information cannot be put in this book. Because prices are likely to increase through the years, specific dollar figures are rarely given for camping; instead, adjectives are used. In 1984, the approximate price range for a "moderate" campground is five to seven dollars per night, with up to six people typically allowed per site (in one or sometimes two vehicles). "Inexpensive" campgrounds cost less money, while "expensive" ones cost more. As mentioned in "A Note on Safety," lake and stream water can rarely be trusted for drinking. To protect the water, toilets should be used where available, or excrement should be buried not less than 100 feet from any stream or lake. A biodegradable soap should also be used.

SEASONS AND WEATHER This is a general chart of the seasonal weather and likelihood of finding good climbing days. Temperatures are given by ten degree intervals with a plus (+) or minus (−) sign designating that temperatures are frequently found either above or below this range. Thus, 70's indicates that temperatures are typically somewhere between seventy and eighty degrees Fahrenheit. 70's+ indicates that the temperature frequently reaches into the eighties. 70's− indicates that often the temperature never reaches seventy degrees. The column "High" is for the typical highest daytime temperature, while "Low" is for the typical overnight lowest temperature. "Likelihood of Precipitation" gives a clue to whether the visitor will encounter rain or snow that will inhibit climbing.

"Frequency of Climbable Days" is a summation of the temperature and precipitation data and some of the "Comments" listed below the chart. It is the best indicator of whether moderate climbers will be able to enjoy themselves during a visit. If an area indicates "low-medium" frequency of climbable days, then a short visit might typically be rained out or the temperatures might be too high or low. A longer visit would probably yield at least a few days to climb in. Of course, zealots will find climbing possible even on hot or wet days.

These charts, based as they are on weather average data, are as variable as any weather.

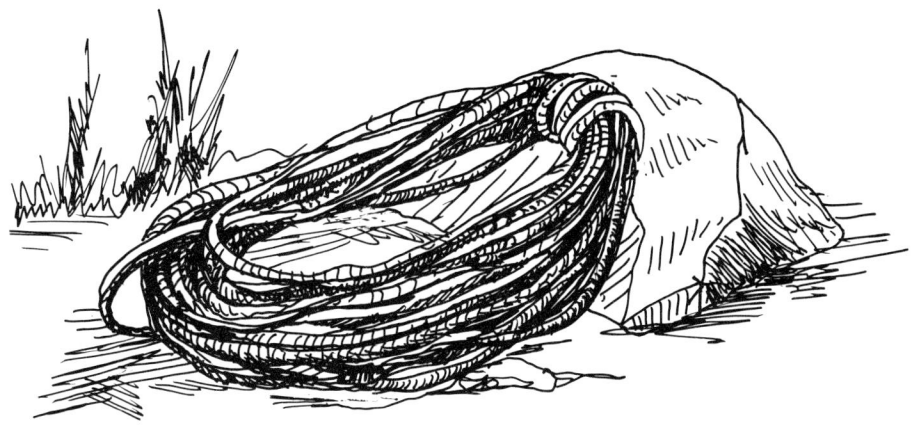

INTRODUCTION

RESTRICTIONS AND WARNINGS Some of the listings here, such as whether one may encounter rattlesnakes, or thieves, are for the reader's personal benefit. More important is such advice as "go slowly through the residential area" because this information is necessary for maintaining access privileges for the entire climbing community. PLEASE READ AND HEED THIS SECTION!

GUIDEBOOKS This section lists the local guidebooks and how to obtain them. A climber on an extended visit may require information for additional routes beyond those provided in this book. In addition, a local guidebook can be invaluable for more information on the area's history and geology.

GUIDE SERVICES AND EQUIPMENT STORES Local equipment stores can be a good source of updated information. The locally based guide services are listed for those in need of either instruction or a well qualified partner.

EMERGENCY SERVICES The nearest hospital and the appropriate contact for rescues is described here. In virtually all cases, the County Sheriff is in charge of coordinating rescues (except in National Parks where the rangers are responsible). Because telephone numbers can change, simply call the operator to make the connection.

Rescues should be called only in case of dire emergencies. Not only does this save the climber and the taxpayer a great deal of money, but self-rescue does not generate the ill-will towards the climbing community that often is the result of very public rescues. A European-style climber's rescue insurance policy is not yet available in North America.

GETTING THERE This section describes the public transportation available to the climbing area.

ROUTE DESCRIPTIONS
Most of the route descriptions in this book are in the form of lines drawn directly onto photographs. Difficulty, fixed protection, and belay notations are written next to the lines. As noted repeatedly in this introduction, this is only a guide. The lines on the photographs are approximate in their placement and route finding skills are a necessity.

On many longer climbs, supplementary drawings—"topos"—are also included. The following drawing explains the symbolism used. Suggested protection is only given when it differs from the standard rack most climbers usually carry with them. In the case of free climbs, assume that the listed protection is in addition to a clean (no pitons) rack with one nut from each of the standard size increments from one quarter inch to two and one-half inches.

INTRODUCTION 5

Unless they are listed in the guidebook, or needed in emergency situations, PITONS OR BOLTS SHOULD NEVER BE PLACED ON ESTABLISHED NORTH AMERICAN ROUTES!

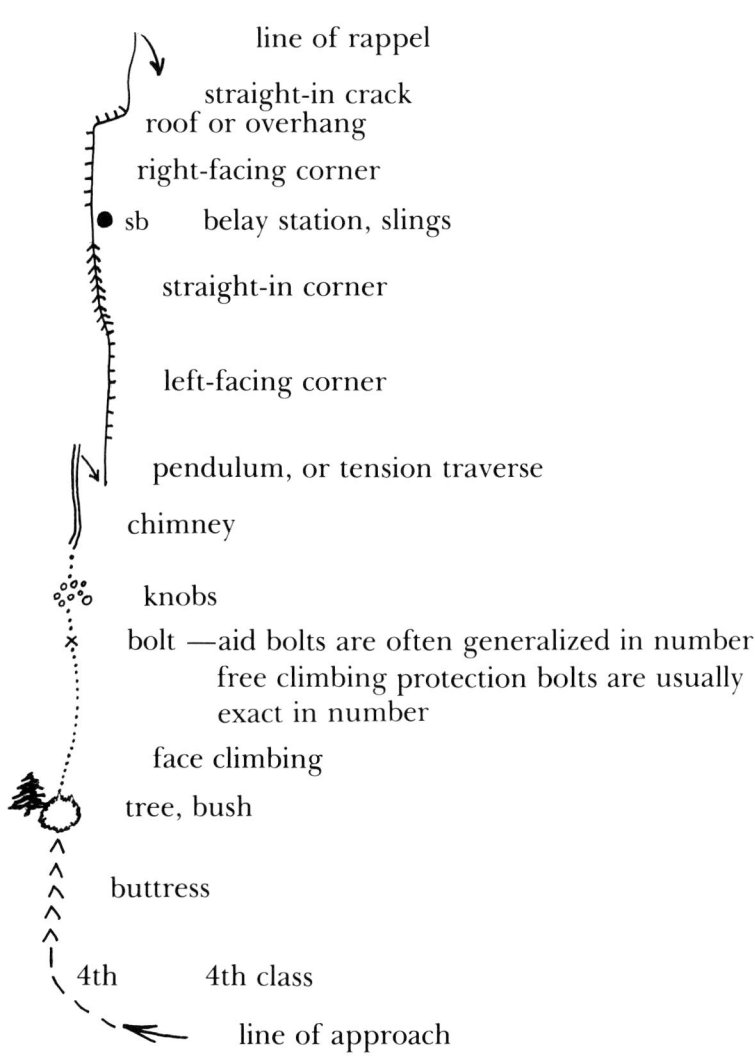

fp	fixed piton
lb	lieback
sb	sling belay
ow	offwidth
chim	chimney
thin	thin crack
165'	165 feet
KB	knifeblade piton
LA	Lost Arrow piton

Key to the maps

freeway	————
major road	═══
paved road	———
unpaved road	- - - -
trail	· · · · · ·
camping	△
area location	✳
mile	mi.

RATINGS

North American climbers use a combination of four rating systems for assessing the difficulty of climbs. The first is a rough classification that distinguishes between the various stages from trail hiking to aid climbing. The next system breaks the technical free climbing category down into much more specific ratings. This Decimal System (widely referred to as the Yosemite Decimal System—YDS—but actually developed at Tahquitz) is the mainstay of rock climbing route ratings. These free ratings refer to the hardest individual moves on a particular section of rock. Sometimes an overall route rating will be raised some if the climbing is extremely continuous, but this practice is not universal. Rarely does a lack of protection affect the free rating of a climb; instead, protection considerations are mentioned more as a footnote to the grade. Aid climbing is also differentiated into various degrees of difficulty; seriousness is a part of the rating.

Many routes are additionally given a roman numeral grade to indicate their length. Thus, an example of an overall route rating might be VI 5.10 A3. Individual pitches might be labelled 5.6, 4th, or A2. An explanation of each category follows.

INTRODUCTION 7

CLASS DESCRIPTION

1   Trail hiking.
2   Rough hiking, frequent use of hands for balance.
3rd   Rock scrambling using hands, sometimes with enough exposure that inexperienced climbers will prefer to use a rope.
4th   Technically more difficult and sufficiently exposed that most climbers use a rope and belay for safety.
5th   Free climbing sufficiently difficult to require the use of a rope and placement of protection for safety.
6th   Artificial (aid) climbing where hardware is not used simply for protection, but also for hand and footholds.

5th class climbing is subdivided by the use of a decimal point. Thus routes are rated 5.0, 5.1, . . . 5.11, 5.12. Currently the most difficult climbs are in the 5.13 category. Routes 5.10 or greater in difficulty usually receive further subgradings in the form of letters (a, b, c, or d) or + and − signs. The following is an approximate comparison of the most popular rating systems used throughout the world.

INTRODUCTION

Decimal	UIAA	English Numerical	Australian	French
5.0	III		4	
5.1	III +		5	
5.2	IV −	3a	6	
5.3		3b	7	
5.4	IV +	3c	8,9	
5.5	V −	4a	10,11	
5.6	V	4b	12,13	4c
5.7	V +	4c	14,15	5a
5.8	VI −	5a	16	5b
5.9	VI		17	5c
5.10a	VI +	5b	18	6a
5.10b	VII −		19	
5.10c	VII	5c	20	6b
5.10d	VII +		21	
5.11a		6a	22	6c
5.11b	VIII −		23	
5.11c	VIII	6b	24	7a
5.11d	VIII +		25	
5.12a	IX −	6c	26	7b
5.12b	IX		27	
5.12c	IX +	7a	28	7c
5.12d				
5.13	X −			

The aid ratings reflect the security of using the latest available technology. The same route climbed with the pitons of the 1960's instead of the modern aid climbing rack would require entirely different ratings. Frequently, difficult modern routes could not be done without the technology of Friends, bashies and hooks.

A1   Easy placements, completely secure.
A2   More difficult placements, less secure.
A3   Even more difficult placements that will usually only hold a short fall.
A4   Each placement will hold body weight but would not sustain a fall.

INTRODUCTION

A5   A series of A4 placements long enough to risk at least a 50 foot fall should one fail.

C1, C2,   ... are used as an aid rating prefix, where known, to indicate the aid rating when the route can be done completely clean—i.e., with no hammer blows.

Roman numerals, intended as a grading of overall difficulty, were designed to reflect many factors about a route, including commitment, difficulty, and length. In current usage, they primarily reflect length in terms of time invested into a climb.

I   About an hour of climbing, usually one or two pitches.
II   Less than a half day of climbing.
III   A half day of climbing.
IV   A full day of climbing.
V   Typically, one overnight is spent on the wall. Since many traditional two-day aid routes are free climbed in a day, this grade on a free climb usually means one very long day.
VI   At least two nights are usually spent on the climb.

WARNING ON ROUTE LINES, SYMBOLS, AND FIXED PROTECTION

The format taken for most of the route descriptions in this book—route lines superimposed on photographs—is helpful only if one keeps in mind the inherent imprecision of route information. In this book, the placement of route lines or protection/belay symbols is not exact. The notations are subject to interpretation, and route finding skills are just as important as ever. Lines on the photos are often drawn next to the feature that is climbed (especially with cracks) so not to obstruct it. The symbols and route lines are guides only.

There are bound to be ways to improve the accuracy of the route line drawings or topos in this book. While any guidebook takes away some of the adventure in climbing, it is not the intent of this guide to mislead. As a user of this guide, your suggestions for better descriptions would be invaluable. A photocopy of a photo with corrections to the route line is ideal. Likewise, feedback concerning the routes selected for this book is appreciated. Suggestions for better routes are welcomed. All route information, corrections and suggestions should be sent to Chockstone Press, 526 Franklin Street, Denver, CO 80218.

As further warning, be aware that fixed pitons and bolts labelled in this guide might have been removed or supplemented. Fixed anchors should always be carefully inspected. They may be weak due to weathering, poor initial placement, or any number of reasons. That they are listed in this book does not imply that they are trustworthy or even exist!

Pitons should not be trusted without testing, preferably with a hammer. Since few climbers free climb with a hammer, fixed pitons are rarely tested and can easily be unsafe.

Bolts should be checked with a strong jerk on the hanger (using a carabiner) and inspected for cracks. They should NEVER be tested with a hammer, as this can severely weaken them! Because defective or poorly placed bolts are a possibility anywhere, no bolt can be fully trusted.

A NOTE ON SAFETY

Those using *The Climber's Guide to North America* as a guidebook are assumed to be competent and experienced climbers. It is not the intent of this book to educate anyone in HOW to climb, but simply to provide suggestions as to where to climb and what it will be like.

It must be noted, however, that many of the places covered by these books are relatively remote. Assistance from fellow climbers, rescues, or hospital facilities may be difficult to obtain quickly. This is a serious

INTRODUCTION

consideration that should be taken into account when deciding just how far to "hang it out" on a particular climb.

Water sanitation can be a problem in some areas. Beware that few streams and lakes can be completely trusted to be safe from contamination—no matter how far away from "civilization." The bacteria Giardia is a common infectious agent and can produce extreme intestinal ills that can completely ruin a climbing vacation. It is best to thoroughly boil and/or treat with purification tablets all stream and lake water.

To avoid further water contamination, all human waste should be buried not less than 100 feet away from the nearest open water.

Theft can be a definite problem in some areas, particularly those with large numbers of people. As a general rule, keep all valuables, including climbing equipment, locked out of sight in a car. Ropes and equipment fixed on routes, or stashed at the base of cliffs, may not be safe.

IF YOU DON'T HAVE A CAR

Public transportation in North America is not nearly as extensive as it is in Europe. Nevertheless, one can certainly reach many of the best climbing areas on the continent without a car. If the climber is willing to hitch-hike, there is almost no place that cannot be reached. Though trains bypass almost everything interesting to climbers, buses connect the major cities with most small communities and some popular recreation sites. From the major airports, it is usually necessary to take a connecting bus to the bus station located downtown.

If you don't have a car, turn to the text under "Getting There" for the area you are interested in visiting. A valuable further reference is the book *How to Get to the Wilderness Without a Car* listed under "Supplementary Information", in this book.

Another option is to rent a car. The major car rental companies found at airports are fairly expensive. The same rental agencies located downtown often offer considerably lower rates. Much cheaper, though riskier, alternatives are the small local companies that rent used cars—sometimes VERY used. By getting together a small group of climbers one of these cars can be rented for very little money and will provide a great deal of mobility. Likewise, even climbers with limited resources can usually afford to buy a suitable used car by pooling their funds. An important fringe benefit to having a car is that the trunk provides a storage place for gear.

If travelling alone or with one other person, consider first visiting one of the more popular areas. There is a good possibility of meeting a climber with a car who can be persuaded to visit new places.

AMERICAN ROCK CLIMBING STYLE AND ETHICS

Traditionally, there has been a difference in free climbing attitudes between Europe and America. These stem in large part from the fact that Europeans have emphasized getting up big mountains fast (crag climbing was often considered practice for the real stuff). Popular American cliffs are low in objective dangers, thus Americans have emphasized the style of the ascent. Now, many Europeans are also concentrating on pure rock climbing and have adopted many similar standards of style. Nevertheless, a short discussion on American attitudes may help visitors from different climbing cultures.

In the United States, the ideal free ascent is a route climbed unpreviewed, unroped, barefoot, and without chalk. Any compromise of this style is just that: a compromise. To provide a greater margin of safety and comfort, few climbers follow such strict guidelines in their climbing style. Many climbers use chalk, most use shoes, and almost everyone uses a rope and protection. They strive simply to climb a route with the minimum number of falls or reliances on equipment, knowing that the further that their style deviates from the ideal, the less the accomplishment of their ascent.

There are many ways of compromising good climbing style, from merely falling, to resting on protection, yo-yoing (making upward progress by lowering to rest, or exchanging leaders), previewing the route by rappel, or pre-placing protection. "Improving" hand or footholds by altering the rock is unthinkable.

Some Europeans consider it good style to practice a route by resting on aid with the intent of finally re-leading the route with no weighting of protection. Most Americans would rather complete the route in one push using their best possible style, even if it means taking falls and lowering to a rest position. Many people prefer to retreat from a short route than to ever rest on aid.

Damaging the rock is the biggest transgression in American rock climbing. Because of their damaging impact on the rock, the use of pitons is discouraged on all free climbs and wherever avoidable on aid routes. On first ascents, any necessary pitons are usually left fixed. The use of bolts on established routes is even more deeply scorned. On the free climbs described in this book, both pitons and bolts should be thought of only as emergency tools.

Chalk is disapproved of by many climbers—both because it is an aid and because it is visually obnoxious on some rock types. It also leaves a "white-dotted line" that shows where to go and where all the hand-holds are. Nevertheless, the stuff works wonderfully in securing grip and is used by most climbers.

Discussions on ethics and style are taken quite seriously by many people. Generally these discussions center on first ascents, because a route that is put up in poor style can take away the thrill and credit for a first ascent by someone who would later do the route in a more accepted style.

Many Americans will be seen bending the "rules" of good style, but when all is said and done, most climbing peers condemn only those who 1) damage the rock, 2) misrepresent their particular climbing style, or 3) grossly deny other climbers a first ascent in better style.

SUPPLEMENTARY INFORMATION

Road Atlas to North America A number of road atlases are available from bookstores and gas stations. A particularly good one is put out by Quaker State and published by Gousha/Chek-Chart, P.O. Box 6227, San Jose CA 95150. These atlases do little that good individual state maps do not do, but they make visiting several states a bit more convenient.

FREE Campgrounds U.S.A. edited by Mary VanMeer, 1983, published by The East Woods Press, Fast & McMillan Publishers, Inc., 429 East Boulevard, Charlotte NC 28203, $9.95. This book lists an incredible number of free campgrounds and can make travelling from one climbing area to another much less expensive. Also, sometimes free alternatives can be found to the more convenient campgrounds listed in *The Climber's Guide to North America.*

INTRODUCTION

How to Get to the Wilderness Without a Car by Lee W. Cooper, 1982, published by Lee Cooper Publisher, P.O. Box 4073, Malibu CA 90265, $7.95. This book describes in detail public transportation to many of the wild areas that have climbing. In appendices, it also lists many of the trail hiking guides to the regions covered. For those without a car and not wanting to hitch-hike, this book may prove helpful.

Let's Go: USA annual, published by St. Martin's Press, 175 Fifth Avenue, New York NY 10010, $8.95. This is only one of many books on travelling in the U.S. that could prove valuable to climbers with interests beyond the rocks. These books usually focus on cities and major recreation areas (e.g. National Parks) and cover historical overviews, interesting sights, hotels, restaurants, transportation. *Let's Go: USA* is written by the Harvard Student's Agencies, and focuses on budget travel for students. By listing Youth Hostels, campgrounds, and budget hotels, it is probably more interesting to climbers than most of the other books available. For the West Coast, there is also a *Let's Go: California and the Pacific Northwest*, which is even more detailed.

American Youth Hostel Handbook, 1332 I St. NW, Washington D.C. 20005, free with membership. Youth hostels are rarely available next to climbing areas, but they can often be relatively cheap and interesting places to stay while travelling or visiting cities (where camping is often not worth the hassle).

Climbing Magazine, PO Box E, Aspen CO 81611. Each issue lists climbing equipment stores that distribute the magazine. This can be a way of locating stores in cities between those listed in the *Climber's Guide to North America*.

50 Classic Climbs of North America by Steve Roper and Allen Steck, 1979, published by Sierra Club Books, 530 Bush Street, San Francisco CA 94108, $10.95. Most of the climbs in this book are also found in *The Climber's Guide to North America*, but since *50 Classic Climbs* concentrates on individual routes, much more historical detail can be learned from it on these particular climbs.

Advanced Rockcraft by Royal Robbins, 1971, La Siesta Press, Box 406, Glendale CA 91209, $3.95. Though not recent enough for the latest technology, this book gives an excellent introduction to big wall techniques.

Climbing in North America by Chris Jones, 1976, published for the American Alpine Club by the University of California Press, and available from the American Alpine Club. 113 East 90th Street, New York, NY 10028. hardback: $19.95, paperback: $9.95, plus $1.25 postage. This is the most comprehensive history to climbing in North America available in print.

WEST COAST ROCK CLIMBS

"Go West" was the call to adventure and opportunity for 19th century North America. The Oregon Trail and other rutted freeways of the 1800's led covered wagons to the coast, where families tested themselves against the land that Indians and Spaniards had found productive for generations.

To rock climbers of the 1960's and 70's the call of the West was equally strong: everyone had to taste the wonders of Yosemite Valley. From around the world, climbers thronged to test themselves against El Capitan's 3,000 feet of vertical granite.

Sometimes, intrepid pilgrims found that they had preceeded the stable weather; Yosemite was still too cold and wet, and ice and waterfalls were cascading down the granite faces. Many climbers went south 500 miles to Joshua Tree National Monument. Huge, coarse-grained granite boulders, scattered through a beautiful desert environment, offered a very Western experience, along with enough climbs to last a lifetime. It was a perfect place to wait for the storm clouds to dissipate and the sun to warm the faces of the place to be—the Valley, of course.

But while these two climbing centers were drawing all the international attention, West Coast residents from San Diego to Vancouver found that their backyards yielded climbs every bit as good as some of those more famous. While some climbers tended to treat the local crags purely as practice for their annual pilgrimages to Yosemite, others were content with the usually quieter home scene.

Even though Tahquitz and the Pinnacles received exploring climbers as early as the 1930's, other areas, such as the Needles and Calaveras Dome, were not touched by technical climbers until the late 1960's or early 70's. Either way, the cliffs are now well developed both by locals and by a few travelling climbers.

An increasing number of people are interested in experiencing many of these once "locals-only" haunts. What will they find? Granite, granite, and a bit more granite. Of the sixteen climbing areas included in this book, twelve are composed of granitic rock. (Variations in chemistry may alter the class in the eyes of a geologist, but from the climber's perspective, they can all be considered granite.) Three of the areas that are not granitic were still formed by igneous processes. Beacon Rock is an exceptionally solid basalt, while Smith Rock is tuff, a consolidation of ash from the nearby volcanoes of the Cascade Mountains. The Pinnacles are also volcanic material, with chunks of other rocks mixed in, yielding a rock type known as breccia.

The reason for all of this igneous activity lies in the interaction between continental plates: as the Pacific Plate was thrust (subducted) under the North American Plate, the moist oceanic material began to melt as it went deeper and deeper underground. Two major igneous rock types were produced: granite and volcanic rock. Generally the igneous activity in California was all granitic, while volcanic rocks dominate Oregon and Washington.

The Leavenworth area of Washington has a few small sandstone cliffs among its more famous granite crags, but the only significant non-igneous rock in this book is the sedimentary cliffs of The Red Rocks in Nevada, somewhat further inland than any of the other West Coast rock climbing centers.

Whether it be granite or otherwise, the West Coast offers a diverse mix of climbing experiences. Despite the vast amounts of climbing from central California south and from northern Oregon north, the landscape in between is virtually devoid of crags. This helps distinguish the very different experiences of climbing in the Northwest and California.

California is famous for sunshine, beaches, mild temperatures and a mellow lifestyle. The climate of such climbing areas as Joshua Tree, Pinnacles, The Red Rocks, and the numerous bouldering areas near San Diego, Los Angeles, and the Bay Area of San Francisco will delight those used to the frigid winter climes that seem to dominate the homegrounds of many European, North American and Asian climbers.

During the spring and fall, most of the diverse crags of California are at their rock climbing prime. In the summertime the lowland areas are too hot for the tolerances of most climbers, but higher altitude areas like Tahquitz, the Needles, Tuolumne, and Lover's Leap can be great, although a bit crowded at times.

Climbers arriving by airplane will most likely land in Los Angeles or San Francisco. While many foreign climbers hop directly onto a bus and head to Yosemite, those arriving in San Francisco would probably find it rewarding to spend a few leisurely days exploring this fascinating city and the beautiful beaches and redwood groves that lie to the north and south.

INTRODUCTION

Most of California's climbing takes place in the Sierra Nevada—often referred to as the Sierra. This north-south running mountain range has a heavily forested western slope that rises to the high peaks, and a sudden precipitous drop on the east side to an arid desert valley. While the crest of the Sierra lies at approximately 14,000 feet, the climbing areas on the western slope range from 4,000 to 9,000 feet in elevation. Most of the east side involves rock climbing routes on exquisite granite mountains. Even though some have 2,000 foot faces, the length of the hike in and the degree of effort necessary for most routes precludes inclusion in this volume.

On the rolling, pine forested hills of the western slope are scattered a vast number of smooth, glacially polished granite domes, cliffs and spires. Many of these are infrequently visited and so are not included in this book. Included, however, are enough easily accessible crags to give anyone a gourmand's taste of what is undoubtedly some of the finest granite in the world. For dome and needle climbing, try the Needles, Tuolumne, or Calaveras Dome. For a different experience, try the small crags at Donner Summit or the outrageously steep—but often jug-laced—600 foot face at Lover's Leap. Then, of course, there is the "Incomparable Valley" of Yosemite. Glacially carved out of the same granite basolith that produced the Tuolumne domes, Yosemite has more high quality granite exposed than anywhere in North America. Though teeming with climbers at times, the climbs are still magnificent.

While the 200 to 900 foot cliffs at Tahquitz also lie in mountainous terrain (the San Jacinto Mountains), they are separated by a few hundred miles from the southern terminous of the Sierra Nevada. Nearby Joshua Tree National Monument is an almost completely flat desert, studded with giant boulders up to about 100 feet in height. While both these areas are granite, Tahquitz climbing is very similar to the smooth domes of the Sierra, while Joshua Tree features coarse-grained crystalline rock.

The Pinnacles are an anomaly in California climbing. The brecciated rock is sometimes frighteningly loose and the landscape of rugged low-altitude hills and jumbled masses of giant boulders are more often described as weird than anything else. But the scenery, especially in the spring, is outstanding. Another anomaly for the West Coast are the sandstone cliffs at The Red Rocks. These 1,000 foot cliffs, carved out of the desert mountains near Las Vegas, provide superb climbing that few visitors fail to appreciate. A few miles away, Las Vegas profers glitter for all and gold for the lucky.

The Pacific Northwest is a vastly different place from California. As in California, a mountain range runs north-south and the western side is wetter than the eastern side, but the similarities virtually stop there.

Smith Rock, Oregon, lies in a desert almost as arid as those of the south. The climbing is on the walls of a river gorge, and from its numerous 200-400 foot cliffs one catches fantastic views of the snow-covered Cascade Mountains. One hundred fifty miles to the north, the 400 foot cliff on Beacon Rock provides steep stemming and crack problems near the waters of the Columbia River. The size of this river and the lush nature of the surrounding forest point out the dominant feature of the Northwest: rain. During the summer months, visiting climbers can expect reasonably good weather at almost all the climbing areas included in this book (except possibly Index, which lies strategically in the path of rising moist air currents). But during the winter, beware. Rain related suicides are not uncommon by residents despondent over months of rain and a sun that seems forever hidden. The rock climber would have to be lucky indeed to stumble on a suitably dry cliff.

In the spring, the weather is often good, though one should hardly count on enough climbing days to justify a long trip. The exceptions are Leavenworth, located on the east (rainshadow) side of the Cascades, Smith Rock—as mentioned above—and, to some extent, Beacon Rock.

Aside from weather, climbers in Washington and British Columbia will be confronted by granite crags of a diverse nature. British Columbia's Squamish Chief is perhaps the only area that has comparisons to California climbing. Here, the main cliff rises to 1,500 feet and offers everything from plumb-vertical wall climbs to slabby apron climbs of a very difficult and committing nature. Unique to Squamish is the view of the fjord—a mere stone's throw away—and of spectacularly glaciated peaks nearby.

Liberty Bell is unusual in this book. It is a true mountain, with rough alpine-granite walls that rise 2,000 feet above a mountain pass. Because a recently built road snakes just beneath its talus slopes, the peak is now accessible to the chalk-bag toting, rock shoe-clad climber, eyes open to the variable mountain weather.

INTRODUCTION

The Index Town Walls perhaps best capture the spirit of the Northwest, though as a consequence they receive the least visitation. When dry, they provide two and three pitch free climbing routes and Grade IV aid routes on vertical granite cliffs that rise out of the lush forests of Western Washington. When wet, Index is usually abandoned as climbers cross the pass to Leavenworth, two hours further east and on the dry side of the state.

Leavenworth is a diverse collection of cliffs. Some are granite and many sections of these cliffs feature fantastic knobs and chickenheads. The granite climbs range up to seven pitches in length. Also in this area are the Peshastin Pinnacles, a group of soft sandstone towers averaging about 150 feet in height. The wonderful thing about these pinnacles is the fact that they lie in one of the driest spots in Washington and hence can be climbed virtually the year-round—though they would hardly be worth a special trip in themselves. A fringe benefit for the Leavenworth climber is the delicious and inexpensive fruit available in the summer and fall.

Just as San Francisco can be recommended for a visit before or after heading off for the climbing in California, so the two major air access points in the Northwest—Vancouver, British Columbia and Seattle, Washington—are each well worth exploration. Both cities are surrounded by snow clad volcanoes, high peaks, and the inland waterways of Puget Sound, and their unique and flavorful character encourage more than a quick pass-through on the way to the rocks.

A BRIEF HISTORY OF ROCK CLIMBING ON THE WEST COAST

The sporting aspects of mountains held little appeal to the early white explorers. During the 1800's a few peaks were climbed by intrepid adventurers out to make a name for themselves—almost invariably, they would declare their summit to be the "highest point in North America." By the late 1800's most of the volcanoes in the Northwest had been scaled and geological surveyors were picking off many of the higher peaks in the Sierra Nevada of California. But these ascents played little role in developing climbing into a popular sport.

In fact, it was not until 1914 that climbing in North America evolved to the stage where a belay was consciously used. Albert Ellingwood, who learned rock climbing on the crags of England (climbing had been popular in Europe for over a century by then) introduced rope handling to America on his climbs in Colorado. In California, however, rope techniques remained little known until Robert Underhill, trained in the Alps and with considerable rock climbing experience in New England, visited the state in 1931 to instruct the local peak scramblers in how to belay. This visit initiated the West Coast into the world of rock climbing—where the difficulty of a route is at least as important as the summit.

Shortly afterwards, Richard Leonard demonstrated the independence of spirit and the technical innovation that was to raise Californians into the top ranks of world climbing. From the English language literature (behind the times from what was actually happening in the Alps), the practice to date was clear: "the leader must not fall." Leonard and his Berkeley cohorts decided that this attitude inhibited their climbing. Recognizing that a long fall could easily break contemporary climbing ropes, they invented the dynamic hip belay to reduce impact force on the hemp rope and the anchors. They practiced belaying first with dummies, then with live falling climbers on Indian Rock and other Berkeley crags.

In 1933, Leonard and the newly formed Rock Climbing Section of the Sierra Club went on the first climbing trip to Yosemite. After their defeat on the Higher Cathedral Spire, they sent away to Germany for pitons and carabiners. With the help of knowledge gained from a German book on "tension climbing" (the current technique for aid) they succeeded on the Spire in 1934, thus ushering the era of modern climbing into Yosemite Valley.

Soon, however, aid climbing went out of fashion and though people were already eyeing some of the larger walls in the Valley, they felt that the necessary amount of aid might be unjustifiable. Thus no great advances were made in California climbing until after World War II. The Pacific Northwest fared no better; interest there centered on getting massive numbers of people up the volcanoes, with no desire for technical difficulty.

The war had a great, though indirect influence on the development of North American climbing. A number of climbers enlisted in the mountain troops of the Army and were instrumental in the development of nylon ropes, angle pitons, and aluminum carabiners. With these items in plentiful supply after the war, climbers set forth onto Yosemite's walls. John Salathe, a Swiss native who lived in California, took things a crucial step further by forging pitons out of steel instead of the soft iron available to date. Furthermore, he made sky hooks, developed a single rope technique in order to save weight, trained himself and his partner Ax Nelson to be able to survive on just over a quart of water between them per day, and learned to tie several weak pitons together to make a placement that would hold body weight. With these avant-garde techniques, they succeeded in climbing the **Lost Arrow Chimney** in five days during the summer heat of 1947—truly a landmark event in North American climbing. A similar epic climb of Salathe's, the **Steck-Salathe Route** on Sentinel Rock, remains a popular route today.

While difficult free climbing was not yet popular in Yosemite, at Tahquitz in Southern California a group of young climbers were developing free climbing past anything yet known in North America. By 1952, Royal Robbins had climbed what was probably the hardest free climb in

INTRODUCTION 21

North America, the **Open Book**. Because the old classification system was far too imprecise to measure the relative difficulties of free climbs, the Tahquitz climbers invented what later came to be known as the Yosemite Decimal System—originally 5.0-5.9, but later expanded into an open ended system, i.e. 5.10, 5.11,.... Robbins' **Open Book** received a 5.9 rating.

In 1953 Robbins and two other Southern Californians, Jerry Gallwas and Don Wilson, visited Yosemite and stunned the locals by cutting the time for the **Steck-Salathe Route** on Sentinel Rock down from five days to two. Yosemite climbers had been living in such awe of their cliffs that they had not developed their skills to the level forced by the intense competition and limited route availability at Tahquitz. The following year Robbins, Gallwas, Wilson, and Warren Harding made the first all-out attempt at the Northwest Face of Half Dome. When Robbins, Gallwas and Mike Shearick succeeded in 1957, they established the first Grade VI in North America.

Warren Harding, disappointed over missing out on Half Dome, embarked on a project that was at the limits of contemporary thought: the 3,000 foot vertical face of El Capitan. He decided to use a series of camps from which he would push further up the cliff in stages. The technique was virtually identical to that used on Himalayan peaks and offered considerable psychological and physical support. It also added immense amounts of time to the climbing, and after several months of effort, the National Park Service forbade them to continue until after the summer tourist season—traffic jams from climber-watchers below El Capitan were simply too much to cope with. In the fall of 1958, Harding, and by now a whole new set of belayer/gear porters pulled over the top of the cliff. A breakthrough in American climbing, the **Nose Route** proved that with enough determination, any rock wall could be climbed.

INTRODUCTION

Events in California were virtually unknown elsewhere in America. The East Coast, centered in the Shawangunks of New York, and the Rocky Mountain states, centered in Colorado, were undergoing parallel evolutions in their own climbing development. But California was ahead in both free and aid climbing skills. When the first visitors from Colorado and New York came to Yosemite in the late 1950's and early 1960's, they were humbled by its walls and the techniques required to climb them.

This period also saw the breakdown of both the social barriers in climbing (until then climbers were generally college educated and employed) and the physical barriers of distance. The full time climbing bums that emerged began travelling widely to experience some of the diversity of climbing on the continent. In the summer of 1960 the notorious Vulgarians from the Shawangunks came to Yosemite, as did Layton Kor from Colorado. Likewise, several Yosemite climbers visited the "Gunks" and Colorado (Dave Rearick and Bob Kamps stole the first ascent of the Diamond from under the noses of Colorado climbers).

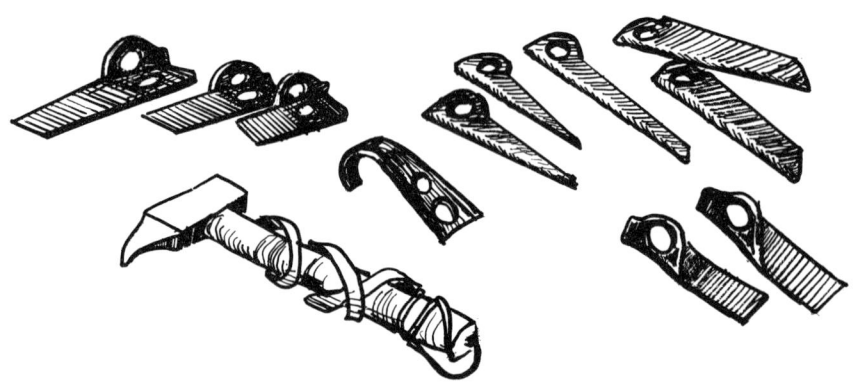

In the late 1950's, Yvon Chouinard, who originated from Southern California but became known for his routes in the Tetons, moved into Yosemite with an anvil in the back of his old truck and began selling his hand-made pitons to Valley climbers. Soon he teamed up with one of Yosemite's leading climbers, Tom Frost, and started a business that would eventually grow into a multi-million dollar corporation: The Great Pacific Ironworks. These two innovators helped usher in the A4 standard of aid climbing, not only with such newly developed equipment as RURPs, but also with aggressive new techniques like nesting and tieing off pitons.

Increased competition and a new willingness to break out of past psychological barriers contributed to a boom in the standards of Yosemite climbing. One of the significant breakthroughs accompanying the introduction of improved nylon ropes was a new attitude towards falling. Where previously falling was to be avoided at all costs, people now realized that with the new equipment and with proper belays, falls were often not as serious an affair on Yosemite's smooth walls. This allowed climbers to push to—and past—their limits.

During this period, Royal Robbins and Joe Fitchen did the first A5 route in North America (**Arches Direct**); Robbins, Fitchen, Frost and Chuck Pratt repeated the **Nose** without fixed ropes in seven days; and Pratt freed the **Worst Error** and the **Crack of Doom**, thus establishing the 5.10 grade.

The Northwest, finally, also experienced an upgrading in its technical climbing standards. Fred Beckey had already launched his prolific climbing career, but his skills on technical ground were limited and he followed a Northwest tradition of fixing ropes on rock that would be considered very easy in any other major climbing center in North America. Though Beckey had already climbed the Squamish Chief, Ed Cooper and Jim Baldwin's 1961 climb of the Grand Wall was a significant step beyond other Northwest routes.

This particular climb may have inspired no locals, but in 1964 Bill Marts, who had climbed with Layton Kor in Colorado, began teaching climbing at the University of Washington in Seattle. Several of his students became leaders in Northwest rock climbing, dispensing with fixed ropes and establishing difficult new routes in the Leavenworth area. During this period, Tom Hargis and Jim Madsen made an early pilgrimage to Yosemite, returning inspired from having seen the vanguard of American rock climbing. In 1965 Steve Marts, Don McPherson and Fred Stanley climbed the **Liberty Crack** (Grade V, 5.8 A3) on the 1,200 foot East Face of Liberty Bell. This was followed by the **Independence Route** (VI 5.8 A4) in 1966 by Alex Bertulis and Don McPherson, and in 1967 Madsen and Kim Schmitz climbed the **Thin Red Line** (VI 5.9 A4), also on Liberty Bell. This quick succession of difficult climbs on Washington's biggest rock wall clearly demonstrated that the new Northwest climbers were of a different breed from those who preceeded them.

But even these climbers considered Yosemite as the place to be. Yosemite was, without question, the most intense climbing scene in North America. Steve Roper's 1964 guidebook to the Valley helped to remove some of the mystery from the big routes, enabling many more climbers to go where before only insiders had the necessary information. Soon, many visitors were doing the biggest routes, often without the fuss that once would have accompanied any such climb. During this period, Yosemite wall tactics were being exported to Europe by the example of Americans like Gary Hemming, Tom Frost, and Royal Robbins who visited the Alps. But it was Northwesterners Jim Madsen and Kim

INTRODUCTION

Schmitz who did as much as anyone to change people's attitudes towards the big walls. Immediately after finishing one wall, they would begin another, then another. Their blitzkrieg style of climbing was stopped only when Madsen rappelled off the end of his rope while checking on friends near the top of El Capitan.

Meanwhile, 5.10 was being developed under the inspiration of Frank Sacherer, who stormed up numerous major routes in his mad-dog style of free climbing. In the early 1970's many more top-notch free climbers emerged. Jim Bridwell, Mark Klemens and others solidified the 5.10 standard and explored the world of 5.11 while reaping an incredible bonanza of first ascents. But Yosemite climbers were no longer head and shoulders above the rest of the nation. Colorado climber Jim Dunn managed the first solo new route on El Capitan in 1972, and Easterner Henry Barber, in 1973, astonished Valley climbers by soloing the **Steck-Salathe Route** on Sentinel in two and one-half hours and doing the first ascent of the much coveted **Butterballs**, 5.11c—still a test piece today.

By the end of the 1960's, climbing had become so popular that even the Yosemite Park and Curry Company—long time arch enemy of the climbing community—decided to open a climbing school in the Valley. Queues were forming at the base of popular routes, and the quantity of climbers at the cutting edge of the sport increased dramatically. Simultaneously, the climbing community spread out to encompass new areas and to more thoroughly explore older ones with new found free climbing skills. Climbers needed an escape from the increasing crowds in Yosemite, but they also needed to make their own marks somewhere and to develop good climbing closer to home.

As the full-time climbing lifestyle became more popular, many people spent winter in the desert sun of Joshua Tree, with the balance of the year in Yosemite. John Bacher and John Long, both Southern Californians, were notable examples of this trend. Bacher, especially, took to climbing with such an intensity that he not only helped to solidify 5.11 and usher in 5.12, but he began free-soloing many routes near the very top levels of difficulty.

INTRODUCTION   25

Many other climbers were active in pushing standards also. Ray Jardine, whose invention of Friends revolutionized the world of climbing protection, showed a proclivity to work out obscure but extremely difficult crack climbs in Yosemite. His 1977 ascent of **Phoenix** and Tony Yaniro's ascent of **Grand Illusion** at Sugarloaf (near Lover's Leap), established 5.13 as new limits of human skill and strength. That Yaniro's test piece did not receive a second ascent until West German Wolfgang Gullich climbed the 40 foot roof in 1983, testifies to the extreme levels that competition and rigorous physical training routines have brought modern free climbers. By the early 1980's, many people were climbing at the 5.12 standard, but only a few managed 5.13. Indeed, as this history is written in 1984, seven years have passed since 5.13 was established, without any sign that 5.14 is around the bend—indicating that perhaps the upper levels of human physical abilities are very nearly being reached.

Though free climbing continues to be the dominant fashion for most climbers, aid climbing has always been of interest to some people. In the early 1970's, Charlie Porter, together with Canadians Steve Sutton and Hugh Burton, greatly expanded the standards of aid climbing seen before 1970, with numerous new routes on El Capitan. Jim Bridwell, a leader in free climbing, was also extremely active over a fifteen year period in developing new aid techniques and in pioneering a new generation of aid climbing horrors that include the hardest walls in North America today. Incidentally, many of the hardest aid routes have become easier with repeated ascents because copperheads get fixed in previously insecure placements; this means that just looking at a current rating does not necessarily indicate how difficult the climb was to the first ascentionists.

Yvon Chouinard once predicted that from the granite walls of Yosemite would spring the great alpinists of the future. Many of Yosemite's most energetic climbers have proved Chouinard accurate. Beginning with himself, and following with Bridwell, Schmitz, Tobin Sorenson, Galen Rowell, and many others, the leaders in Yosemite's mixed free and aid climbing have gone on to distinguish themselves in the world of big mountains and harsh conditions far removed from the idyllic climate of California.

In this history, Yosemite has been stressed, possibly to the detriment of the many other top quality rock climbing areas on the West Coast. This is because, however fine the climbing at the other areas, they played little direct role in the advancement of climbing standards on the West Coast. Even if people from the Northwest played an interesting part in establishing the cutting edge of climbing, their marks were mostly felt in Yosemite first. Peter Croft's 1981 free ascent of the **University Wall** on the Squamish Chief was a significant feat, but similar freeing of Grade V aid climbs had been taking place in Yosemite for many years

INTRODUCTION

already. Perhaps the greatest role for this brief historical essay is to form a rack on which the local histories—given in each area chapter—can be hung. Each area has its own individual story, but almost all somehow intertwine either directly with Yosemite or indirectly through the standards first established by Yosemite's climbing community.

Chris Jones' book, *Climbing in North America,* offers the only comprehensive history of climbing on the continent. Because this fascinating book presents history by tracing the flow of events instead of simply reciting the facts, it provides very entertaining reading, at home or by fire-light. Everyone interested in the historical development of climbing on this continent is urged to read the book. Published for the American Alpine Club by the University of California Press, Berkeley CA, 1976. Available from the American Alpine Club, 113 East 90th Street, New York, NY 10028, hardback: $19.95, paperback $9.95, plus $1.25 postage.

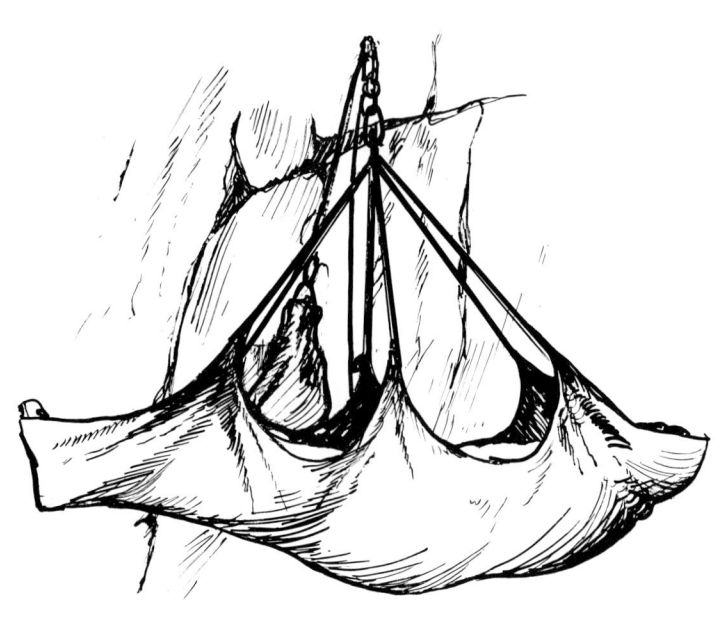

INTRODUCTION

John Harlin on Baby Robbins - Mt. Woodson photo: Dick Shockley

THE RED ROCKS

The Red Rocks

The thousand foot face of Rainbow Mountain

THE RED ROCKS

HIGHLIGHTS
Untouched until 1968, and only known to a few climbers for another fifteen years, The Red Rocks is nevertheless one of the finest rock climbing areas in North America. Located in the desert near Las Vegas, Nevada, The Red Rocks is a complex system of canyons and cliffs cut into a 3,000 foot escarpment. Though short climbs abound, Grade IV and V free climbing routes are the area's specialty. Several faces of 1,000 feet and larger are found. The rock is steep sandstone, usually very solid, with both excellent crack and face climbing. Camping is available nearby, and in Las Vegas one can find diversions from gambling to cabarets. The usual climbing season is fall, winter, and spring.

CLIMBING
The Red Rocks holds a great variety of cliffs in a dozen or more separate canyons. Select routes from three of these canyons are included in this guide, plus the small crags at Willow Springs. Juniper and Black Velvet Canyons both face east and are ideal for warmer desert days. During cold spells, Oak Creek Canyon offers a south facing wall that is well worth the longer hike in. Approximate approach times are five minutes to Willow Springs, forty-five minutes to Black Velvet, one and one-half hours to Juniper, and two hours into Oak Creek Canyon.

The rock is an extremely solid sandstone that does not usually suffer from natural rockfall. The climbing is often in cracks that have been compared to the quality found in Yosemite; one route even follows a

700 foot crack. Just as often, the rock is coated with "desert varnish," a very hard surface plate that provides many excellent edges. These holds can be sharply lipped, making ascents of vertical and even overhanging walls surprisingly easy.

Although small sections of aid are occasionally encountered, most of the climbing at The Red Rocks is free and fairly difficult. Relatively few routes go at less than 5.8 and there are many excellent climbs of Grade III to V on cliffs in excess of 1,000 feet. Though a standard rack should be carried on all climbs, fixed protection is plentiful on some routes. Many descents involve rappels, sometimes of the entire route. In fact, the treacherous nature of the descents is considered by some to be the major drawback to climbing at The Red Rocks.

ENVIRONMENT

The Red Rocks are more than just red. They are a complete artist's palate where someone mixed a liberal dash of red into each of the colors. The variations come from different rates of leaching in the sandstone layers. As one climbs, or waits on a belay ledge, the surrounding rocks are a kaleidoscopic marvel to watch, especially in the morning or evening hours. The approach to the Black Velvet Canyon involves a more forgiving version of the famous desert dirt roads that can destroy a car. Then, as for all cliffs at The Red Rocks, comes a trail-less hike through the desert. Lush with cactus, yucca, sage, and, after a spring rain, with flowering annuals, the desert is a beautiful place that belies its harsh reputation.

Twenty miles to the east is Las Vegas—wholly living up to its glittery renown. Be sure to drive the "Strip" at night; it boggles the senses.

CLIMBING HISTORY

Although the surrounding peaks had received earlier exploration, the cliffs that lure climbers today were not touched until 1968. Then, a teenager from Las Vegas who appreciated the neighboring hills, made several visits to Yosemite and decided that his backyard had some potential as a climbing area. A few more routes were done in the meantime, but in 1973 he let loose a burst of route exploration that lasted until the 1980's. As the 1970's progressed, new figures entered the scene, but a few names (mostly Las Vegas residents) always dominated the first ascent list. Only an elite few outsiders even knew about this area, though around the winter campfires at Joshua Tree one could occasionally hear a tale of this remarkable place. In 1982, a well known climber wrote in *Climbing* magazine that **Levitation 29** was "probably the most incredible face climb I've ever done." Although this stimulated people's interest, meeting another climber in one of the canyons remained a rare event. Perhaps the publication of the first guidebook (and this one) will change that sense of solitude somewhat, but the sheer

THE RED ROCKS

quantity of rock will absorb climbers for years to come.

CAMPING

Undeveloped car camping is permitted only at the head of the Oak Creek Canyon Road. Bring your own water. Water found in rivers is considered safe by most climbers, but it can disappear in dry spells. For more rules and regulations, check with the Nevada State Park Division, Red Rock Spring Mountain Ranch, Blue Diamond, telephone: 875-4141.

While Las Vegas is most famous for its gambling, protein-starved climbers on a budget may enjoy the casinos' "all-you-can-eat" buffets—breakfast, lunch and dinner—at very reasonable prices. Circus-Circus advertises "the largest buffet in the world."

During the day, the best place to meet other climbers is probably the Willow Springs area.

THE RED ROCKS

SEASONS AND WEATHER

Approximate Months	Typical Temperatures High	Low	Likelihood of Precipitation	Frequency of Climbable Days
Nov-Mar	60's	30's+	med-low	high
Apr-May	80's+	50's	very low	very high
Jun-Sep	100's	70's	very low	low-med
Oct	80's	50's	low	very high

Comments: Flash floods are possible during any season, especially summer. Spring and fall can be extremely variable in temperature, and at least one big storm is likely in the spring. High temperatures during this period must be endured only during a very short period of the day. Considerable differences in temperatures will be found depending on whether or not the route is exposed to the sun.

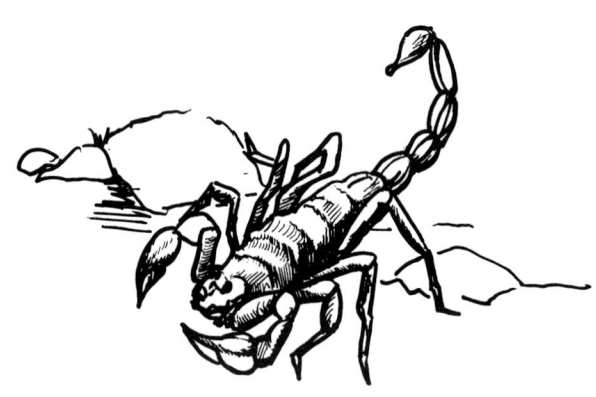

RESTRICTIONS AND WARNINGS

In the summer, be prepared for extremely hot temperatures and know its effects on a long day's climb. During the other seasons, a wide variation in temperatures is possible. Be aware of rattlesnakes. More insidious are the thefts and vandalism that have been known to occur while climbers are on the rocks. Please be especially careful not to litter The Red Rock's beautiful canyons. Exceptionally vicious cacti lurk about—if you have a dog, be prepared to pull spines out of its tongue with pliers.

THE RED ROCKS

GUIDEBOOKS
The Red Rocks of Southern Nevada (1984) by Joanne Urioste. Available from many equipment stores including those in Las Vegas, or from the American Alpine Club, 113 East 90th St, New York, NY 10028.

GUIDE SERVICES AND EQUIPMENT STORES
While there is currently no guide service for the Red Rocks, equipment stores in Las Vegas include the Highland Outfitting Co., at 600 S. Highland Drive, and the Vegas Ski Chalet, at 2111 S. Maryland Parkway.

EMERGENCY SERVICES
The nearest hospital is the Southern Nevada Memorial Hospital at 1800 West Charleston Blvd; telephone: 383-2000. For rescues contact the Sheriff Jeep Posse at 386-3111.

GETTING THERE
Las Vegas is served by airlines from most major Western cities. Greyhound Bus Lines also serves Las Vegas. The road from California to Las Vegas is well travelled and thus a prospect for hitch-hiking, but one needs to be cautious not to be dropped off in the middle of nowhere. Hitch-hiking to the climbing areas could be very slow.

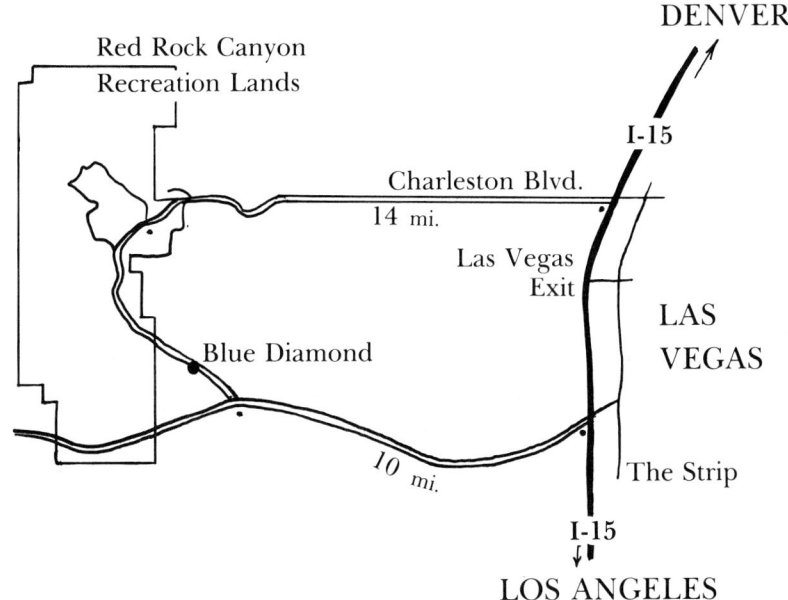

The Red Rocks

THE RED ROCKS

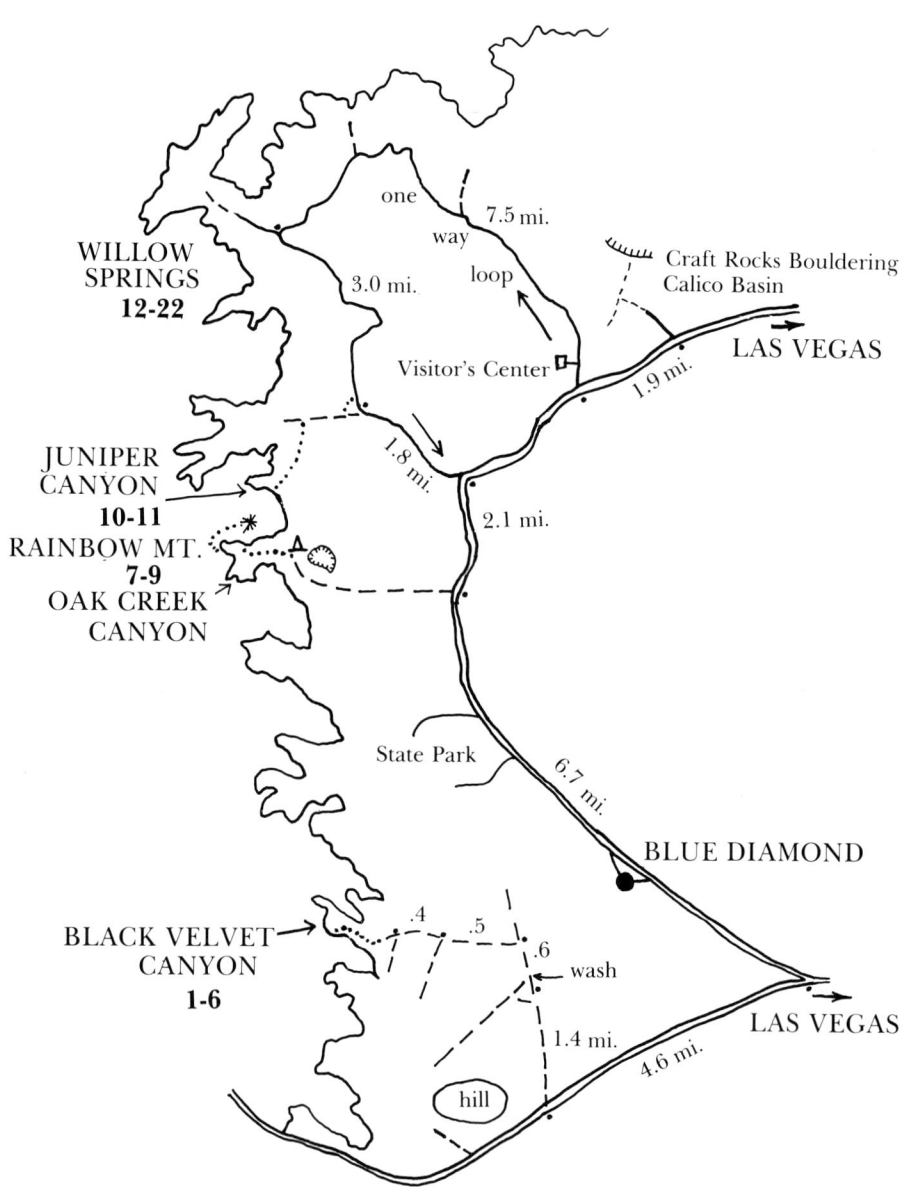

The Red Rocks

Bill Bradley on pitch 9, Levitation 29 photo: Jorge Urioste

Black Velvet Peak

The wrong road to Black Velvet Canyon

THE RED ROCKS

BLACK VELVET CANYON
1 Frogland III 5.8 Mike Gilbert, Joanne and Jorge Urioste, 1978.

2 Misunderstanding II 5.9 Dave Anderson and partner, 1975. Bring several large nuts to 5".

3 Ixtlan IV 5.11 Jorge and Joanne Urioste and Dan Goodwin, 1981. Features diverse climbing.

4 Triassic Sands III 5.10+ Joe Herbst and Larry Hamilton (via lower aid variation), 1972. FFA: Augie Klein, Tony Kaufman, Randy Grandstaff, Chris Robbins and Joe Herbst all participated, 1979.

BLACK VELVET CANYON
Black Velvet Peak

5 Rock Warrior IV 5.10 Jay Smith, Richard Harrison and Nick Nordblum, 1983. Bring many small-medium wired nuts and Friends to #2 (nothing else should be needed). Face climbing.

6 Dream of Wild Turkeys V 5.10 Jorge and Joanne Urioste, 1980. Superb face climbing.

7 Epinephrine V 5.9 Jorge and Joanne Urioste and Joe Herbst, 1978. Diverse climbing.

THE RED ROCKS 39

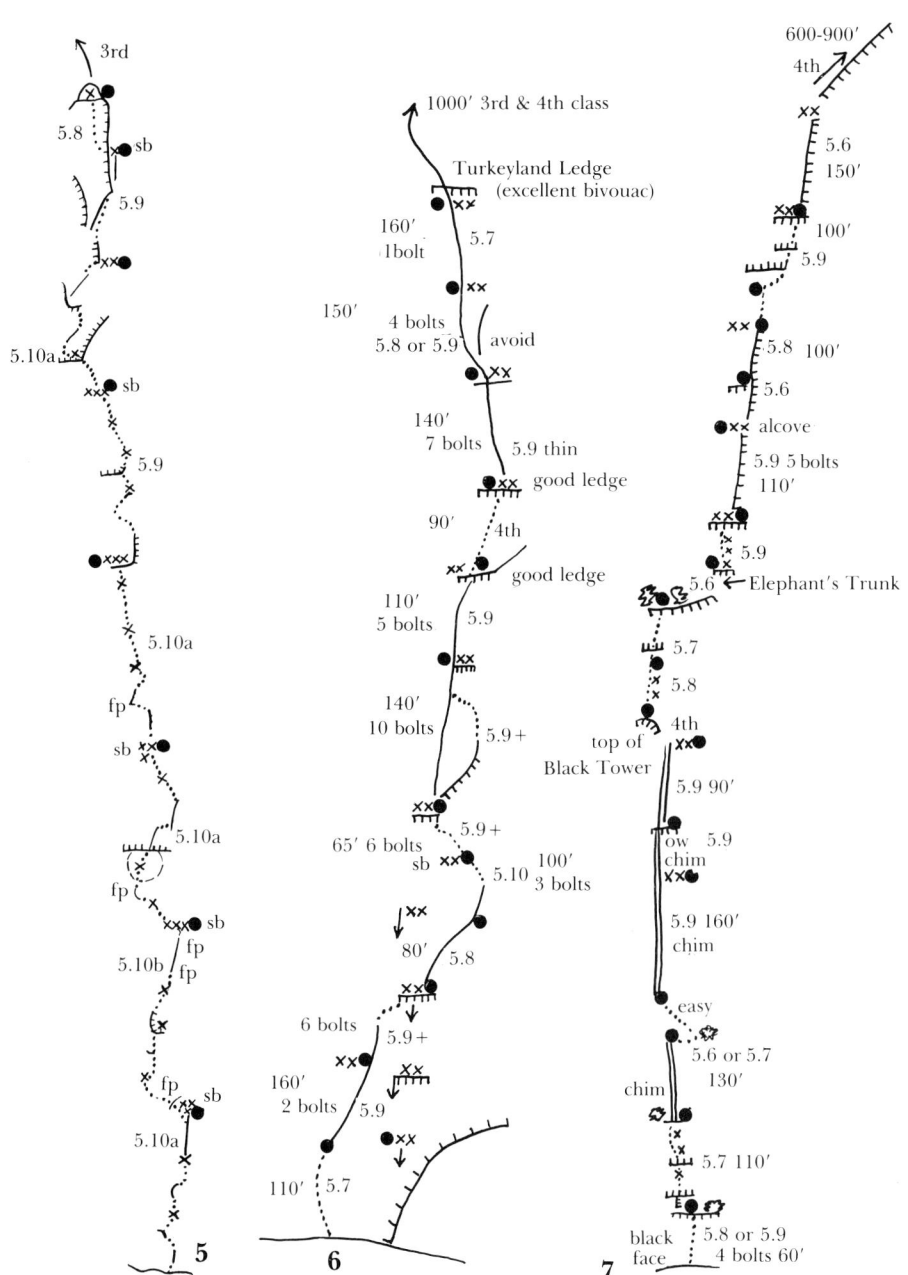

Black Velvet Peak

OAK CREEK CANYON
Rainbow Mountain
  8 Eagle Dance V 5.10 A1 Jorge and Joanne Urioste, 1980. Steep face climbing.
  9 Levitation 29 V 5.11 Jorge and Joanne Urioste with Bill Bradley on the lower section, 1981. FFA: Lynn Hill, John Long and Joanne Urioste. Steep, strenuous and superb face climbing.
10 Rainbow Buttress IV 5.8 Joe Herbst and Joe Frani, 1975. Clean crack systems.

THE RED ROCKS

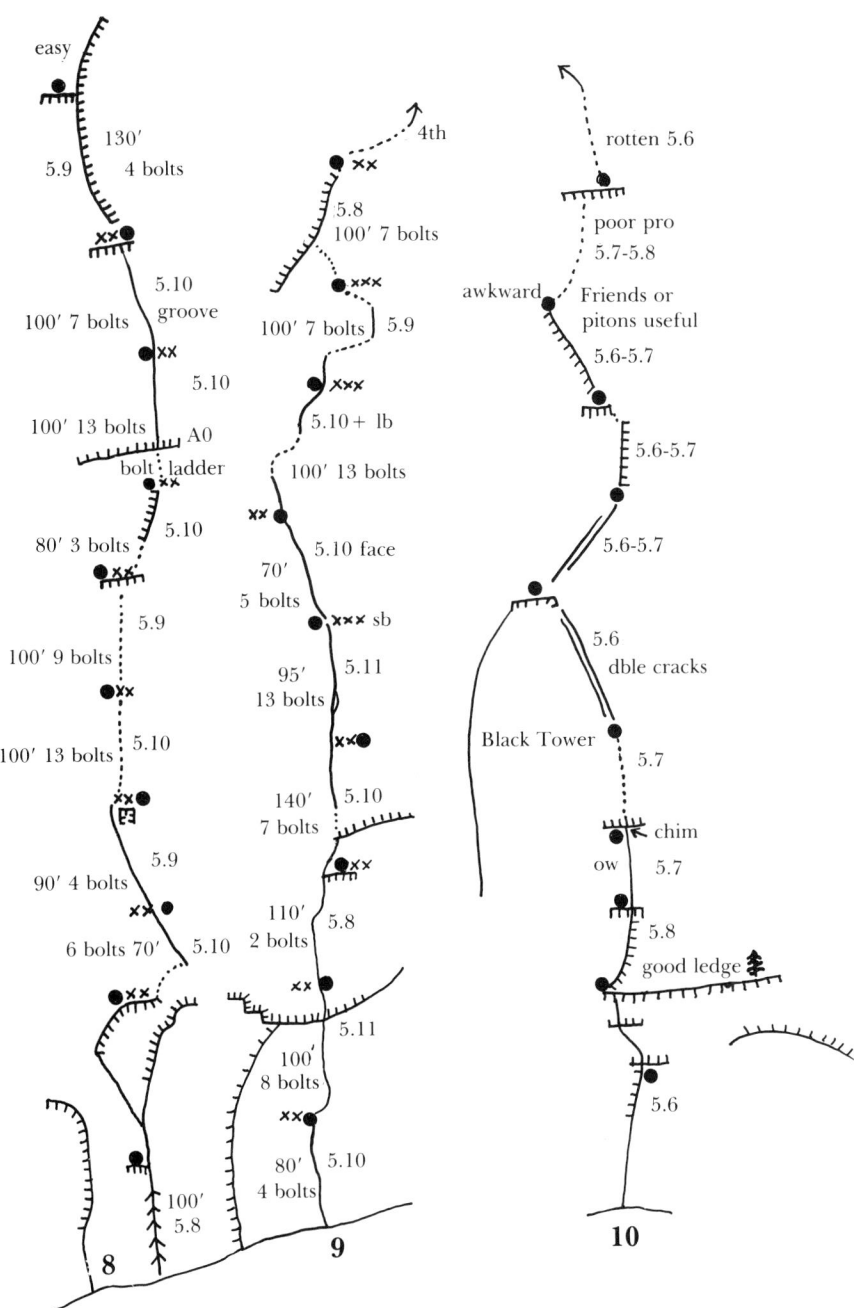

Rainbow Mountain

The first free ascent of Levitation 29, Rainbow Mountain.
photo: Jorge Urioste.

THE RED ROCKS

Lynn Hill on Levitation 29 photos: Jorge Urioste

44 THE RED ROCKS

Crimson Chrysalis

Juniper Canyon
11 The Pachyderm II 5.8-5.9 Jorge and Joanne Urioste, 1980.
12 Crimson Chrysalis IV 5.9 Jorge and Joanne Urioste, 1979. Sustained and diverse climbing.

THE RED ROCKS

Willow Springs
13 Black Track 5.9
14 Grippity Gravity 5.10
15 Cochise 5.7
16 Gray Matter 5.7
17 Crack of Infernity II 5.8+
18 Theme Book 5.9
19 Ragged Edges 5.8
20 Walk to School 5.7
21 The Graduate 5.9-5.10
22 Territorial Imperative 5.10
23 Hard Case 5.8 Climb the obvious crack.

Tahquitz (Lilly) Rock, and Tahquitz Peak

TAHQUITZ SUICIDE

HIGHLIGHTS
Though Tahquitz is now considered fully developed and climbers go elsewhere for first ascents, it offers some of the finest climbing in Southern California. The area consists of two crags of impeccable granite set in the pine forested hills east of Los Angeles at an elevation of about 8,000 feet. While Tahquitz itself is almost 1,000 feet tall, many climbers find the 200 foot routes at Suicide more appealing. The tourist town of Idyllwild is within a few miles of the rocks and offers all the normal conveniences. Despite its low latitude, Tahquitz is often buried in snow during the winter. But spring, summer and fall, it ranks as one of the finest crags to be found.

CLIMBING
Tahquitz and Suicide granite is ideal for climbing: it is completely solid (except on some North Face routes, loose holds are extremely rare) and the rock is neither excessively polished nor rough. The many face climbing routes ascend either friction or small edges on low to medium-high angle faces. This is especially true on Suicide; Tahquitz has a few excellent high-angle jug-hold routes, but most climbs are mixed crack and diverse "broken face" climbing. On both Tahquitz and Suicide,

superb pure crack climbs can also be found. Tahquitz is 900 feet tall on its main North Side and tapers to about a third that on the South Side—where the angle increases considerably. At about 200 feet in height, Suicide is a complex cliff band that faces mostly south—making it ideal for late or early season climbing. Approaches to both rocks are about one-half hour, though Suicide is considerably easier to reach because the hill is less steep. Most routes are descended by walking off the back of the cliff.

ENVIRONMENT

Located high on a pine forested hillside, Tahquitz and Suicide command beautiful views westward over the Los Angeles basin. Though smog rarely reaches as high as these rocks, the view of the sun setting into it (the "smog-set") can actually appear quite lovely. Snow usually blankets the hillsides in winter, though on a good day, climbing at Suicide is still quite possible. The town of Idyllwild (just a few miles from the rocks) is a fairly attractive tourist town. Since Tahquitz is in the San Jacinto Wilderness, an excellent hiking trail leads near the rock and into the wilds. Numerous publications in town will describe the available recreation and will also detail the Indian legend of Tahquitz: rumblings are said to still be heard from the devil who has a collection of maidens trapped beneath the rock.

Incidentally, government publications refer to the climbing crag as Lilly Rock—reserving Tahquitz for the peak behind it.

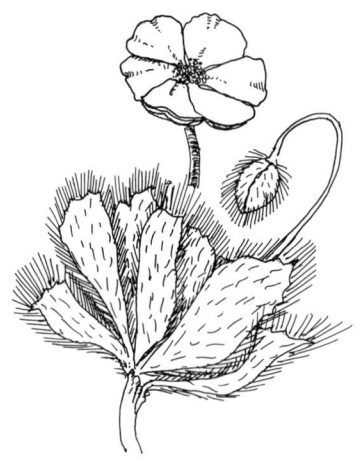

CLIMBING HISTORY

Technical climbing at Tahquitz began when members of the newly formed Southern Chapter of the Sierra Club hiked past the rock in 1936 and were struck by its climbing potential. Routes on the shorter South and West faces were soon established. As Tahquitz became known as an

TAHQUITZ/SUICIDE 49

excellent "practice" area, the number of routes gradually increased. It was in the 1950's that rock climbing truly took off as a sport of its own, and several climbers from Los Angeles who climbed primarily at Tahquitz were instrumental in raising the standards of free climbing in California. In fact, the 1952 free ascent of the **Open Book** is considered the first 5.9 in America. And what is now widely referred to as the Yosemite Decimal System (YDS), was actually developed at Tahquitz during this period.

Tahquitz so dominated the early climbing scene that the smaller Suicide was not explored until 1966. Since then, the potential of Suicide was increasingly developed, so that by the mid 1970's, Suicide was at least as popular as Tahquitz itself. Numerous updatings of Chuck Wilts' guidebook have occured through the years, but by 1979, Wilts stated "this may be the last edition." The consensus seemed to be that the area was climbed out. Many of those who played important roles in its development now rarely climb here. In fact, excellent new routes continue to be established, albeit infrequently. And for those who have not climbed all 200 available routes, there is much to do at Tahquitz/Suicide.

CAMPING

Though many climbers stay illegally at the day use parking area (Humber Park), this is not a good idea. Best is the county-run Idyllwild Park Campground just outside of town. With restrooms, showers, hiking trails and boulders, this campground is worth its modest price. Up to eight people can share a site. Most climbers stay at the end of the road where some fine bouldering can be found. Reservations are occasionally necessary; call (714) 787-2553. Laundromats and all other facilities including a library can be found in town.

SEASONS AND WEATHER

Approximate Months	Typical Temperatures High	Low	Likelihood of Precipitation	Frequency of Climbable Days
Dec-Mar	40's	20's−	med-high	low-med
Apr-May	60's+	30's	low-med	med-high
Jun-Sep	80's−	40's	low	very high
Oct-Nov	70's−	30's+	low-med	high

Comments: Decrease the temperatures for north-facing Tahquitz routes, and increase them for south-facing Suicide routes.

RESTRICTIONS AND WARNINGS

Free wilderness permits are not required for rock climbing at Tahquitz or Suicide, but are necessary for any other hiking into the Wilderness Area. Obtain them at the Forest Service Ranger Station in the center of Idyllwild.

GUIDEBOOKS
Topo Guide to Tahquitz & Suicide (1980) by Randy Vogel. Available locally from Dee's Booknook and the Town Crier, in Idyllwild, or from Bonehead Publishing, 1252 Peacock Hill Drive, Santa Ana, CA 92705. *Tahquitz and Suicide Rocks* (1979) by Chuck Wilts, is available from some climbing stores nationwide and from The American Alpine Club, 113 East 90th St., New York, NY 10028

GUIDE SERVICES AND EQUIPMENT STORES
There are no local services.

EMERGENCY SERVICES
The nearest hospital is the Hemet Valley Hospital at 1116 E. Lataham Ave., Hemet; phone: 652-2811. For rescues call the Riverside County Sheriff: dial the operator, ask for Zenith 7-8000 or call the sheriff at the Banning Station (714) 849-6744. Litters for carrying injured people are located at the bottom of the Eagle's Nest Pinnacle and just right of the Sunshine Face at Suicide; also at the base of the South Face of Tahquitz.

GETTING THERE
There is no public transportation to Idyllwild.

The Fiend photo: Chris McDivitt

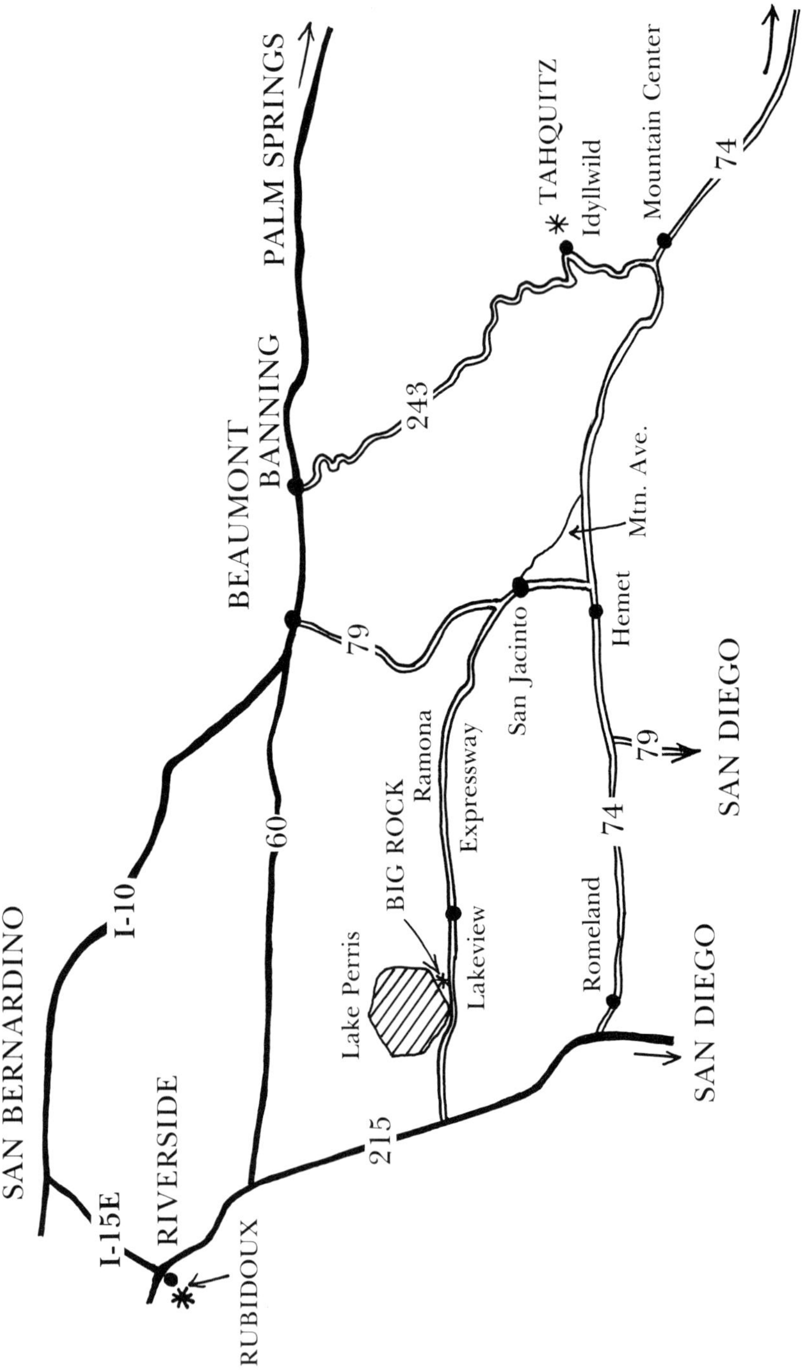

TAHQUITZ/SUICIDE

Tahquitz/Suicide

TAHQUITZ/SUICIDE

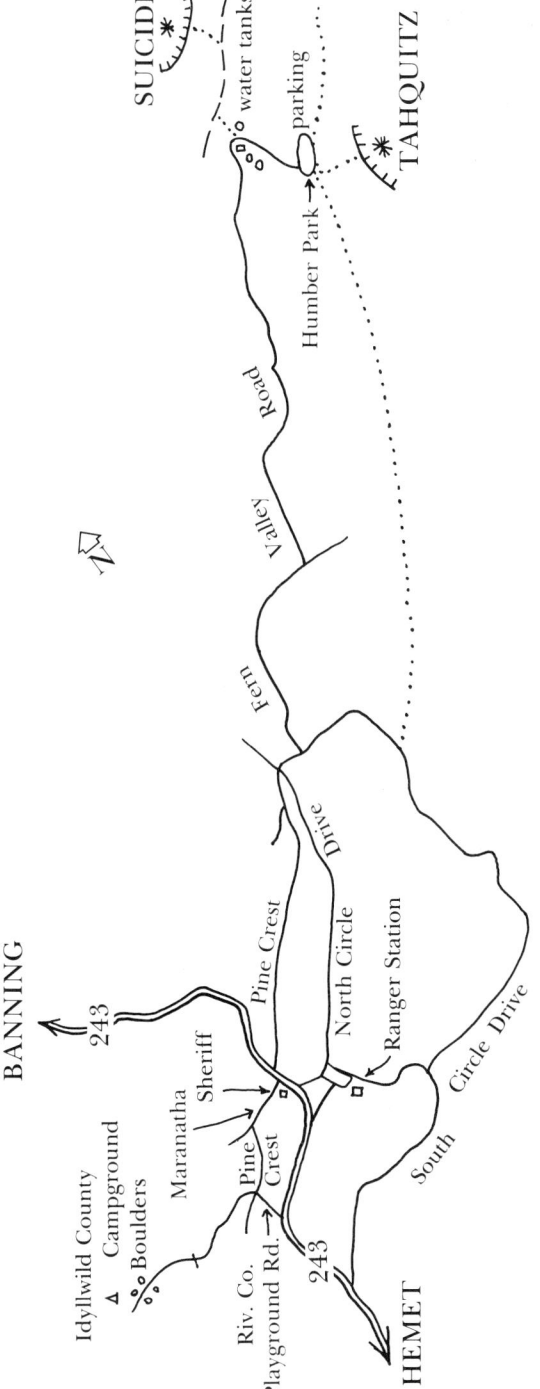

Tahquitz/Suicide

TAHQUITZ/SUICIDE

Suicide Rock

Suicide Rock - The Smooth Sole Wall

1 **The Fiend 5.9** Jim Wilson and Phil Warrender, 1972.

2 **Mickey Mantle 5.8+** Jim Wilson and Phil Warrender, 1972.

3 **The Ultimatum 5.10b** John Long and Gibb Lewis, 1972. Bring a long sling to tie off a knob.

Suicide Rock - The Sunshine Face

4 Paisano Overhang 5.12 or A3 Pat Callis and Charlie Raymond, 1968. FFA: John Long, 1973. Horizontal roof and a 4" crack.

5 Drain Pipe 5.7 A1 or 5.11 L. Harrell and Charlie Raymond. FFA: John Long and Richard Harrison, 1973.

6 The Iron Cross 5.11 Charlie Raymond and Pat Callis, 1968. FFA: Gibb Lewis and Tobin Sorenson, 1973.

7 Sundance 5.10b Pat Callis, Charlie Raymond and L. Herrill, 1967. Bring some larger nuts (to 3").

8 Valhalla 5.11 − Bud Couch, Larry Reynolds and Mike Dent, 1970. Probably the first 5.11 at Suicide.

9 Insomnia 5.11 Pat Callis and Larry Reynolds, 1967. FFA: Jim Erickson, 1972.

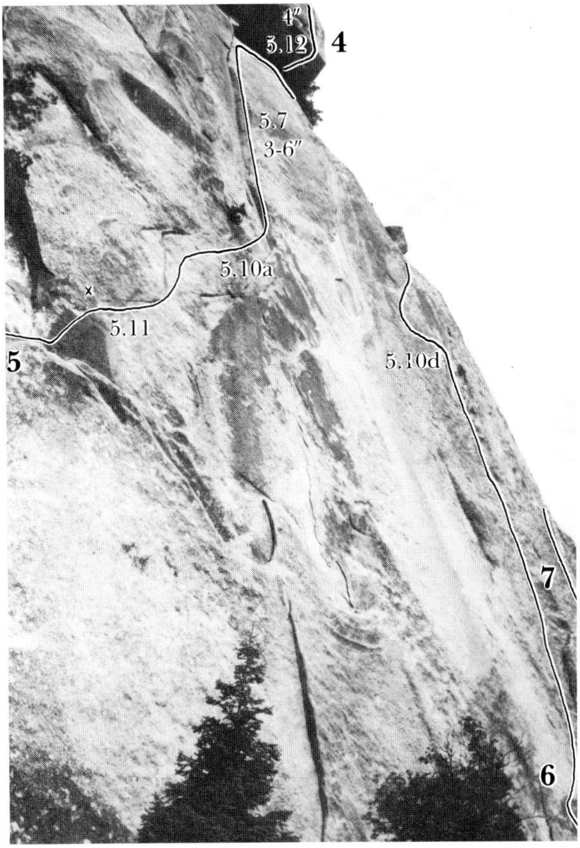

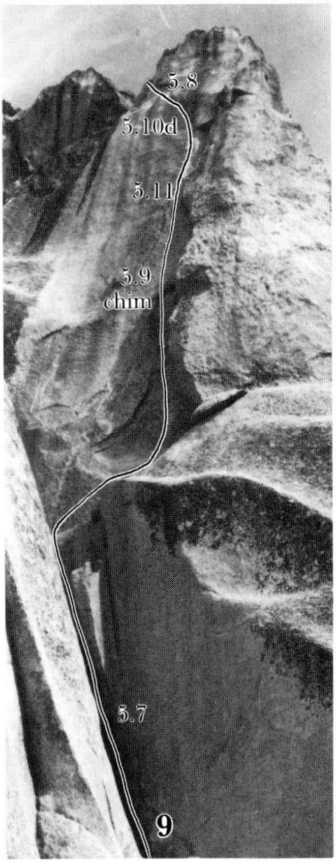

TAHQUITZ/SUICIDE

Suicide Rock - The Sunshine Face

Suicide Rock - The Weeping Wall

10 Surprise 5.8 (or 5.9) Pat Callis and Larry Reynolds, 1966. Variation: Pat Callis and Mike Dent, 1966. The first significant face route at Suicide, it is not nearly as difficult as it looks. Bring nuts.

11 Revelation 5.10a Bud Couch and Mike Dent, 1970. Very continuous face climbing.

12 Serpentine 5.9 Pat Callis and L. Harrell, 1967.

13 Ten Karat Gold 5.10a John Long, Richard Harrison, Rick Accomazzo and D. Watson, 1973. Continuous and runout on the last pitch.

14 Rebolting Development 5.11 D. Wert, M. Kaeser and G. Bander, 1971.

15 Delila 5.8 Pat Callis, Charlie Raymond and P. Raymond, 1968. Crack climb.

Suicide Rock - Northern Area

16 Flower of High Rank 5.9 Rob Muir and Mike Graham, 1972.

17 Graham Crackers 5.6 D. Lashier and P. Raymond, 1968. Crux on the second pitch.

18 The Guillotine 5.8 Allen Steck and Chuck Wilts, 1969. Second pitch is 5.7.

19 The Superfluous Bolt 5.10a Bud Couch, Mike Cohen and Mike Dent. Second pitch joins Guillotine, 5.7.

Tahquitz - North Face
20 Sahara Terror 5.7 William Shand, R. Gorin and P. Flinchbaugh, 1942.
21 The Swallow 5.8 Chuck Wilts and Royal Robbins, 1952.
22 The Consolation 5.9 John Mendenhall and Chuck Wilts, 1953. FFA: Royal Robbins and TM Herbert.
23 The Long Climb 5.7 Royal Robbins and Don Wilson, 1952.
24 The Illegitimate 5.9 TM Herbert and Royal Robbins, 1959.

Tahquitz - North Face

Tahquitz - Northwest Face, Left
25 From Bad Traverse 4th Bob Brinton and H. Fuller, 1939.
26 Super Pooper 5.10a Chuck Wilts, Don Wilson, John and Ruth Mendenhall, 1952. FFA: Bob Kamps and Mark Powell, 1967.
27 The Flakes 5.11 Royal Robbins and Don Wilson, 1953. FFA: John Long, Tobin Sorenson, Richard Harrison and William Antel.
28 The Vampire 5.10d Royal Robbins and Dave Rearick, 1959. FFA: John Long, Mike Graham, Rick Accomazzo and William Antel.
29 The Jam Crack/ Piton Pooper 5.7 (5.9 variation) Upper: R. Brinton and A. Johnson, 1936. FFA: Chuck and Ellen Wilts and S. Austin, 1949. Lower: Don Wilson and Royal Robbins, 1959.

Tahquitz - Northwest Face, Right
30 Human Fright 5.10a John Mendenhall and Royal Robbins, 1952.
31 Blanketty-Blank 5.10c Tom Frost and Harry Daley, 1959. FFA: Bob Kamps and Tom Higgins, 1963.
32 Fingertrip 5.7 Chuck Wilts, D. Gillespie and J. Rosenblatt, 1946.
33 Jensen's Jaunt 5.6 C. Jensen, J. Smith and D. MacDonald, 1938.
34 Traitor Horn 5.8 J. Smith, A. Johnson and M. Holton, 1938. FFA: R. Gorin and William Shand, c. 1941.

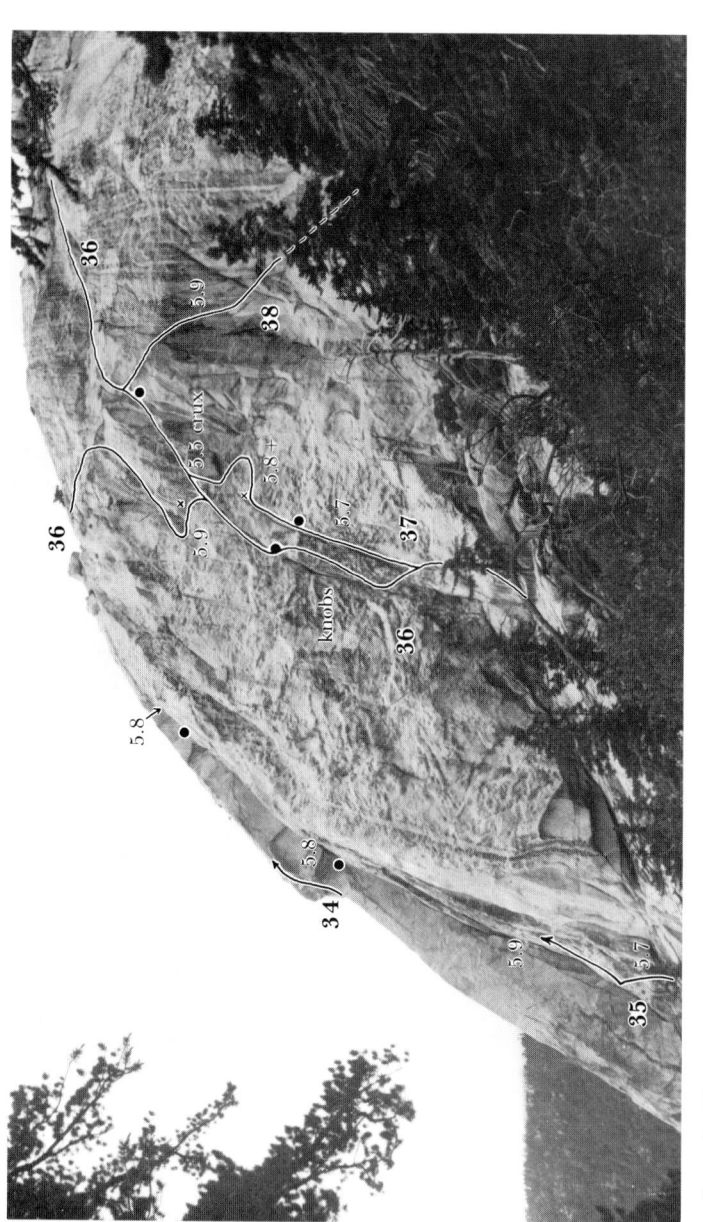

Tahquitz - South Face

35 Open Book 5.9 John Mendenhall and H. Sutherland, 1947. FFA: Royal Robbins and Don Wilson, 1952. Probably the first 5.9 in North America.

36 Left Ski Track 5.5 (and 5.9 variation) Chuck Wilts and R. Van Aken, 1947. Variation: Bob Kamps, Chuck Wilts and Mark and Beverly Powell. Vertical climbing on huge face holds.

37 Right Ski Track 5.8+ G. Harr and W. Dixon, 1957.

38 The Innominate 5.9 Chuck Wilts and G. Bloom, 1947. FFA: Royal Robbins and Jerry Gallwas.

Del Johns on Valhalla, Suicide Rock

Hidden Valley Campground and Old Woman Rock

Eric Perlman in a Joshua Tree Crack

JOSHUA TREE

HIGHLIGHTS
Joshua Tree National Monument has a special beauty of its own—small crags scattered almost randomly through the desert environment. Though foreigners often pass through the area in the mid-summer, most climbers come here to escape the cold of an otherwise unclimbable winter or spring. The rock is a coarse, sometimes painfully crystalline granite that provides numerous high quality crack, face and friction climbs among the more than 1,400 routes in the Monument. Camping is free and the campground is an excellent place to meet people and pick up partners.

CLIMBING
The crags in Joshua Tree resemble overgrown granite boulders twenty to 200 feet high. They come in all shapes, some with clean platelike rock, others with coarse, grainy rock that gives good friction by sinking its crystalline teeth into the climber's hands and feet. The short nature of the crags permits most routes to be climbed—depending on one's mood or boldness—top-roped, lead climbed, or free soloed. All three styles are commonly practiced, though most routes are led. Indeed, the short routes allow one to push harder on the lead than one is often willing to do on a big climb. To counteract the painful nature of the rough rock, some climbers protect the back of their hands with tape. Finger tips simply go raw before toughening into leather. While there are many crack climbs at Joshua Tree, friction and small edge climbing are also common.

ENVIRONMENT

The pleasure of climbing in Joshua Tree is in large measure due to its weird and wonderful environment. The low angle light of winter combines with the bizarre contortions of the Joshua Trees and the strangely shaped rocks that lie scattered over the open Mojave desert to create a colorful and friendly atmosphere that is as much a joy to explore as to climb in.

Winter can be surprisingly cold—it may even snow—but within a few days things are usually back to normal: days that start with frost but quickly warm to pleasant climbing temperatures. Spring and fall provide the most consistent weather for climbing, and when the weather in Yosemite is poor, a VW van convoy might be spotted on its way to Joshua Tree. During the week one will find climbers from around the world, but open space remains plentiful. On weekends the Los Angeles crowd moves in to queue for the popular routes.

CLIMBING HISTORY

Until recently, climbing histories placed only a few disparate groups from Los Angeles climbing at Joshua Tree National Monument during the 1950's and 1960's and held that standards lagged well behind those at nearby Tahquitz, where a technical revolution was taking place. In

JOSHUA TREE

fact, many of the leading climbers at Tahquitz were also climbing at Joshua Tree, doing free ascents of many of the routes whose first recorded ascents were made years later with aid.

The publication of the first climber's guide in 1970 alerted a broader public to the potential of the area. Soon the warm winter weather lured a regular contingent of climbers that rapidly expanded into an international group. Joshua Tree is still popular among travelling climbers as a hang-out until the weather improves sufficiently for them to move into Yosemite.

Most new routes are put up on the weekends by climbers from Southern California; many are at the top of the difficulty spectrum. Joshua Tree is still a place for considerable new route exploration and development—150 to 200 new routes are done every year. Some locals even choose to free solo most of their climbs, including 5.12's. Local phenomena include "Half Dome days" (2,000 feet of climbing—usually unroped and above 5.10) and "El Cap days" (3,000 feet of climbing in a day).

CAMPING

Most climbers stay at the Hidden Valley Campground (different from the nearby "real" Hidden Valley where many climbs are found). Indeed, climbers often outnumber tourists, providing a concentration of kindred spirits rarely found outside of Camp 4 in Yosemite. Fortunately, the campground holds campers far more discreetly than Camp 4—avoiding the Yosemite ghetto appearance. There is a fourteen day camping limit at Hidden Valley that is often strictly enforced. Joshua Tree camping is free, but one must bring water and firewood. The towns of Joshua Tree and Twenty-nine Palms, located about fifteen miles away are the only sources of food, showers, laundry, and all other services.

SEASONS AND WEATHER

Approximate Months	Typical Temperatures		Likelihood of Precipitation	Frequency of Climbable Days
	High	Low		
Dec-Feb	60's	30's−	low	high
Mar-May	80's	40's	very low	very high
Jun-Sep	100's	70's−	low	low-med
Oct-Nov	80's−	50's−	low	very high

Comments: Snow and wind are possible in winter and early spring.

RESTRICTIONS AND WARNINGS

The prickly dangers of both cacti and rattlesnakes can be avoided with a little caution.

GUIDEBOOKS
Joshua Tree Climber's Guide (1984) by Randy Vogel. This is available from climbing stores or Bonehead Publishing, 1252 Peacock Hill Drive, Santa Ana, CA 92705. Also available in some stores: *A Climber's Guide to Joshua Tree National Monument* (1979) by John Wolfe and Bob Dominick.

GUIDE SERVICES AND EQUIPMENT STORES
No equipment stores are available, but the California Mountaineering School can provide guiding. They are reached at Box 1099, Joshua Tree, CA 92252; telephone: (619) 366-9452. Big-5 Sporting Goods in Palm Springs sells a limited selection of climbing hardware.

EMERGENCY SERVICES
The nearest hospital is the High Desert Memorial Hospital, next to the Sheriff Station at 6601 Whitefeather Road, Joshua Tree. For rescue assistance, visit the ranger station if other climbers cannot help.

GETTING THERE
Greyhound Bus Lines serves Palm Springs, from which the High Desert Stage can be taken to Joshua Tree and Twenty-nine Palms. From there it is necessary to hitch-hike. The nearest airport is in Palm Springs.

Beth Bennett on Run For Your Life, Tumbling Rainbow Rock

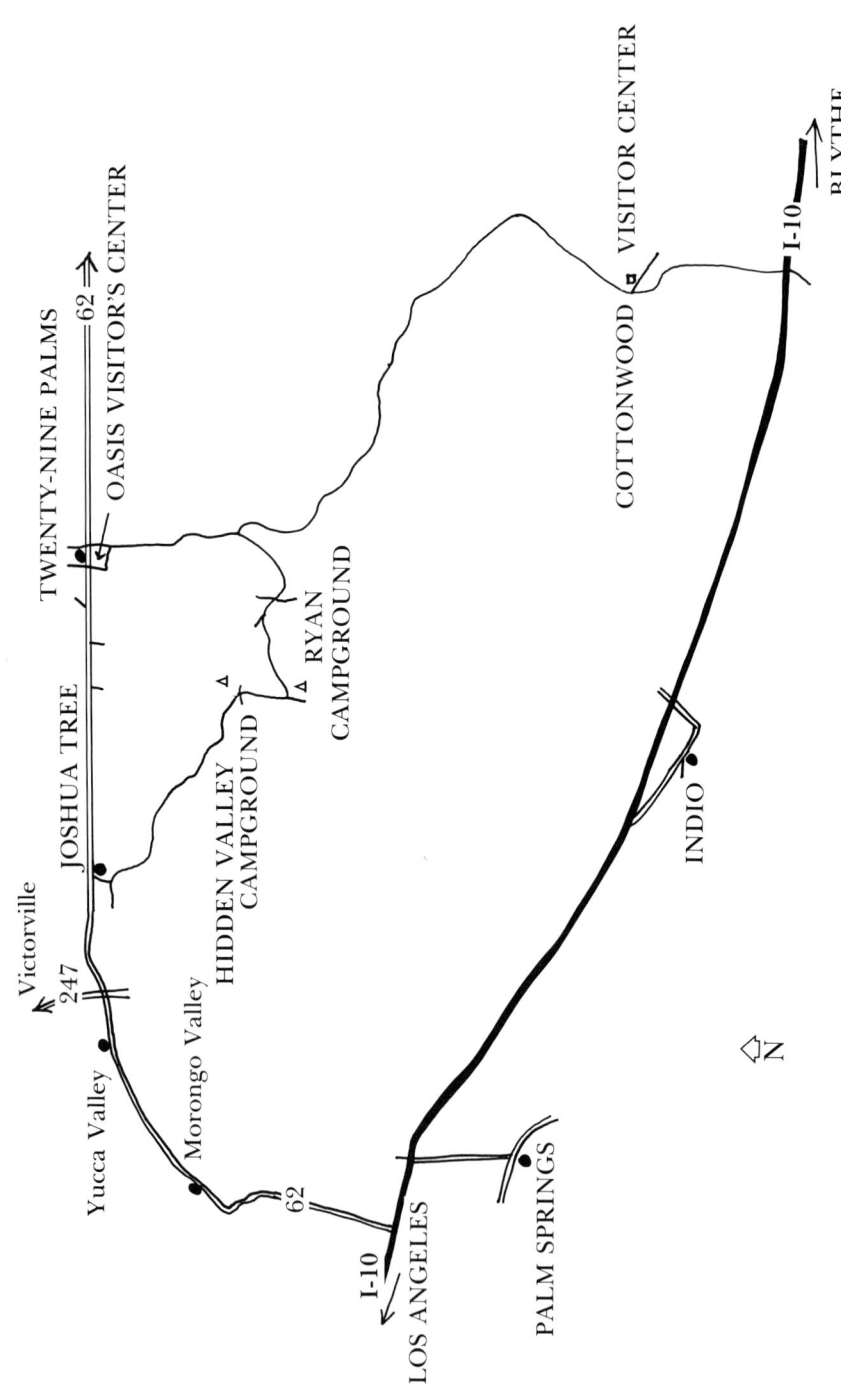

JOSHUA TREE

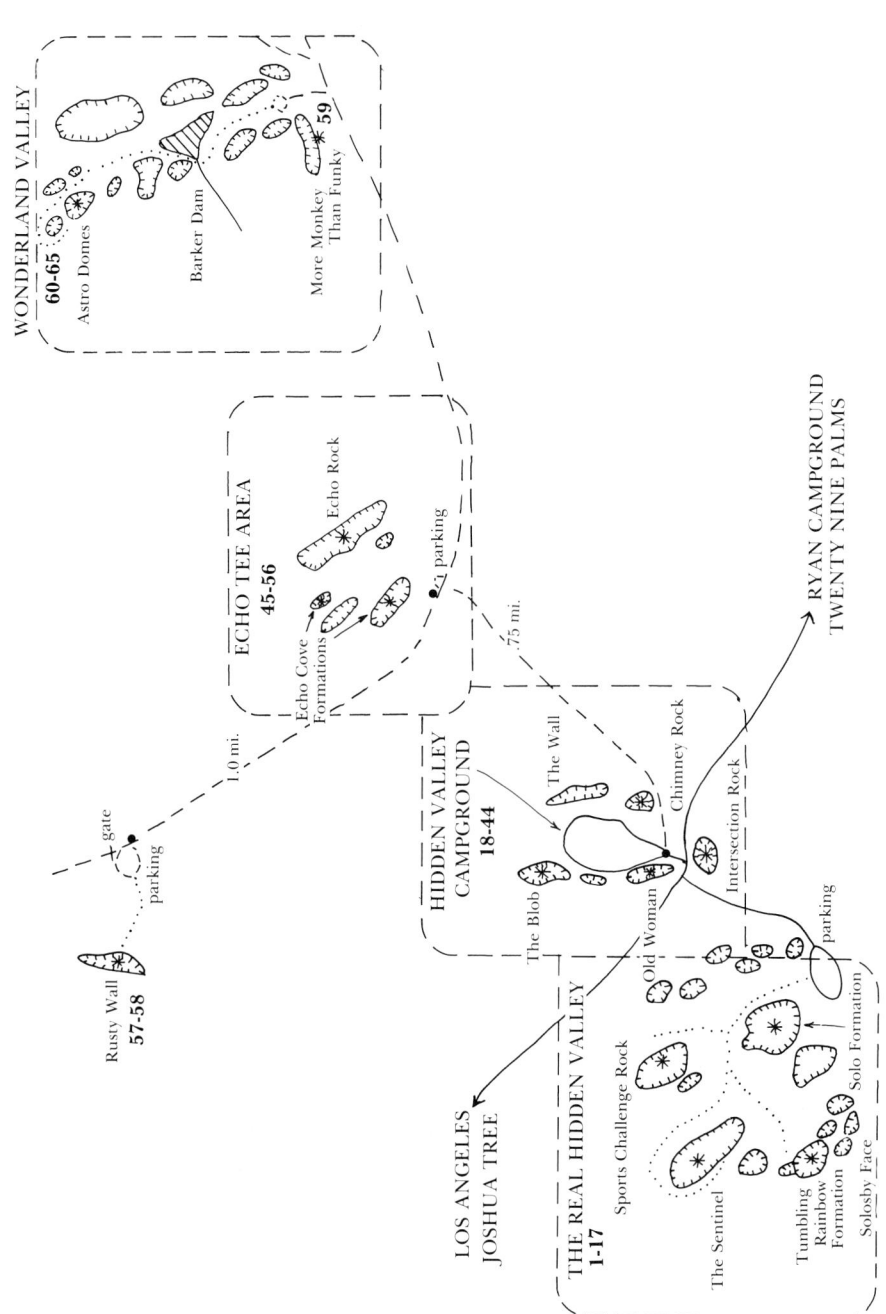

Joshua Tree National Monument

74   JOSHUA TREE

The Real Hidden Valley

The Real Hidden Valley

JOSHUA TREE

Solo Formation
1 In the Pit 5.10c
2 Semi Tough 5.11a

Solosby Face
Shady and cool top rope climbing
3 Solosby 5.10b
4 Latin Swing 5.11c
5 Bebop Tango 5.11a

Tumbling Rainbow Formation
6 **Run For Your Life** 5.10b
7 **Tumbling Rainbow** 5.9 John Long, Richard Harrison, Rick Accomazzo and Ging Gingrich, 1973.
8 **Rainy Day Dream Away** 5.11 top rope
9 **Fisticuffs** 5.10b John Long and Rick Accomazzo, 1973.

JOSHUA TREE

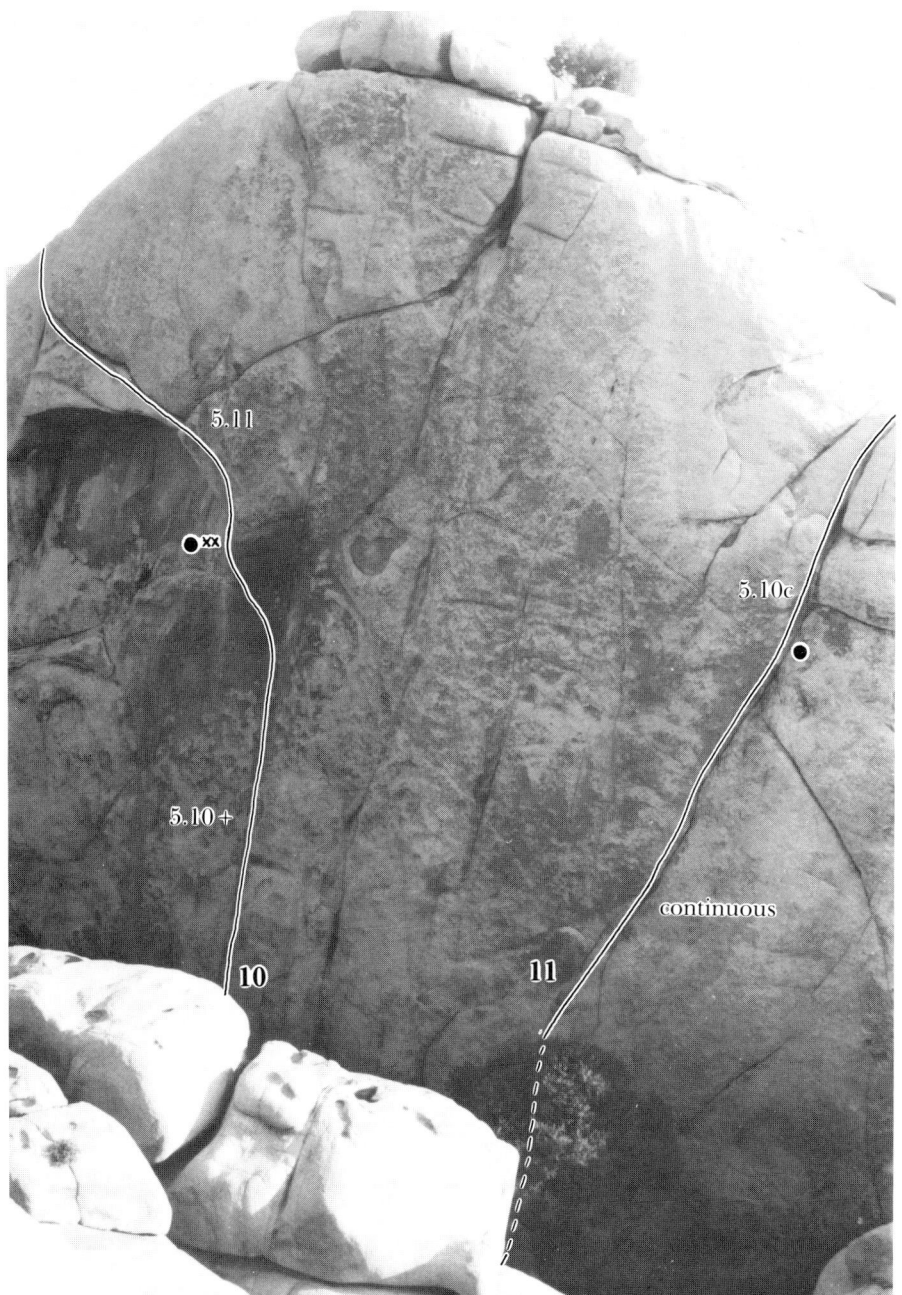

The Sentinel
10 Desert Song 5.11 John Bachar, 1977.
11 Illusion Dweller 5.10c Matt Cox, Spencer Lennard and Gary Ayres, 1973. Can be done as one pitch.

Sports Challenge Rock
12 Sphincter Quits 5.9 Dave Evans and Randy Vogel, 1978.
13 Top Rope 5.10d
14 Ride a Wild Bago 5.10a Randy Vogel and Dave Evans, 1978.
15 Clean and Jerk 5.10b Kevin Powell and Dan Ahlborn.
16 Dick Enberg 5.10d
17 Leave It To Beaver 5.12 Dave Evans and Jim Angione, 1978. FFA: John Bachar, 1978 top rope. A popular top rope problem, occasionally led or free soloed.

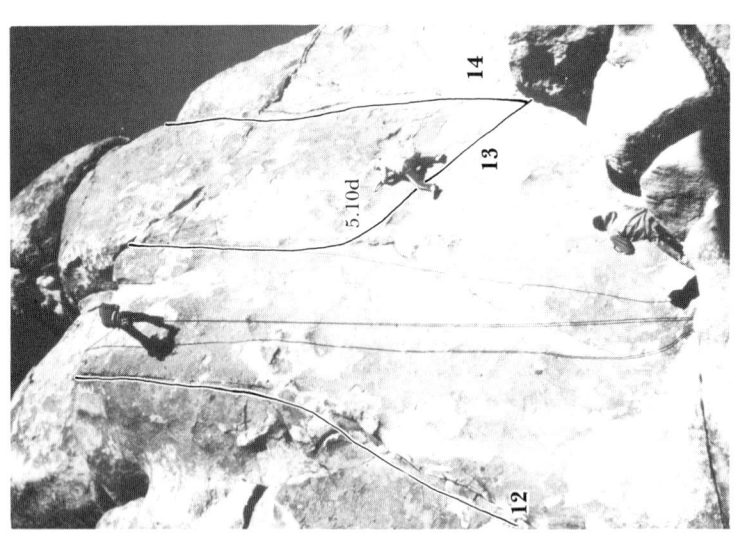

JOSHUA TREE

Tourist spectators at Intersection Rock photo: Tom Rogers

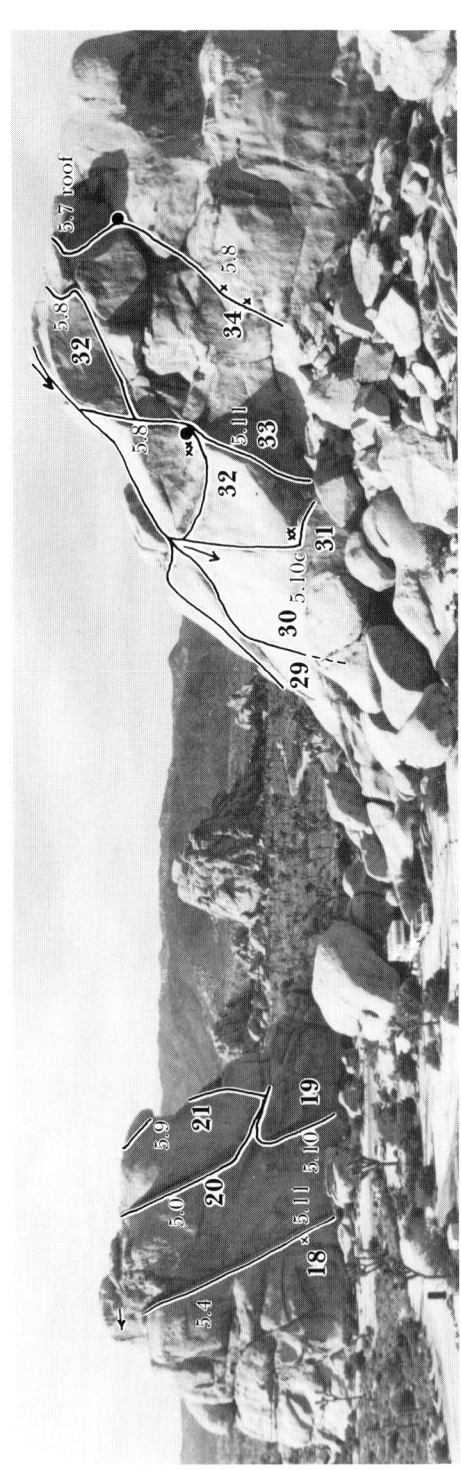

HIDDEN VALLEY CAMPGROUND
Intersection Rock
18 **Left Ski Track Direct 5.11** John Bachar and John Long, 1973.
19 **Right Ski Track Direct 5.10b** Al Ruiz and Rich Wolfe, 1966. FFA: John Long and Oliver Moon, 1972.
20 **Upper Right Ski Track 5.0**
21 **North Overhang 5.9** John Wolfe and Howard Weamer, 1969. FFA: John Long and Rick Accomazzo, 1972.
22 **Overhang Bypass 5.7** FFA: John Wolfe and Howard Weamer, 1972.
23 **The Flake 5.8** Dick Webster and Woody Stark, to top of flake, 1967; Jim Wilson and Dick Shockley, upper face, 1971.
24 **Billabong 5.10c** John Wolfe and Al Ruiz, 1969. FFA: John Long, Bill Antel and Rick Accomazzo, 1973.

Old Woman Rock
25 **Dogleg 5.8** John and Rich Wolfe. FFA: Dick Webster, Bill Briggs and Woody Stark, 1967.
26 **Double Cross 5.7** John, Rich and Mike Wolfe, 1967. FFA: Woody Stark, Dick Webster and Bill Briggs, 1967.
27 **Orphan 5.9** FFA: John Wolfe and Al Ruiz, 1970.
28 **Dandelion 5.10a** Don O'Kelley and Dave Davis, 1971. FFA: John Long, Richard Harrison, Kevin Worrall, Bill Antel, Rick Accomazzo, John Bald and America Pizzo.

JOSHUA TREE

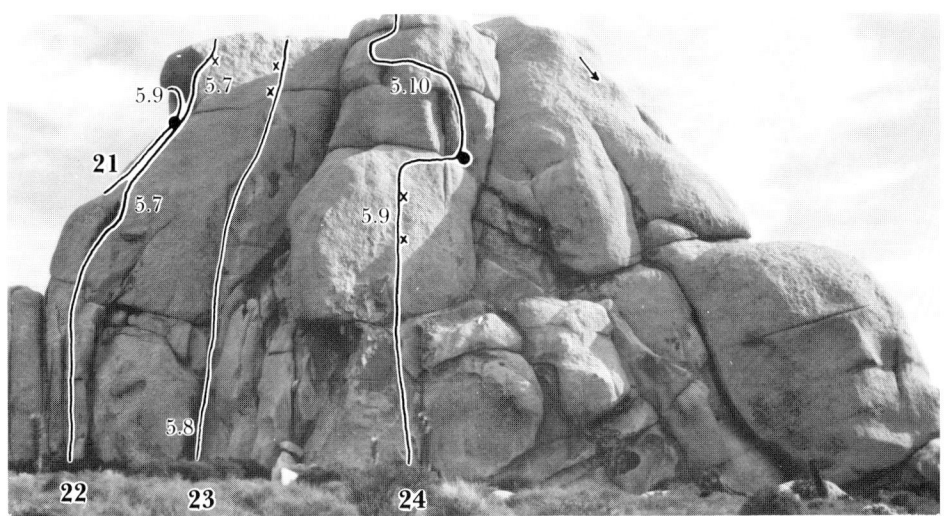

HIDDEN VALLEY CAMPGROUND
Old Woman Rock
29 Toe Jam 5.7 Kevin Smith and Dick Webster, 1959.
30 Judas 5.10b John Wolfe, 1967. FFA: John Long and Oliver Moon, 1972.
31 Bearded Cabbage 5.10c John Long and Richard Harrison, 1973.
32 Spider 5.8 John Svenson and George Karsh, 1968. FFA: Don O'Kelley, 1969.
33 Spider Line 5.11 Woody Stark and Dick Webster, 1967. FFA: John Yablonski, free solo, 1978. Usually top-roped.
34 Deviate with Geronimo finish 5.8 Dick Webster, Dick James and John Wolfe, 1969. Geronimo finish: Phil Haney, Mokri and Bob Dominick, 1970.

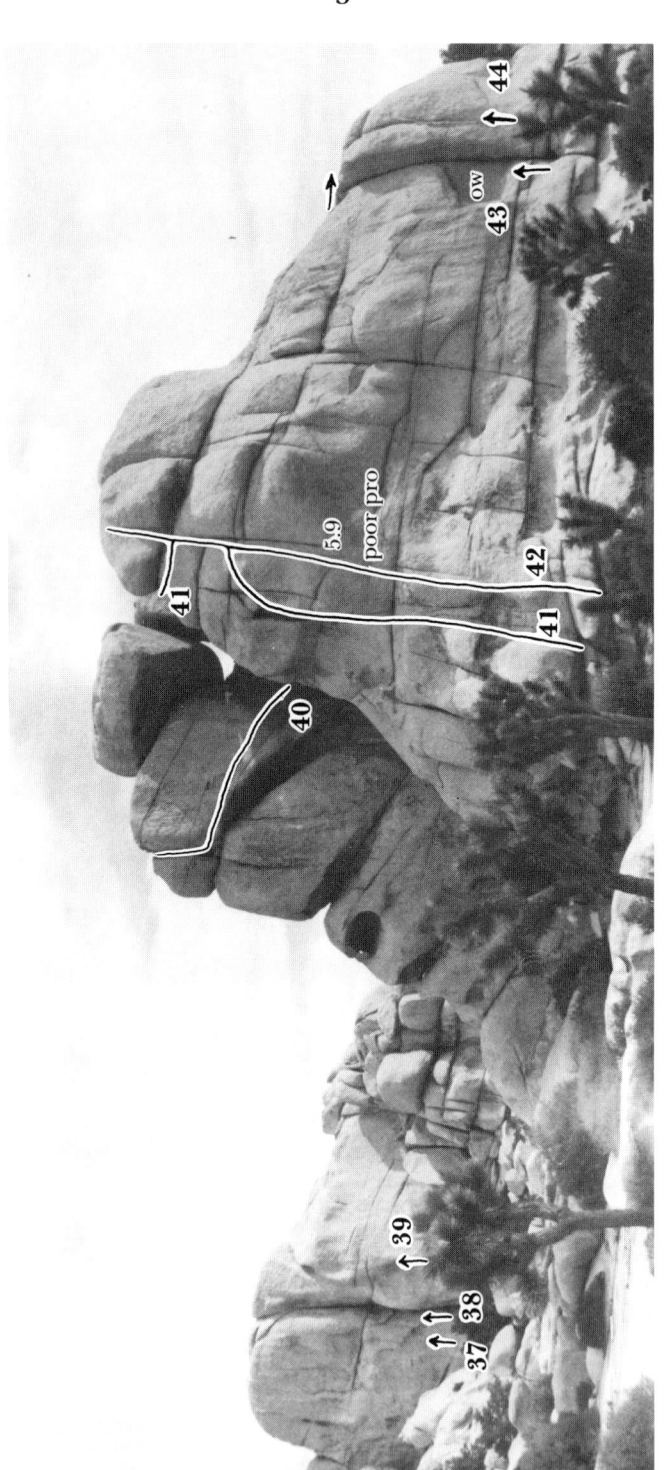

HIDDEN VALLEY CAMPGROUND
The Wall

37 **Good to the Last Drop 5.9** Mike Waugh, Jan McCollum and Dave Houser, 1977. Three bolts.
38 **Damn Jam 5.6** Dick Webster, Bill Briggs and Woody Stark, 1967. Bolt at crux.
39 **Chalk Up Another One 5.9** Jan McCollum, Hank Levine and Dave Houser, 1978. Bolt protection.

Chimney Rock

40 **Loose Lips 5.11** Tobin Sorenson, Gibb Lewis and Dean Fidelman, 1975. FFA: unknown.
41 **West Face Overhang 5.7**
42 **Ballet 5.9** John Wolfe and Dick Webster, 1970. FFA: Tobin Sorenson and Gibb Lewis, 1975.
43 **Damper 5.9**
44 **Pinched Rib 5.8** Roy Naasz, 1973. Bolt protection.

HIDDEN VALLEY CAMPGROUND
The Blob
35 Papa Woolsey 5.10b Mark Powell, 1972. Bolt protected.
36 Surrealistic Pillar 5.10b Craig Parsley.

ECHO TEE AREA
Echo Cove Formation
45 Halfway to Paradise 5.10a Herb Laeger, Mike Waugh, Jan McCollum and Dennis Knuckles, 1978. One bolt.
46 Effigy Too 5.10a Matt Cox and Dave Evans, 1975.
47 Touch and Go 5.9 Matt Cox, Bobby Kessinger and Dan Ahlborn, 1976.

JOSHUA TREE

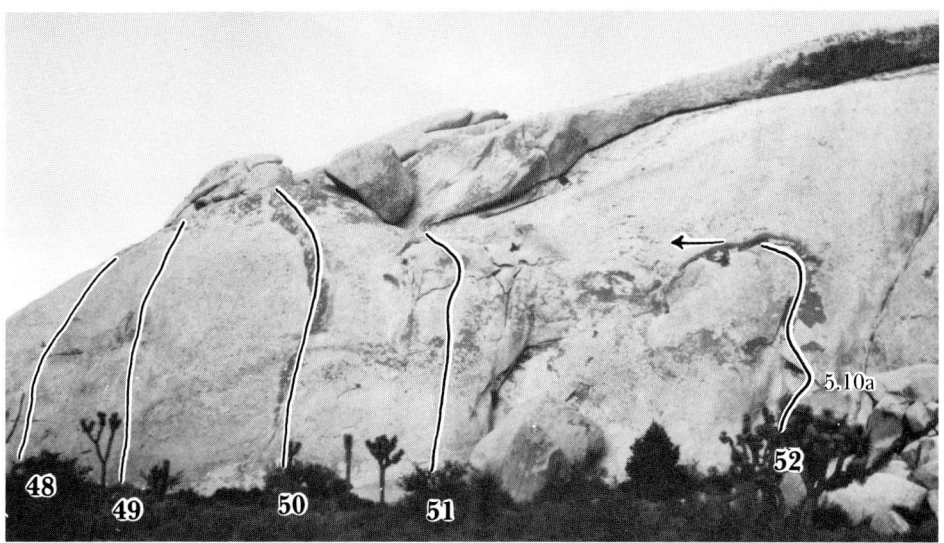

ECHO TEE AREA
Echo Rock
48 Double Dip 5.7 Chris Gonzalez and Mona Wolfe, 1973. Bolt protected above flake.
49 Try Again 5.10c Bill Antel, Darrell Hensel and Bobby Kessinger, 1976. Three bolts in lower section.
50 Black Tide 5.7 Ken Stichter and John Wolfe, 1972. Four bolts.
51 Stick to What 5.9 Mike Jaffe and Larry Thaxton, 1974. Four bolts.
52 Heart and Sole 5.10a Herb Laeger, Rich Smith and Jai Watts, 1978. Bolt protected to flake.

ECHO TEE AREA
Echo Rock
53 EBGB's 5.10c Dave Houser, Mike Waugh, Jan McCollum and Nick Badyrka, 1977.
54 Pope's Crack 5.9 Craig Parsley and Mike Pope, 1975.
55 Swept Away 5.11 Dave Evans and Randy Vogel, 1977. Bolts on route.
56 T.S. Special 5.9 Mike Graham, Rick Accomazzo, Tobin Sorenson, Pete Wilkening and Jim Wilson, 1973. Very runout after the crux.

JOSHUA TREE

Rusty Wall

Rusty Wall
57 Wangerbanger 5.11+ Tobin Sorenson, 1975.
58 O'Kelley's Crack 5.10c Don O'Kelley, 1974. FFA: Tobin Sorenson, Jim Wilson, Dean Fidelman and Gary Ayres, 1975.

JOSHUA TREE

Dan Michael and Beth Bennett on O'Kelley's Crack

WONDERLAND VALLEY
59 More Monkey Than Funky 5.11b John Bachar, 1976. Usually top-roped.

Barney Sheafor climbing

JOSHUA TREE

WONDERLAND VALLEY
South Astro Domes
60 Hex Marks the Root 5.7

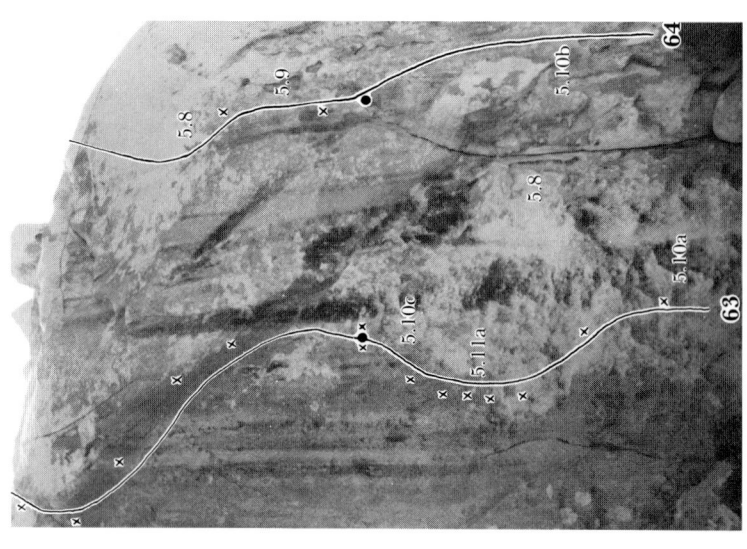

WONDERLAND VALLEY
South Astro Dome

61 My Laundry 5.9 Jim Wilson and Herb Laeger, 1976.

62 Solid Gold 5.10a Herb Laeger, Jon Lonne, Jim Wilson and Mike Jaffe, 1977.

63 Such a Savage 5.11a Spencer Lennard and Craig Fry, 1977.

64 Piggle Pug 5.10b Spencer Lennard and Chris Robbins, 1977.

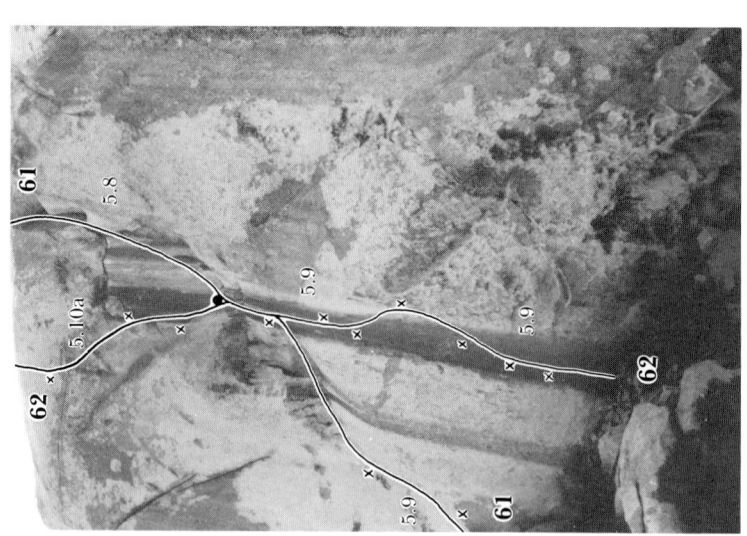

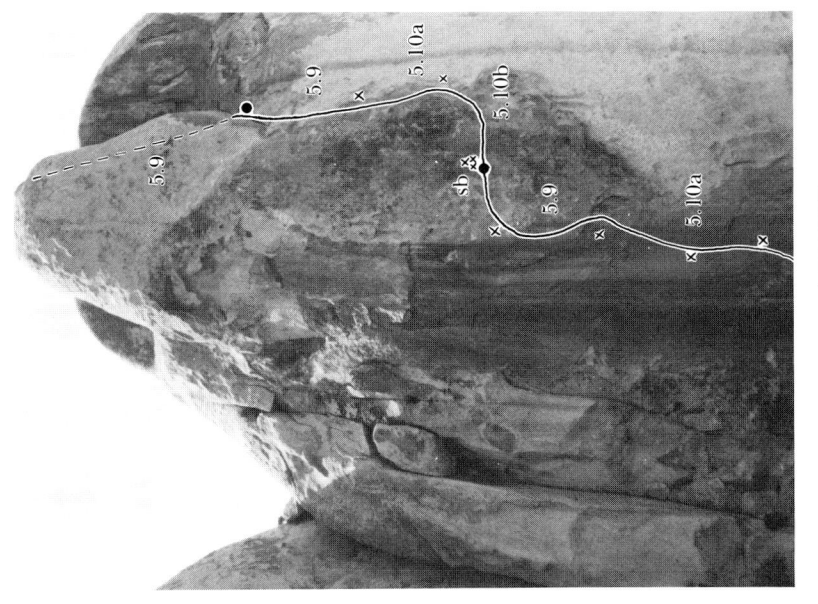

**WONDERLAND VALLEY
North Astro Dome
65 Figures on a Landscape 5.10a** Randy Vogel and Dave Evans, 1978.

Eric Perlman on Illusion Dweller

NEEDLES

The Needles from the lookout on Magician Needle

NEEDLES

HIGHLIGHTS
Superb granite, thrust steeply out of a forested hillside characterizes the Needles, offering tremendous views and unsurpassed crack and face climbing of all difficulties. Nearby Dome Rock adds a number of interesting routes, including many that follow giant knobs that can be tied off for protection. Climbs average around 400 feet, though a thousand foot low angle face does exist. In addition, this impeccable climbing is set in the beautiful coniferous forests of the southern Sierra Nevada. With a lovely approach hike, a mild climate, and quiet, scenic camping, the Needles are a great destination.

CLIMBING
The Needles are ten semi-independent summits, each with at least two good-sized faces exposed to view. Since they sit on a hillside, a pinnacle summit may be reached by routes that can vary tremendously in length—from as few as two to as many as twelve pitches in length. The vast majority of routes, however, lie in the three to six pitch range, and climb east and west faces. Though most routes follow crack systems up steep walls, some hard climbs have been worked out on the few sections of cliff without a crack. Free climbing is almost the rule at the Needles, with excellent crack climbs from 5.5 to 5.12 in difficulty, though CLEAN aid can be employed on the harder routes by those not quite up to the standard.

The approach is a gentle walk of about two and one-half miles from the car, along a scenic ridge which leads to and then through the Needles. Descents are generally made by rappel down the shorter, "uphill" side of the rock.

The route descriptions in this book are less detailed than usual. This is to keep in character with the Needles guidebook which seeks to maintain the heightened sense of adventure befitting this wild area.

Dome Rock is separate from, but even easier to approach, than the Needles. Since the Dome protrudes from the hillside, one can simply walk from the car down around to the front. Confronting the climber at this point is a cliff 400 feet high by 800 feet long. It can be subdivided into several sections, each with its own character: low angle, steep & plastered with knobs of all sizes, mixed knobs and cracks, and almost blank. For Dome Rock, one should carry a number of light slings for tying-off knobs—9/16" webbing is ideal.

ENVIRONMENT

From the freeway, two hours of driving up a winding, paved mountain road leads through chapparal covered hillsides and into the coniferous trees of Sequoia National Forest. At about 8,000 feet in elevation, the Needles protrude from a long and narrow ridgetop—permitting panoramic views of the distant Sierras and forested hills. Other than a road that snakes up the Kern River valley below, no sign of human activity can be seen from the cliffs. The open forests permit pleasant walking almost anywhere, and a few trails can provide long hikes—including into the Golden Trout Wilderness Area. Streams large enough for fishing do flow through the region, but are not close enough to the climbing for very convenient access unless one camps below the Needles near the Kern River.

In evening light, the golden-colored granite of the Needles takes on a magical appearance befitting the names of the individual Needles: Magician, Sorcerer, Wizard, Warlock, Voodoo,.... Winter temperatures are sometimes mild enough to permit climbing on sundrenched faces reached by several miles of ski touring from the end of the plowed road. But since it is normally fairly cold, very little climbing is done in that season. During the spring, summer and fall, temperatures are generally comfortable, though wind can sometimes be a problem.

CLIMBING HISTORY

Because of its distance from established California climbing centers, it was not until the 1960's before the Needles were explored by climbers and most of the summits reached. It was not until 1969 that more serious routes were attempted. During the early 70's a gradually increasing number of ascents were made, and with the publication of a glowing article about the area in 1974, more climbers filtered into this mysterious place. A small number of people, however, dominated the first ascent list until the publication of the first guidebook in 1983. That the area received many routes of the highest standards testifies to the quality of its climbing: news about this area spread by word of mouth among an small group of climbers, many of whom lived within a three hour drive of the climbs. By 1983 the guidebook recorded two dozen routes from 5.11 to 5.12. Part of the allure of the Needles is its peaceful remoteness from the climbing masses—including the fact that one can leave a rack of Friends safely at the base of a route, to be retrieved hours later. It is hoped that visitors will respect this tradition.

CAMPING

Several camping locations are available, each with a radically different character. For maximum convenience to the Needles, the best choices are either at Needles Springs—the end of the dirt road, where there is an excellent flat and open area—or at the Needles themselves—which involves carrying one's water and equipment in for two and one-half miles, but which is rewarded by maximum exposure to the beauty of the Needles. Neither site has water of any kind. Another free site is the Peppermint campground. It is within walking distance of Dome Rock, but is least convenient to the Needles themselves. All of these campsites require free fire permits for any open fires—see Restrictions and Warnings. The Quaking Aspen Campground is the most comprehensive in the area and is the only camping with potable water; it also charges Forest Service rates. A final choice involves completely different access considerations. It is possible to camp on the Kern River valley road BELOW the Needles. From a fisherman's perspective, this is best. But for climbers to reach the rocks, it involves a strenuous uphill hike on faint game trails. Nevertheless, camping down by the river is a popular alternative. The Ponderosa Lodge, between the Needles and Dome Rock, offers several amenities, including a grocery store, restaurant, and gas station. It does not have showers or laundry facilities (except for guests at the lodge).

SEASONS AND WEATHER

Approximate Months	Typical Temperatures High	Low	Likelihood of Precipitation	Frequency of Climbable Days
Nov-Apr	40's	20's	medium	low
May-Jun	60's+	30's	medium	high
Jul-Aug	80's−	50's	low	very high
Sep-Aug	70's−	30's	med-low	high

RESTRICTIONS AND WARNINGS

Campfire permits are required for all sites except the Quaking Aspen Campground. They may be obtained from the U.S. Forest Service in Springville, California Hot Springs, Kernville, or Bakersfield. The Forest Service maintains regular business hours during the week and is closed on Sunday.

Rattlesnakes are found in the area, but are not common.

GUIDEBOOKS

Stonemasher Rockclimbing Guide to the Kern River Canyon and Environs (1983) by E.C. Joe and Dick Leversee. It is available from E.C. Joe, P.O. Box 1164, Tehachapi, CA 93561.

GUIDE SERVICES AND EQUIPMENT STORES

No services are available locally. Bigfoot Mountaineering, at 2594 Brundage Lane in Bakersfield, is the nearest complete climbing equipment store.

EMERGENCY SERVICES

The nearest hospital is the Sierra View District Hospital at 465 W. Putnam Ave, Porterville; phone: 784-1110. For rescues, contact the Tulare County Sheriff by calling (209) 784-4670.

GETTING THERE

Public transportation will take you to Bakersfield or Porterville (Greyhound or Orange Belt Stagelines), but from there one must rent a car or hitch-hike a lightly travelled road. By car one has a choice: access from Porterville on the north or through Lake Isabella on the south. The southern road is much less contorted and makes for more pleasant driving.

Airy Interlude photo: Adele Hammond

NEEDLES

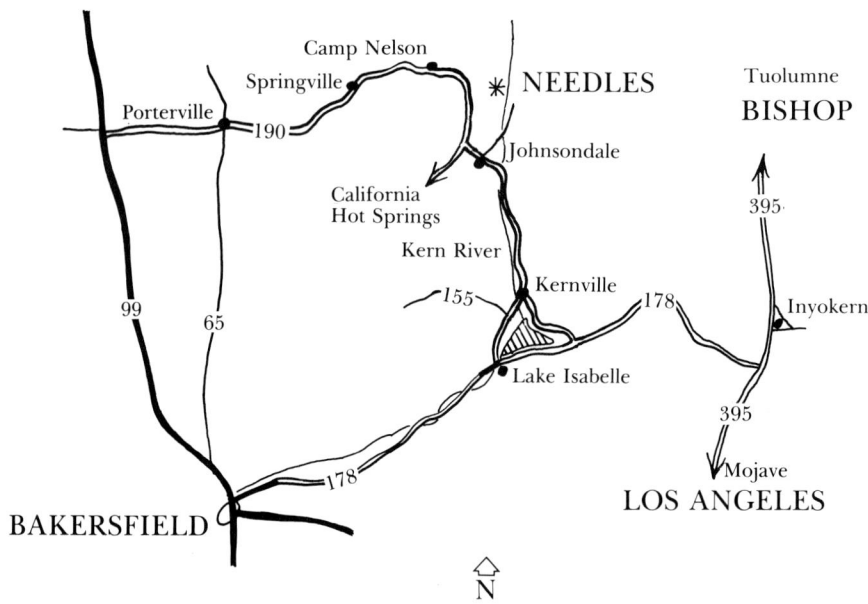

Needles

NEEDLES

Needles

The Needles
A Magician Needle
B Djin Needle
C Wizard Needle
D Sorcerer Needle (Routes 2-4)
E Charlatan Needle (Routes 5-6)
F Witch Needle (Routes 7-11)
G Warlock Needle (Routes 12-16)
H Necromancer Needle
I Voodoo Dome (Routes 18-19)

The Needles

NEEDLES 103

Dome Rock photo: U.S Dept. of Agriculture

Magician Needle photo: Patrick Paul
1 Black Magic IV 5.8 Greg Bender and Phil Warrender, 1974.

Sorcerer Needle

2 Don Juan Wall III 5.11 or A1 Ed Ehrenfeldt and Mike Pope, 1976. FFA: Mike Waugh, Tony Yaniro and Randy Leavitt, 1981.

3 Thin Ice III 5.10 Dennis Johnson and Ted Heath, 1975. FFA: Pete Steres and Paul Clark, 1976.

4 Atlantis III 5.11 Randy Leavitt and Tony Yaniro, 1981.

Charlatan Needle

5 Spooky II 5.8 Rich Smith and Herb Laeger, 1976. Bring a 4" nut and long slings.

6 Horrorscope II 5.9 Paul Clark and Charlie Manfredi, 1977.

Witch Needle
7 North Face I 5.5 Mike and BJ Heath, 1970. The rappel route.
8 Airy Interlude II 5.9 Eve Viga and Pete Steres, 1976. Bring a 4" nut.
9 Igor Unchained II 5.9 Herb Laeger and Paul Clark, 1976. Bring a 4" nut and 165' rope.
10 Spook Book III 5.10+ Bob Kamps and Herb Laeger, 1978. Bring many small nuts.
11 Innersanctum III 5.8/5.9 Fred Beckey, David Black and Steve Eddy, 1974.

Warlock Needle
12 The Howling II 5.8/5.9
Herb Laeger, Eve Viga and Mike Jaffe, 1981.

Witch Needle

White Punks on Dope, Voodoo Dome photo: Eddie Joe collection

NEEDLES

Warlock Needle

Warlock Needle

Warlock Needle
13 The 'S' Crack IV 5.9 Herb Laeger and Dick Saum, 1976.
14 South Face IV 5.9 Fred Beckey, Dan McHale and Mike Heath, 1970. FFA: Jeff Dozier, Steve Gerdsen and David Black, 1976.
15 Fate in Place III 5.10 Kevin Lindgren, Chris Bort and Dick Leversee, 1977.
16 The Spell II 5.9 Paul Clark and Pete Steres, 1976. Bring large nuts to 5".

Necromancer Needle
17 No More Mr. Nice Guy III 5.10 Mike Lechlinski, Tom Gilje, Randy Vogel, Dave Evans, Mari Gingery and Maria Cranor, 1982.

Voodoo Dome

18 White Punks on Dope III 5.8 Todd Burrill, Dick Leversee, EC Joe and Scott Edmiaston, 1976. Considered by some to be the finest moderate route in Southern California.

19 The Skull III 5.11 Charles Haas and Greg Cloutier, 1974. FFA: Tobin Sorenson and Dean Fidelman, 1976. Bring extra medium nuts and long slings.

Michael Forkash on Tobin's Dihedral, Dome Rock photo: Forkash

NEEDLES

Dome Rock

NEEDLES

Dome Rock

20 Between Nothingness and Eternity III 5.10+ Eric Erickson and Dick Leversee, 1979. Continuously difficult face climbing. Bring knob tie-off slings and a 165' rope. Nuts are not needed.

21 Tobin's Dihedral III 5.10+ Tobin Sorenson. Sustained and strenuous offwidth. Many extra large nuts to 5".

22 The Arch Bitch-Up (right crack) **III 5.8** First ascent unknown.

23 Windjammer II 5.9 Neil Carlos, Dick Leversee, Herb and Eve Laeger, 1975. Protection for the first pitch is tied off knobs. Bring many tie-off slings and a 165' rope.

24 The Spectrum II 5.10 Dick Leversee, 1979.

25 More Raisins II 5.7 (or 5.8 var.) Todd Burrill, Dave Steres and Dick Leversee, 1976. Bring knob tie-off slings and a 165' rope.

26 Anti-Jello Crack 5.9/5.10 FFA: pitch one, Tony Yaniro, Tom Murley, 1974. Finish, Todd Burrill and Dick Leversee, 1976.

27 The Tree Route II 5.6 First ascent unknown.

PINNACLES

The Pinnacles in fog photo: Carl W. Smith

PINNACLES

HIGHLIGHTS

The Pinnacles are as much hated as loved. Coarse volcanic rock that ranges from rotten to reasonably solid instills terror in the hearts of most uninitiated climbers. But many routes are excellent, protection is usually fixed and climbs average one or two pitches in length. Good routes, combined with the weird and beautiful scenery created by the giant volcanic "boulders," have made many a climber fall in love with the Pinnacles. Fall and the spring are the principle climbing seasons. Except for the influx of weekend crowds from San Francisco, campgrounds are rarely full and the rocks are even less busy. With the coast of Monterey and the Big Sur only an hour away, the Pinnacles is a delightful area to visit—if you don't mind climbing on pebbles more or less solidly cemented together.

CLIMBING

Except for an occasional abrasive chimney, cracks are rare at the Pinnacles. Instead, the climbing is almost entirely on coarse chunks of rock protruding from tuff (hot volcanic ash that has consolidated and solidified). The difficulty of the climbing is usually a factor of how large these protrusions are and how far apart they are spaced. On the lesser quality routes, one also has to be concerned with how solidly welded in place the rock chunks are.

The Pinnacles deserve their name: rising from fifty to 500 feet high (but averaging less than 200 feet), they frequently come to a narrow summit. But more often, the rocks are overgrown boulders that take on every shape under the sun. Sometimes the rocks permit scrambling descents down the "back" side, but equally often, rappels are the only way down.

Because of the virtual absence of cracks, protection is almost entirely from bolts. Still, a small rack of nuts are sometimes useful, and slings are handy for tying off knobs and a necessity for reducing rope drag on the sometimes wandering route lines. Although protection may seem adequate, the Pinnacles is still often considered a "no falls" area—no one wants to come crashing into chunks of protruding rock.

The rocks cover a large and complex hill about 1,200 feet high and three miles across. Excellent climbing can be found on top of the hill (the "High Peaks"), but the regions covered in this guide lie in the valleys on each side—within easy walking distance from the road.

ENVIRONMENT

Almost 150 miles south of San Francisco and fifty miles inland from the Pacific, Pinnacles National Monument is covered with the infamous Coast Range chaparral. For the uninitiated, chaparral is dense brush that grows in the "Mediterranean" climate of Southern California—hot, dry summers and cool, moist winters. It blankets the hillsides, provides an excellent home for wildlife and keeps hikers from straying from the trails. Summer heat at the Pinnacles is intense—over 100 degrees F—but during this season most climbers are off to the Sierra Nevada.

The Pinnacles are located next to the San Andreas Fault, well known to Californians for its propensity to shift with earthquakes. Sliding north at one and one-half inches per year, the Pinnacles are now 195 miles north of where its lava originally spewed out of the earth. In six million years, the Pinnacles are expected to be an island off the coast of Northern California. Currently, Pinnacles National Monument is located in an extensive range of 2,000 foot hills separating two of California's huge, rich, agricultural valleys.

CLIMBING HISTORY

First spotted by Europeans in 1792, the Pinnacles were later explored by the bandit Vasquez, who is said to have buried a treasure near his hideout during the 1870's. Legend also has a lost mine somewhere in the heart of the Pinnacles. But climbing received an especially slow start for such a significant area close to the major climbing community of San Francisco. The main problem was the lack of cracks. The use of bolts was discouraged until the later 1950's. This, combined with the strange rock, encouraged few climbers to venture seriously into the Pinnacles. Thus, even though the Sierra Club made the first roped climb there in 1933, it was not until the 1950's that frequent excursions placed the Pinnacles on the California climber's map. By the end of the decade most of the spires and faces had been climbed. The 1960's brought a high standard push to the Pinnacles, including a proliferation of new routes and exploration of offshoot areas. After the 1966 guidebook, most climbers wrongly considered the area climbed out, and first ascents were rare for several years. But this changed in the 1970's when a new breed of climbers descended on the Pinnacles. Many first free ascents were made during this period, including the 1978 freeing of the bolt ladder on **Machete Direct** (5.11). Even though considerable room still exists for route explorations, the early 1980's have, as yet, seen little route development.

CAMPING

Camping for the Pinnacles inherently involves a significant choice between the East or West Side climbing. While it is less than four miles by trail to connect the two road ends, climbers will tend to do the routes nearer camp, often ignoring those on the other side of the hill. Because of the radically different nature of the routes near each end of the road, both are included in this guide. The East Side is the most popular for tourists. As a consequence, the campground has been turned over to private management and moved to just outside the National Monument boundaries. Food and other supplies are available at its Camper Supply Store. But it is an expensive drive-in campground as compared to the moderately priced, but less popular walk-in campground on the West Side. Those wishing to experience both sides might consider staying on the East Side during the week and making the two hour drive to the West Side on Friday before the weekend crowds arrive. A pleasant diversion would be to make a two day trip out of the drive and visit the city of Monterey and the spectacular coastline from Point Lobos to Big Sur, where one can camp. If plans include Southern California, the drive down Highway 1 south of Big Sur is well worth the extra time it takes.

From the West Side, the nearest showers and laundromat are located in Soledad, thirteen miles away. From the East Side, showers are available at the campground, and laundry facilities are thirty-five miles away in Hollister. No camping is allowed outside of the designated sites.

SEASONS AND WEATHER

Approximate Months	Typical Temperatures		Likelihood of Precipitation	Frequency of Climbable Days
	High	Low		
Dec-Feb	60's	30's+	medium	medium
Mar-May	70's+	40's+	low-med	very high
Jun-Sep	90's+	60's−	very low	low
Oct-Nov	70's−	40's+	low	high

RESTRICTIONS AND WARNINGS

The National Monument imposes no restrictions on climbers other than an admonishment not to leave slings behind on routes, especially where visible to hikers. A voluntary registration system has been instituted to provide the park with resource management data. Climbers are encouraged to cooperate with the Park Service and to register. When bouldering next to a trail, it is suggested that chalk use be avoided. Most important is to follow the climber's access trails, marked with signs featuring carabiners, in order to reduce impact on the fragile grasslands near some of the cliffs. Poison oak and rattlesnakes are not uncommon throughout the Monument.

GUIDEBOOKS

A Rock Climber's Guide to Pinnacles National Monument, (1983) by Paul G. Gagner. Available in many climbing stores or from Paul G. Gagner: Pinnacles Guide. 5000 Shady Ave, San Jose CA 95129.

GUIDE SERVICES AND EQUIPMENT STORES

No services are available locally. The nearest equipment stores are Bugaboo Mountaineering in Monterey, and Western Mountaineering in San Jose and Santa Cruz.

EMERGENCY SERVICES

The nearest hospitals are located as follows:

East Side:
Hazel Hawkins Memorial
911 Sunset Dr.
Hollister 637-5711

West Side:
Mee Memorial
300 Canal
King City 385-5491

Report accidents to the nearest ranger, who will arrange the suitable rescue or medical services.

GETTING THERE

No public transportation serves the Pinnacles. Greyhound Bus Lines serves Soledad and Hollister, from where one can hitch-hike in. Be forewarned that traffic can be very light, especially during the week, so hitch-hiking may not be terribly efficient.

PINNACLES

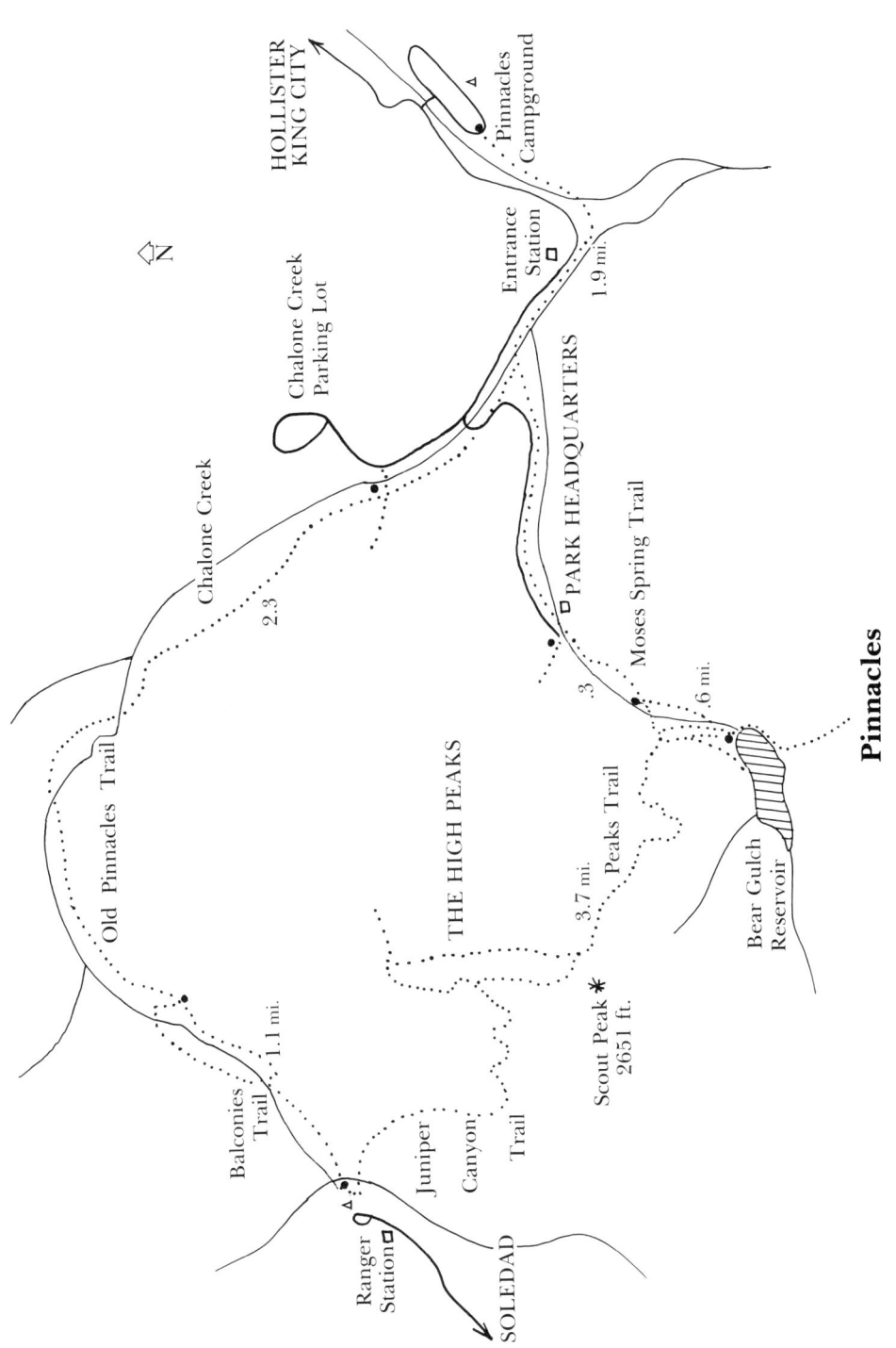

PINNACLES

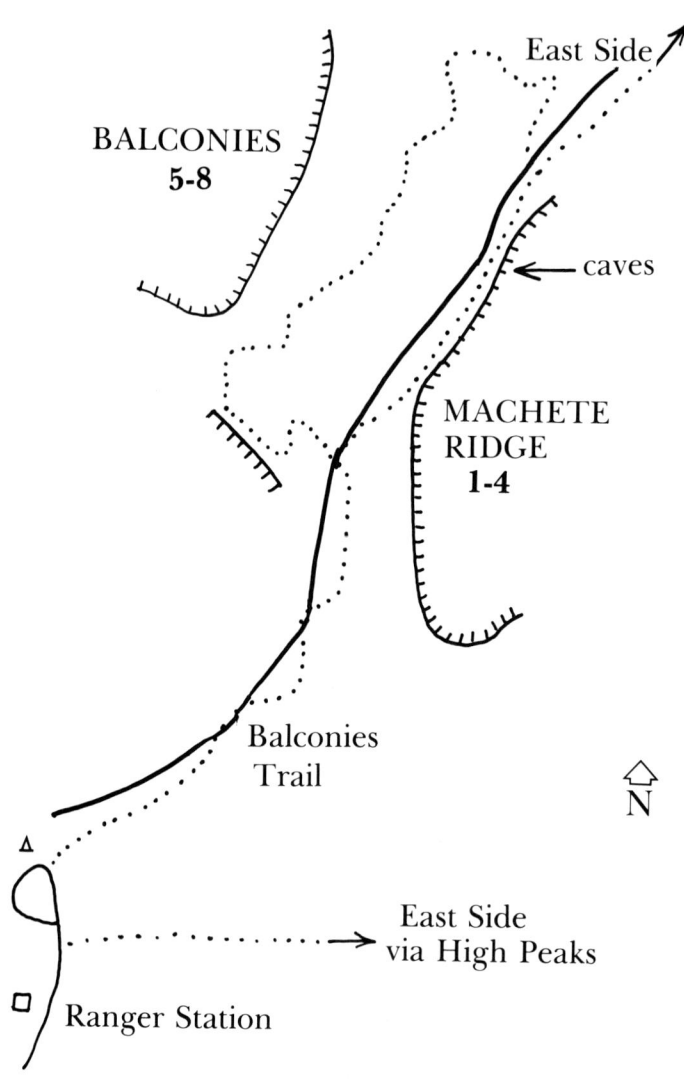

Pinnacles - West Side

PINNACLES

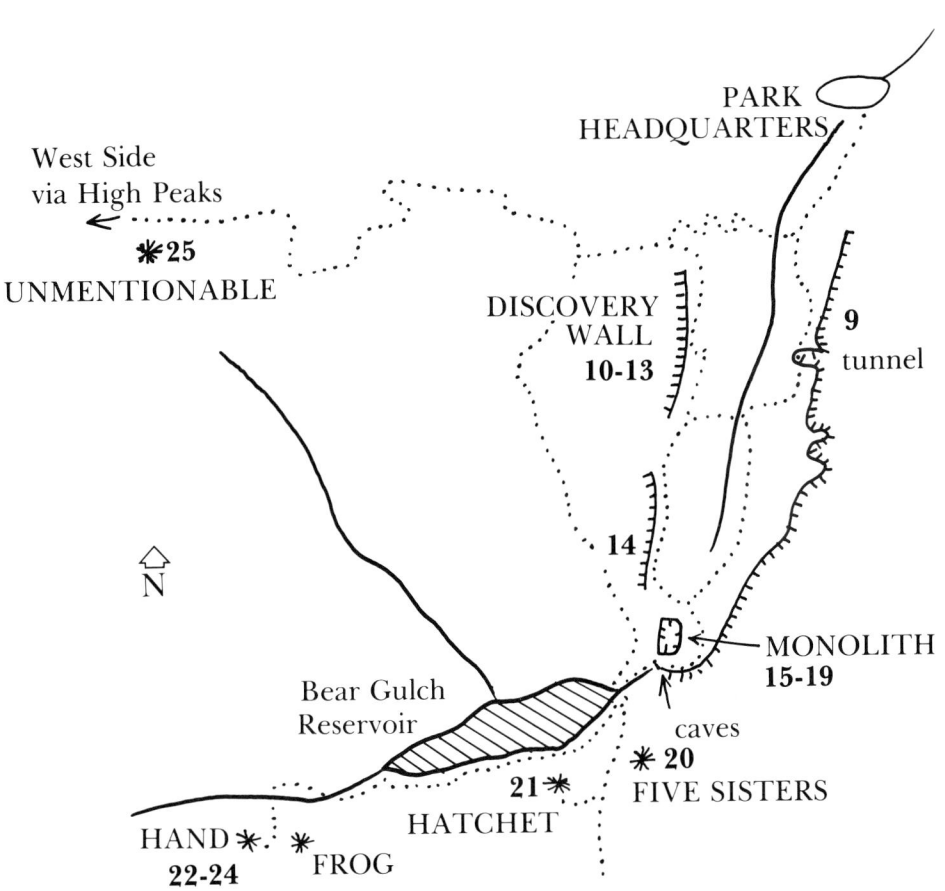

Pinnacles - East Side

PINNACLES

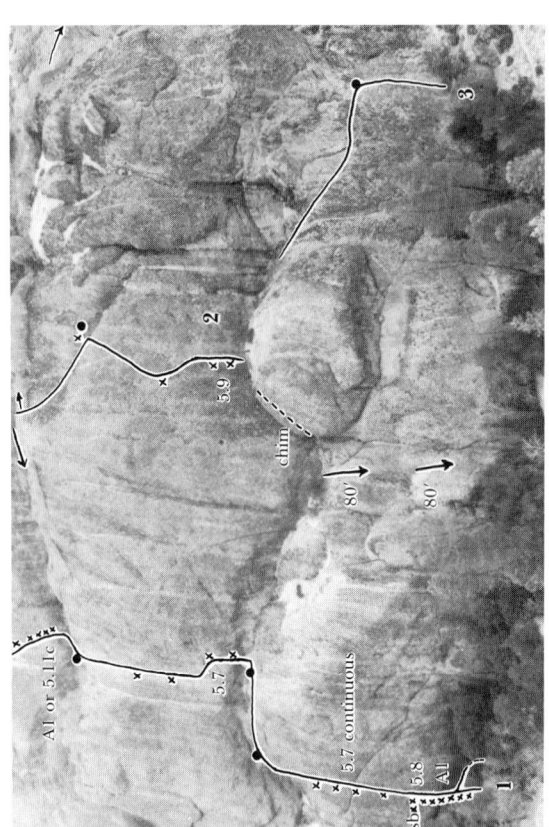

WEST SIDE
Machete Ridge

1 Machete Direct 5.8 A1 or 5.11c/d Gary Colliver and Glen Denny, 1974. Final two pitches: Lee Donaghey, Bruce Edwards, Dave French and Jim Smith, 1963. FFA: Barry Bates and Glen Garland, 1978; lower variation: John Barbella and Chris Bellizzi, 1982. One of the longest routes in the Pinnacles.

2 Upper Bandits Bench 5.9 First ascent unknown.

3 Twinkle Toes Traverse 5.5 Seth Boatright and Chuck Richards, 1972.

4 Destiny 5.8 First ascent unknown.

PINNACLES

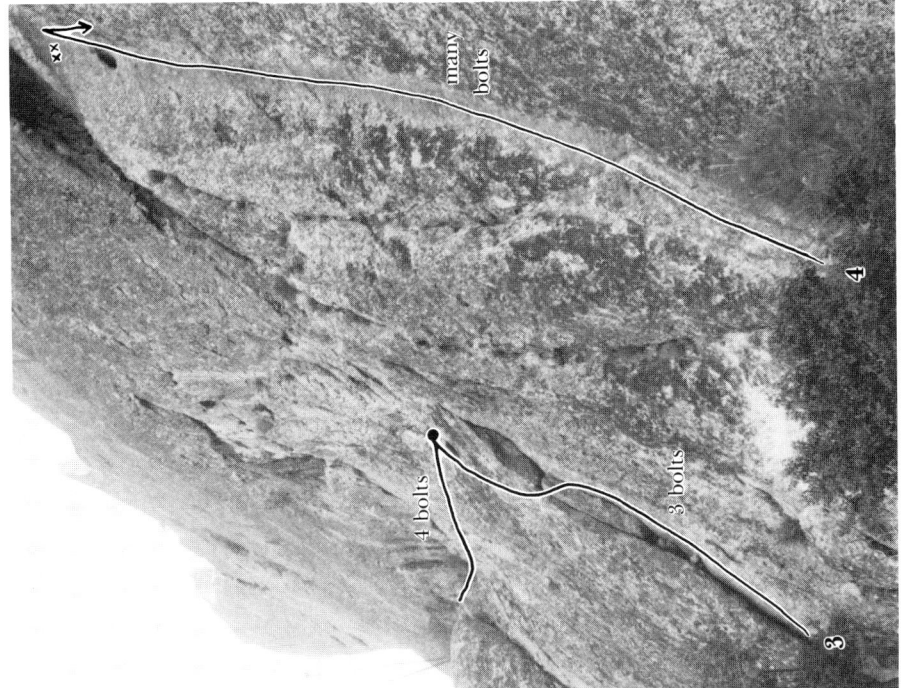

Machete Ridge

Janet Tornow on Machete Ridge photo: Tom Rogers

The Balconies *photo:* Carl W. Smith

PINNACLES

Tom Rogers on Shake and Bake
photo: Janet Tornow

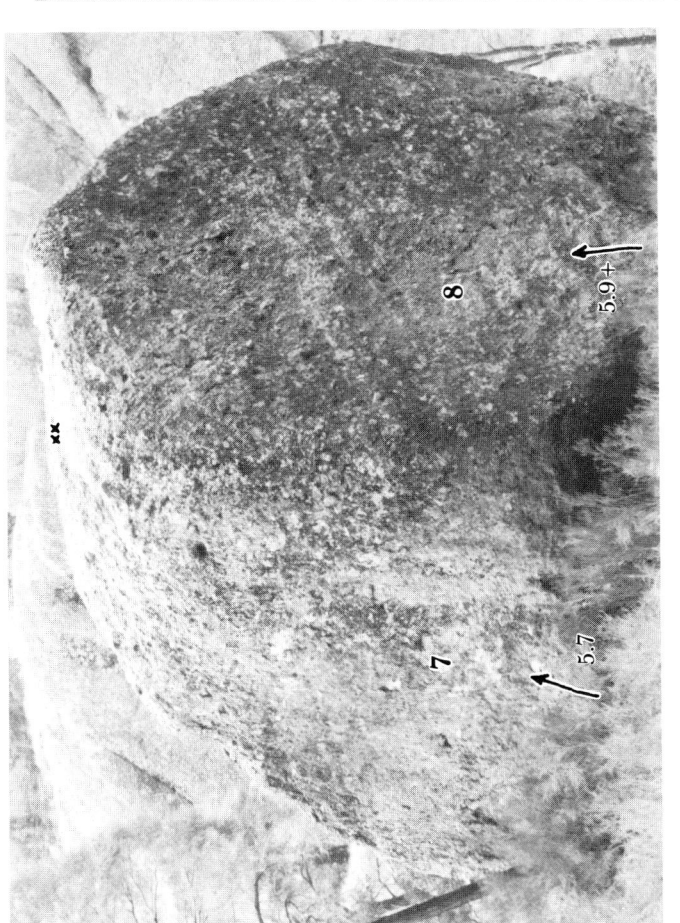

WEST SIDE
The Balconies

5 **Shake and Bake 5.10a** Tom Higgins and Chris Vandiver, 1976. Inspect bolts before trusting them—erosion occurs in these water chutes.
6 **Regular Route 5.9 A1 or 5.10b** Howard Bradley, Steve Roper and Frank Sacherer, 1961. FFA: Tom Higgins and Chris Vandiver, 1979.
7 **Smiling Simian 5.7**
8 **No Smiles 5.9** Bruce Cooke and Tom Higgins, 1976.

The Ordeal photo: Carl W. Smith

EAST SIDE
Discovery Wall
10 **Ordeal** 5.8 Dave Bircheff, Jim Bridwell and Wayne Steinert, 1965.
11 **Swallow Crack** 5.6 Dave and Phil Bircheff, 1965.
12 **Fly-By** 5.9 Dave Coates and Wayne Steinert, 1965. FFA: Dave Bircheff, Jim Bridwell and Mike Kilmer.
13 **Portent** 5.5 Andrew Emery and Steve Roper, 1965.

EAST SIDE
9 **No Holds Barred** 5.10a or 5.10c Jim Bridwell, 1965.

PINNACLES

Monolith Regular Route
photo: Tom Rogers

EAST SIDE
14 Agrarian 5.8 Jim Beyer and Janice Linhares, 1977.

EAST SIDE
Monolith
15 Piton Traverse 5.6 A1 or 5.11c Al Baxter, Bud Gates and John Hood, 1947. FFA: unknown.
16 Post Orgasmic Depression 5.11a First lead: Chris Bellizzi, 1981.
17 Indirect Traverse 5.8 Doug Cardinal and Blake Hinman, 1974.
18 Direct Route 5.6 Dave Hammack and John Whitmer, 1965. Poor protection.
19 Regular Route 5.7 Craig Holden and John Whitmer.

Bear Gulch Caves

The Sisters photo: Carl W. Smith

EAST SIDE
The Sisters
20 First Sister 5.4 First ascent unknown. Possibly the most popular route in the Pinnacles.
21 Hatchet 5.5 A1 or 5.10a Jim Moore FFA: unknown.

EAST SIDE
The Hand
22 The Snail 5.7 First ascent unknown. South ridge past bolt.
23 Salathé (with Burnette Bolt Variation) 5.6 First pitch: Robin Hansen, Dick Houston and John Salathé, 1947. Second pitch (var.): Floyd Burnette and Allen Steck, 1949.
24 Back of Hand 5.6 Bill Kyle and John Whitmer, 1958.

PINNACLES

EAST SIDE
25 **The Unmentionable 5.5** First ascent unknown.
photo: Carl W. Smith

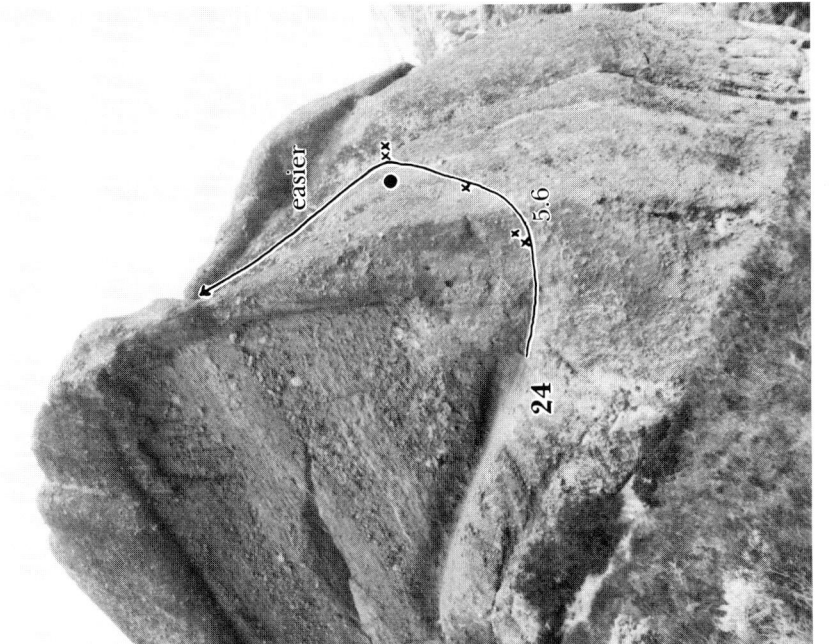

The Hand

The Valley from the North Rim

YOSEMITE VALLEY

HIGHLIGHTS
In the rock climbing world, Yosemite Valley is unequaled. With a tremendous concentration of steep walls that rise to 3,000 feet in height, hundreds of shorter routes, and superbly clean and smooth granite, Yosemite has provided the impetus for the establishment of contemporary rock climbing standards. To this climber's Mecca, people flock from around the world. The one mile wide by seven mile long valley, lined by more giant walls than one could hope to climb, exceeds all expectations. But there can also be disillusionments: it is expensive, crowded, legal stay limits seem short, and the weather can sometimes be uncooperative. Still, few climbers will not want to experience this famed valley for themselves.

CLIMBING
Yosemite's popularity stems in part from its conveniently accessible climbs; routes one to thirty pitches long are minutes from camp. In the spring and fall, the weather is generally very comfortable for climbing. The granite has become a reference point worldwide for the finest, cleanest, most solid rock a climber could ask for. But contrary to some people's expectations, the weather can turn foul at any time, forcing climbers to retreat from high on a multi-day route and to remain tent-bound for days. The glacially polished rock is so smooth that jamming its cracks can take weeks of retraining for climbers unaccustomed to the style.

Though Yosemite is generally known for its crack climbing, there are several big cliffs that offer superb face and slab routes, notably Glacier Point Apron and Middle Cathedral Rock. Routes up to twenty pitches long involve face climbing on thin or rounded edges and difficult friction on smooth rock. Bolts on these routes are often widely spaced, making long falls a frightening possibility.

Short crack routes are generally found along the base of the bigger walls or just outside the main valley. The many smaller crags in the Lower Merced Canyon provide some of the best cracks in Yosemite. Climbers interested in short, hard, free routes sometimes climb here to the exclusion of the massive walls that dominate the main valley.

El Capitan, with its forty or more Grade VI routes, is the big brother to the dozen other walls offering Grade V and VI climbs. Before attempting El Capitan, climbers unfamiliar with multi-day routes are advised to learn about exposure and practice wall techniques on smaller cliffs. This is especially important on the popular El Cap routes because a slow party can be a nuisance to the other climbers that are likely to be following close behind.

Among the unexpected difficulties can be the oven-like qualities of the south-facing El Cap. Two quarts of water per day are all that most climbers ration themselves on a multi-day route, but this can seem far too little during hot weather. Conversely, one must also be prepared for the possibility that an ice storm could move in, trapping T-shirt clad climbers high on a wall. There are also many "big-wall techniques" to learn that will radically increase climbing efficiency.

To guarantee reaching the belay bolts on many routes, the use of l65 foot ropes is strongly recommended. For any route that requires rappel descents (or where an escape might be necessary), two l65 foot ropes are usually mandatory.

On free routes, clean climbing is the rule. Many walls (notably the **Nose** of El Capitan) can easily be climbed clean with an occasional use of unhammered pitons and crack-n-ups. Crack-n-ups are very useful for clean-aiding piton scars. Any route involving A4 climbing will require pitons and often copper heads, hooks and other specialized paraphernalia. Among the requirements for many multi-day routes are hammocks and trusted rain gear with wool or pile insulation. Once climbers have made friends in the Valley, they can often borrow the needed equipment for a big wall. A bolt kit in the bottom of the haul sack is a good idea to facilitate self-rescue in an emergency situation.

While queues can form at the base of popular climbs, one can always find many excellent routes to experience alone. Passing another climbing party should ONLY be done with their permission because of potential rock fall from the party in the lead. Despite Yosemite's solidity, rockfall is still a definite possibility.

YOSEMITE

ENVIRONMENT

Yosemite Valley is only a small segment of the 1,200 square mile Yosemite National Park. This valley, deeply sculpted by glaciers out of the gentle alpine mountains of the surrounding Sierra Nevada, is the primary point of interest for most of the two and one-half million people who visit the Park every year. From a distance—especially from its rim—Yosemite Valley appears as wild and beautiful as the surrounding peaks. On entering the Valley itself, however, one discovers that hidden by the trees is a small city, complete with everything from residential neighborhoods to bars and grocery stores. The air pollution from campfires and automobiles can be quite startling to someone gazing down from a bivy high on a wall. The many large campgrounds can be very crowded in the summer.

   This is said not to discourage, but to forewarn. Yosemite is indeed the "Incomparable Valley," and its walls are fantastically beautiful, its meadows and river wonderful to frolic in, and the hikes that lead from the forested valley floor (at 4,000 feet in elevation) to the less trampled back country are lined with spectacular waterfalls. As long as climbers recognize that the Valley floor receives millions of tourists every year and therefore cannot possibly be a wilderness experience, they will not be disillusioned. Should one want to escape the crowds, it is only necessary to start hiking.

CLIMBING HISTORY

Not until 1933 did members of the newly formed Sierra Club Rock Climbing Section in Berkeley (near San Francisco) feel competent to attempt any of the so far untouched walls and spires in Yosemite. Though the Valley stayed isolated from other climbing communities in America and abroad, those who climbed here included a number of truly innovative people.

The size of the Yosemite walls and the solidity of its rock forced the development of many new techniques and specialized tools. Pitons were made from alloy steel instead of the soft iron available from Europe, hauling techniques were invented that greatly increased efficiency on multi-day routes, free climbing skills were eventually found to ascend the smooth, parallel-sided cracks.

Competition within a small group of Valley regulars drove skills so high, that by the time the outside climbing world discovered the Valley in the early 1960's, Yosemite had developed the highest American rock climbing standards. Indeed, during the 1960's many of the wall techniques developed here were exported to Europe's mountain walls and beyond. Climbers from around the world came to the Valley to learn the techniques and to climb the increasingly famous walls in California's even more famous mild climate. In the climber's campground, one will often see more foreigners than Americans, attesting to the area's international popularity.

While some people still do a majority of their climbing in the Valley, fewer Americans than in earlier times treat it as the dominant influence in their own climbing careers. Instead, they come to Yosemite for what it has to offer—big walls, excellent free climbing, and generally good weather—but they might well do a majority of their climbing in the dozens of other important areas that have developed around the continent. Still, for many, an annual trip to Yosemite is a must.

CAMPING

Camping in Yosemite Valley can be a trying experience. While everyone has heard stories of climbers living in the Valley for months at a time, few seem to know that doing that in the 1980's may involve fees, evading the law, and other hassles.

Most climbers want to experience the famous climber's campground: Camp 4, now known as the Sunnyside Walk-In Campground. Besides the social environment, this campground offers bouldering, more sunshine than other campgrounds, and is accessible to the Yosemite Lodge complex—especially its large lounge, where one can read at night and during rainy spells. But this campground is so densely packed with climbers in the spring and fall that some prefer to stay in other, less congested sites that are safer from gear theft. Sunnyside does not allow reservations in advance. Though the campground is usually officially full by mid-April, some sites will often not have all six people allowed by the law. By asking around, one can often find a site. Registration should be done in the morning in an attempt to get a spot as they are vacated. Because Sunnyside charges by the person (two dollars per day in 1984), groups of more than three people will find it cheaper to use another campground that charges by the site and allows up to six people to share the cost.

Be cautious about using the excuse "I was on a wall" for not paying camping fees. Tents have frequently been confiscated until all back fees are payed. If this situation must be confronted during a rainstorm, after days on a wall, it is no fun at all.

Yosemite's numerous drive-in campgrounds are available first come, first served from October through April. May through September they are available by reservation only, from Ticketron, Ricon Annex, P.O. Box 7416, San Francisco, CA 94102. Reservations cannot be made more than eight weeks in advance. Climbers with a family or unwilling to endure the hassles of Sunnyside Campground, will probably prefer reserving a drive-in site.

Between June 1st and September 15, the camping limit is seven days in the Valley. During the rest of the year the limit is thirty days. Other options include renting tent cabins or hotel rooms.

In order to increase the likelihood of finding a site, one should plan to arrive in the Valley during a weekday morning. For more information on camping, write to The National Park Service at the address under "Guidebooks."

Mail can be received addressed to "your name", General Delivery, Yosemite CA 95389 USA.

All the services one would expect from a small city are available in the Valley. The concessionaire providing these services is The Yosemite Park and Curry Company. Showers and laundry are found in Curry Village. The grocery store is in Yosemite Village. Climbers on a tight budget may save money by buying food before entering Yosemite.

SEASONS AND WEATHER

Approximate Months	Typical Temperatures High	Low	Likelihood of Precipitation	Frequency of Climbable Days
Nov-Feb	50's	20's	med-high	medium
Mar-May	70's+	30's+	medium	high
Jun-Aug	90's	50's	very low	high-med
Sept-Oct	70's+	40's	low	very high

Comments: Spring storms are common. In the summer it is often comfortable on north facing climbs, while south facing cliffs are sometimes warm in winter.

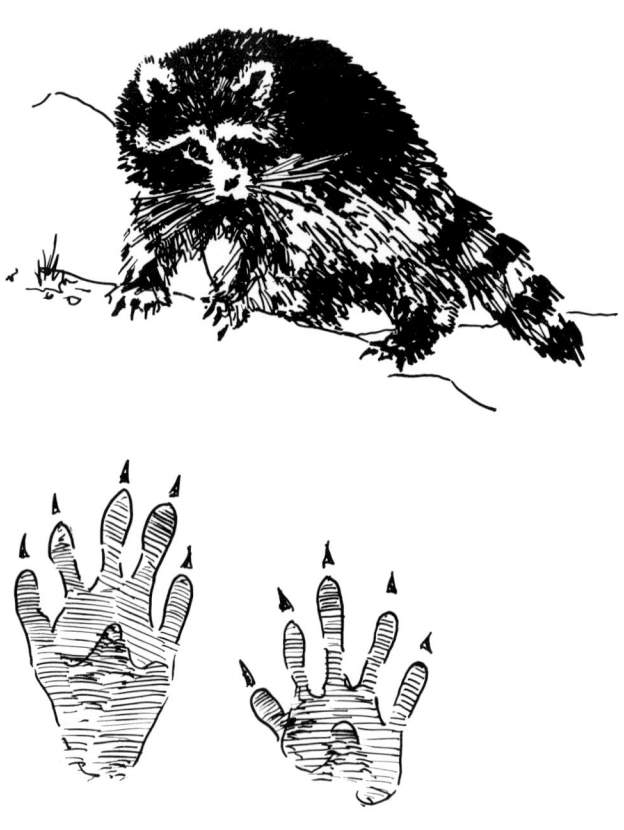

YOSEMITE

RESTRICTIONS AND WARNINGS

Note the restrictions on camping. Theft is a definite possibility. Expensive equipment should be stored out of sight in a car trunk, if that is available. Everything should be labeled clearly with your name. Record serial numbers if available. If camping at Sunnyside, small storage lockers are available at the nearby gas station. Carry travelers checks instead of money. There is a Wells Fargo branch bank located in Yosemite Village. Do NOT leave gear at the base of—or on!—a route. Report stolen equipment and suspicious people immediately. Other thieves include bears. All food must—by law!—be stored in a car or suspended out of bear's reach.

Do not use the Yosemite Lodge as a drying room for wet gear. Thievery or abuse of National Park Service and Curry Company property and personnel only creates animosity towards climbers. Since climbers often request special treatment not accorded other visitors (such as extensions of legal stay limits), good relations are important in the long run.

A voluntary climbing registration is available at the main visitor's center and climbers without watchful friends are encouraged to use this service, but be sure to sign back in after a successful climb.

Do not defecate behind flakes or on ledges on routes. While best is to let it drop on a sunny area well away from where others will ascend, many climbers use paper bags, then throw them from the side of the wall. This way it will break down in the sun and wash away relatively quickly.

DO NOT throw haul-bags or other objects (especially litter) from the walls. There is the very real possibility of hitting someone on the ground with your haulbag, and littering is disgusting.

For more information, write the Park Service at the address under "Guidebooks."

GUIDEBOOKS

Yosemite Climbs (1982) by George Meyers. Available in most climbing stores or from Chockstone Press, 526 Franklin, Denver, CO 80218. Topo format. *Climber's Guide to Yosemite Valley* (1971) by Steve Roper. Available in many climbing stores or from the Sierra Club, 530 Bush Street, San Francisco, CA 94108. Written descriptions and out of date, this book does have a good history section (to 1971).

For more details on camping and other guidelines for climbers, write for the pamphlet: Rock Climbing in Yosemite National Park, The National Park Service, P.O. Box 577, Yosemite CA 95389.

GUIDE SERVICES AND EQUIPMENT STORES

Instruction, guiding and equipment is available from the Yosemite

Mountaineering School, Curry Village, Yosemite CA 95389. Telephone: (209) 372-1244.

EMERGENCY SERVICES

Though rescues in Yosemite are often efficient and reliable, they are also expensive to the Park and generate ill-will toward the climbing community. The Park Service is pursuing a policy of charging fines and/or rescue costs to those who get themselves in trouble through negligence, or request a rescue frivolously. If you are being rescued by helicopter, ropes will be lowered to you and someone will rappel to your location. BE SURE NOT TO ATTACH THE ROPES TO THE WALL!

For rescues contact any park ranger or dial 911 in an emergency. There is a medical clinic in Yosemite Village.

GETTING THERE

The Yosemite Transportation System provides daily bus service into Yosemite Valley from Merced throughout the year. Daily bus service from Fresno is available June through August and from Lee Vining July and August. Connections with Greyhound Bus Lines can be made in any of these cities and serves the major airports in San Francisco, Los Angeles, or the rest of the United States. Hitch-hiking may be improved by displaying your climbing gear and a sign saying "Yosemite." If you are a foreigner, a flag displaying your nationality may help.

YOSEMITE

El Capitan photo: George Meyers

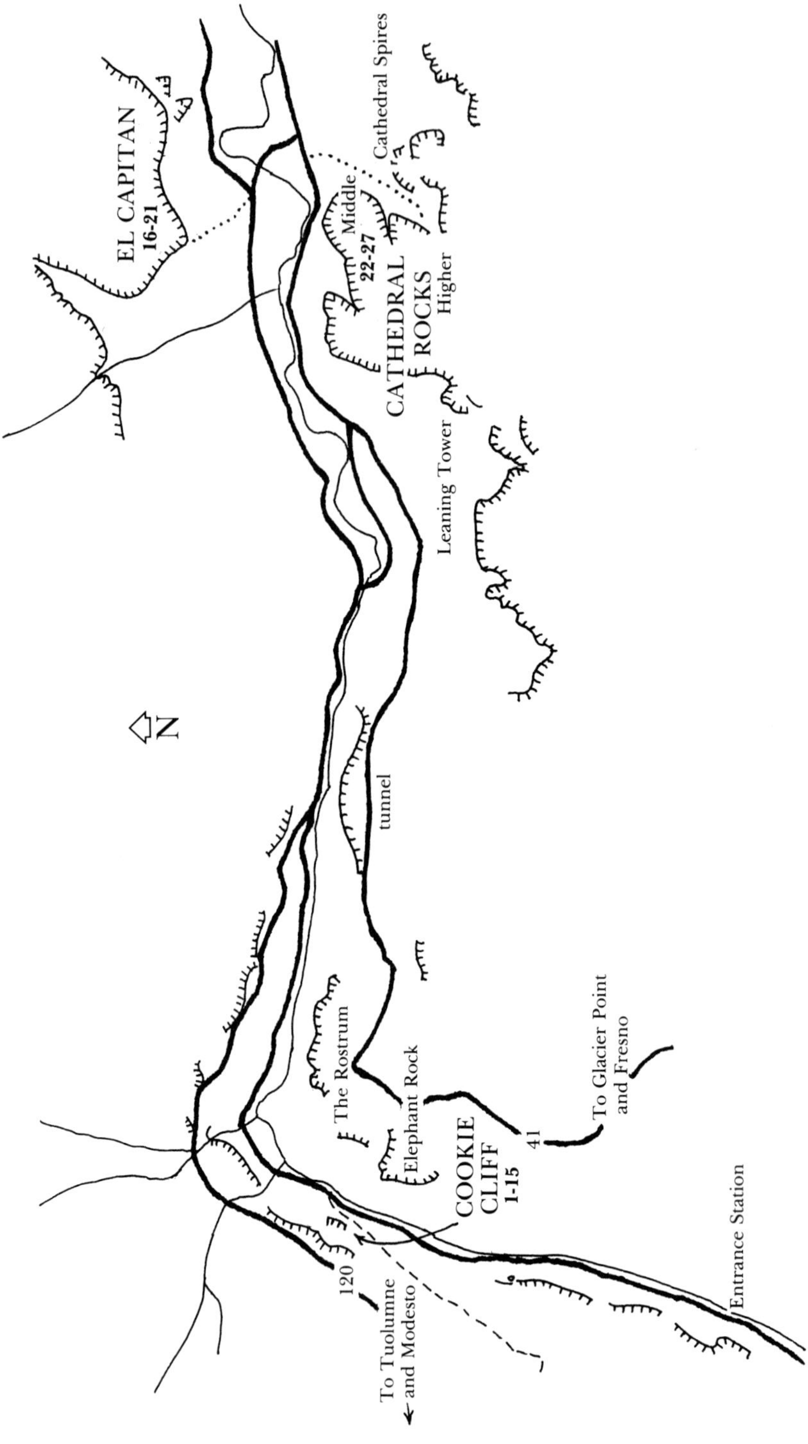

YOSEMITE

Yosemite Valley - Lower Merced Canyon

YOSEMITE

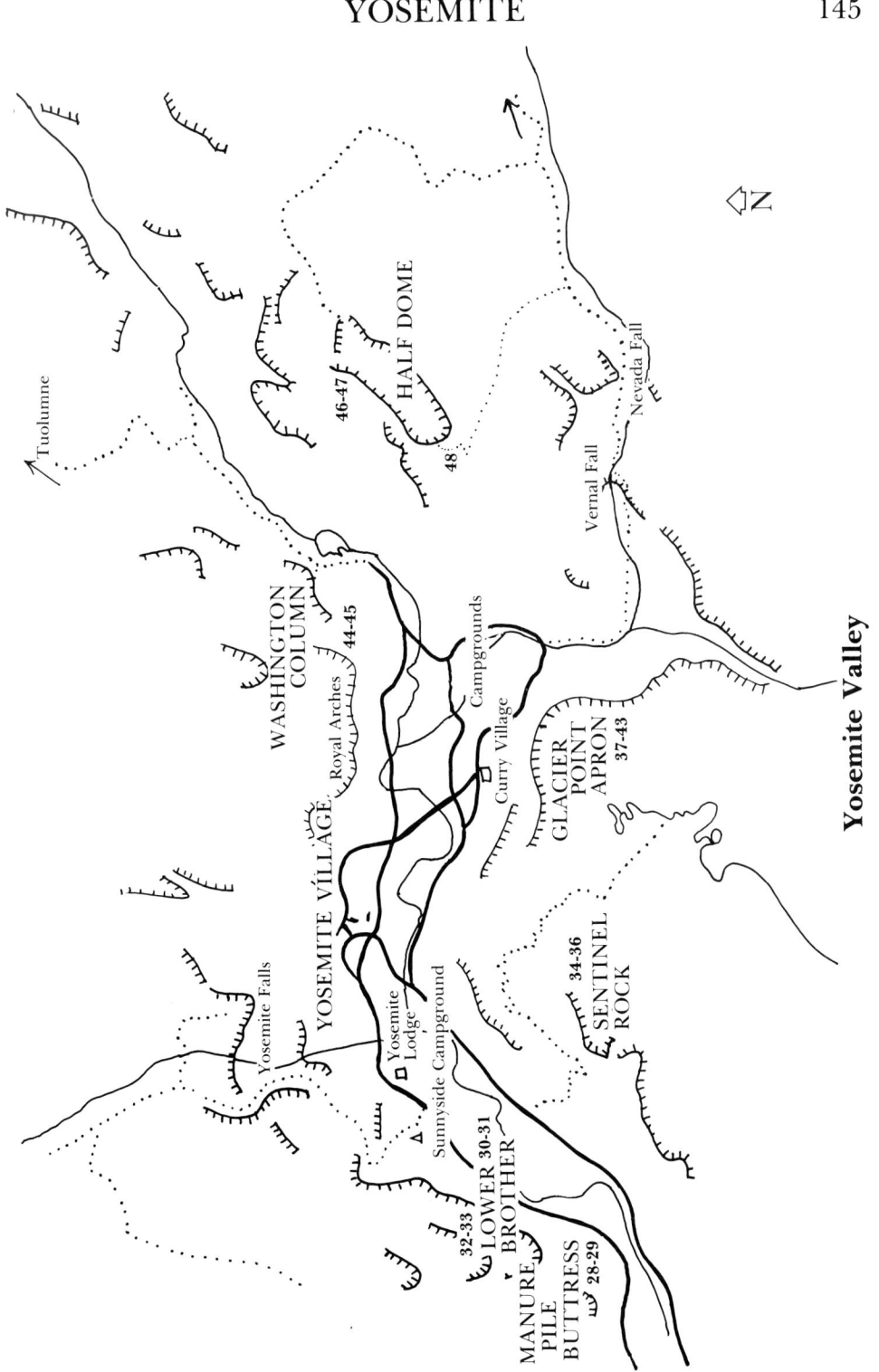

146 YOSEMITE

The Cookie Cliff photo: George Meyers

YOSEMITE

The Cookie Cliff

1 **Hardd** 5.11b Henry Barber and Ron Kauk, 1975. Small nuts.
2 **Crack-A-Go-Go** 5.11c Harvey Carter and Pete Pederson, 1967. FFA: Pete Livesey and Ron Fawcett, 1974. Small nuts.
3 **Outer Limits** 5.10b Jim Bridwell and Jim Orey, 1971. Bring nuts to 3½".
4 **Meat Grinder** 5.10c Royal Robbins and TM Herbert, 1968. Bring nuts to 3½".
5 **Waverly Wafer** 5.10c Jim Bridwell, Barry Bates and Beverly Johnson, 1970. Bring a 3" nut.
6 **Butterballs** 5.11c Henry Barber et al., 1973. Bring extra 1" to 1½" nuts.
7 **Wheat Thin** 5.10c Peter Haan and Jim Bridwell, 1971. Bring nuts to 3".
8 **Butterfingers** 5.11a Jim Bridwell and Charley Jones, 1971. Small wired nuts.
9 **The Cookie, Center** 5.9 Tom Kimbrough, Tom Hargis and Roman Laba, 1965. FFA: Loyd Price and Roger Gordon, 1967.
10 **The Cookie, Right** 5.9 Royal Robbins and Loyd Price, 1968.
11 **Vendetta** 5.10b Loyd Price and Roger Gordon, 1967. FFA: Royal Robbins and Galen Rowell, 1968. Bring nuts to 5".
12 **The Cleft** 5.9 Chuck Pratt and Wally Reed, 1958. FFA: Chuck Pratt and Chris Fredericks, 1965.
13 **Catchy** 5.10d Jim Pettigrew, Jim Bridwell and Mark Klemens, 1971.
14 **Catchy Corner** 5.11a Jim Bridwell and Dale Bard, 1974. Bring extra ½"–¾" nuts.
15 **The Enigma** 5.9 Barry Miller and Ray Barlow, 1964.

Hidetaka Suzuki on Outer Limits

Barney Sheafor on the last pitch of the Nose Route

YOSEMITE

El Capitan from Middle Cathedral Rock

Descents: The most popular descent follows the East Ledges and involves two rappels. The Valley floor can be reached in about 2½ hours. Another possibility is top hike five miles (gently downhill) north to the Tuolumne road at Tamarac Flat Campground, where a car can meet the climbers. It is also possible to hike east to the Yosemite Falls Trail, but this is long and strenuous.

16 West Face V 5.11b TM Herbert and Royal Robbins, 1967. FFA: Ray Jardine and Bill Price, 1979. The first entirely free route on El Capitan. Not a good route to haul a bag on. Bring tiny wired nuts.

17 Salathe Wall VI 5.10-5.12 A3 Royal Robbins, Chuck Pratt and Tom Frost, 1961. This route has been widely referred to as "the finest rock climb in the world." Pitons: 1 KB, 3 LA, 1 each ½"-1½" angles.

18 Free Blast IV 5.11b Jim Bridwell, John Long, Kevin Worrall, Mike Graham, John Bachar and Ron Kauk, 1975. The first 10 pitches of the Salathe are often climbed as a free route with a rappel descent from Mammoth Terraces.

El Capitan photo: George Meyers

YOSEMITE

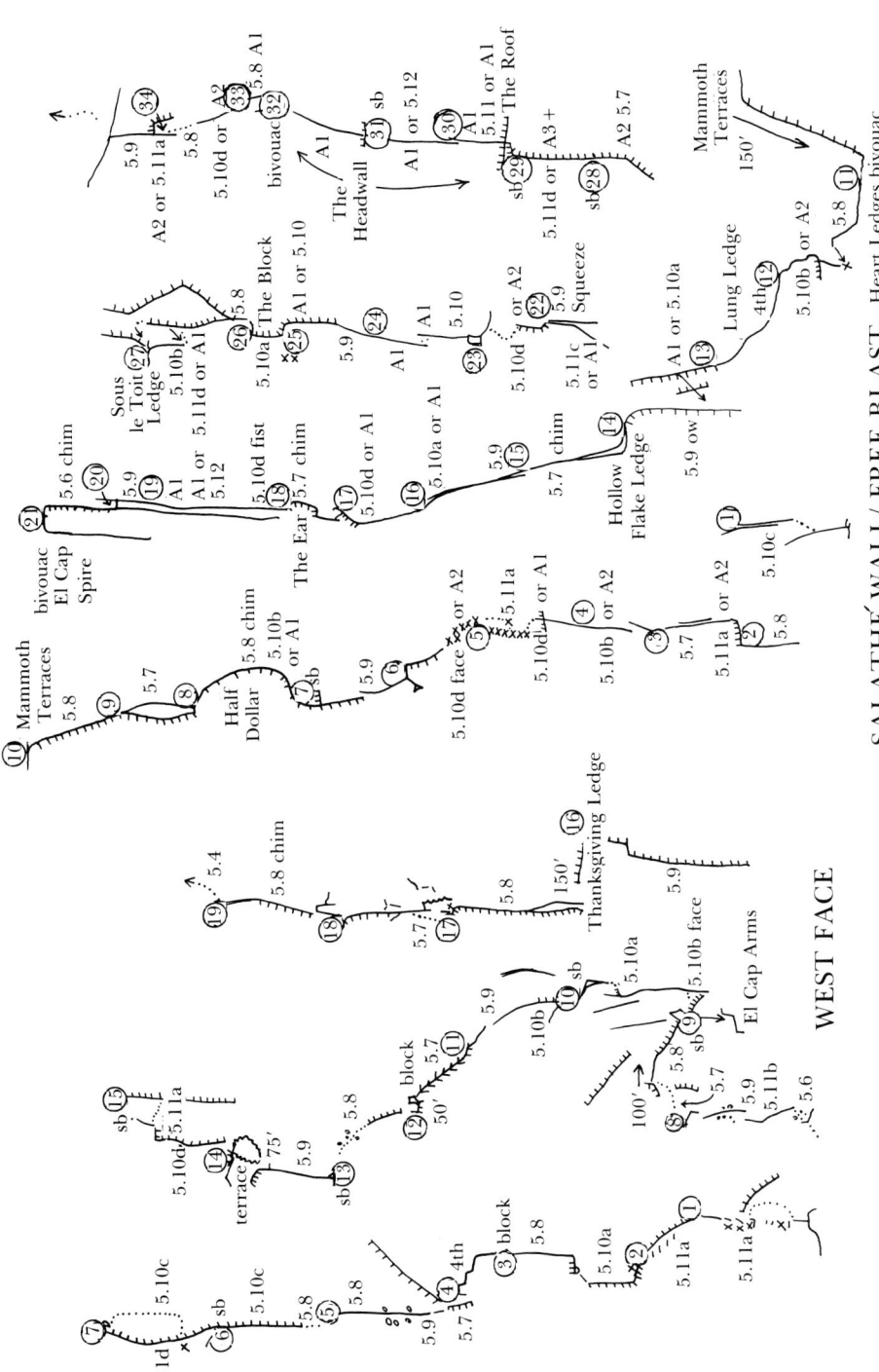

El Capitan

19 Nose Route VI 5.9-5.11 C3 Warren Harding, Wayne Merry, George Whitmore et al., 1958. The first route on El Capitan and still one of the most popular. If done mostly free, there are 20 pitches 5.9 or harder. Bring nuts to 4". Pitons: A few small angles and LA's can be useful to slot as nuts or for use when the weather is bad.

20 Mescalito VI 5.9 A4 Charlie Porter, Hugh Burton, Steve Sutton and Chris Nelson, 1973. Pitons: 5 RURPS, 15 KB, 20 LA; angles: 6 each ½"-1½", 3 each 2", 2 each 2½"-4"; many small copperheads, rivet hangers, keyhole hangers, hooks, ring angle claw.

YOSEMITE

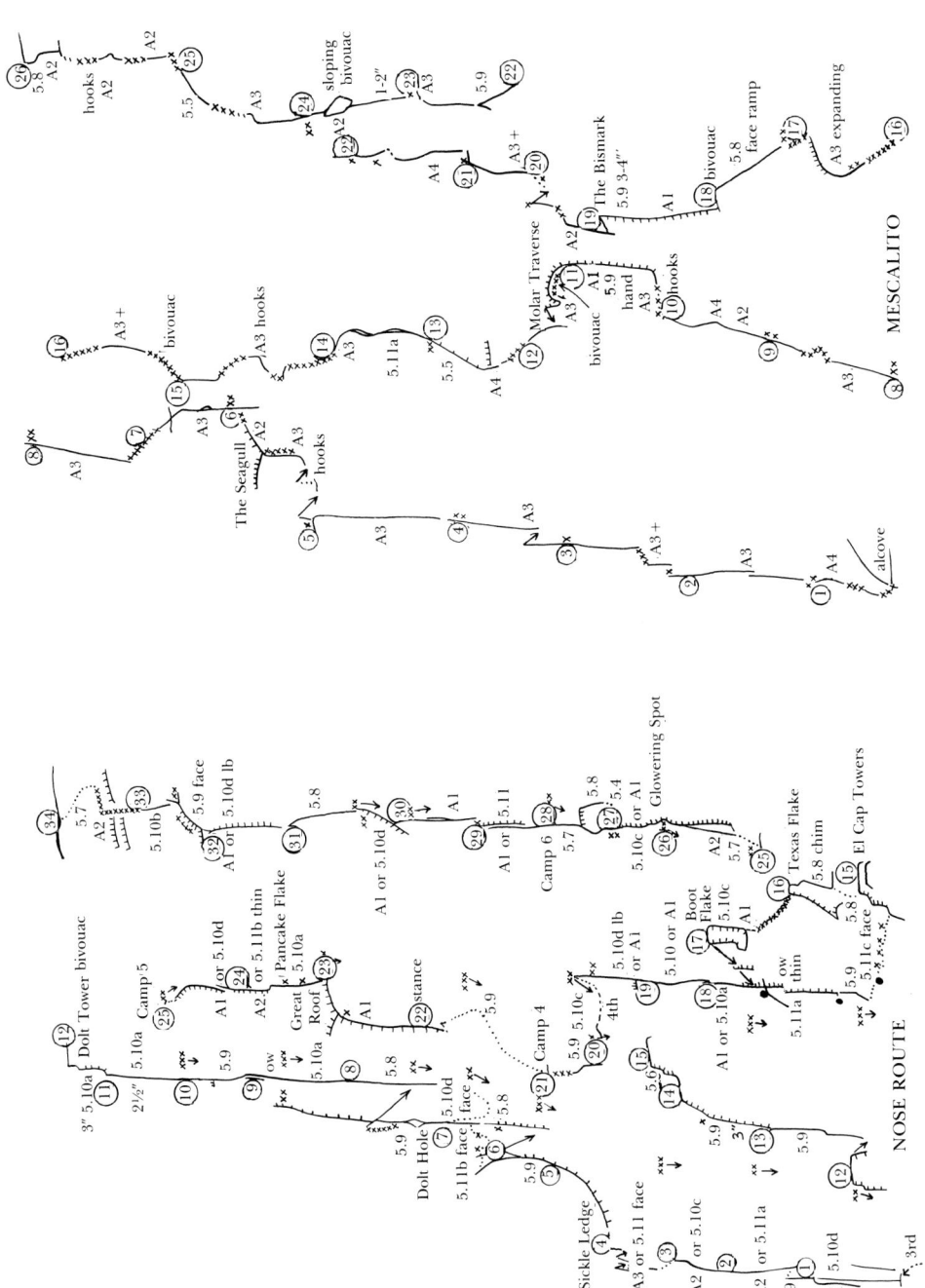

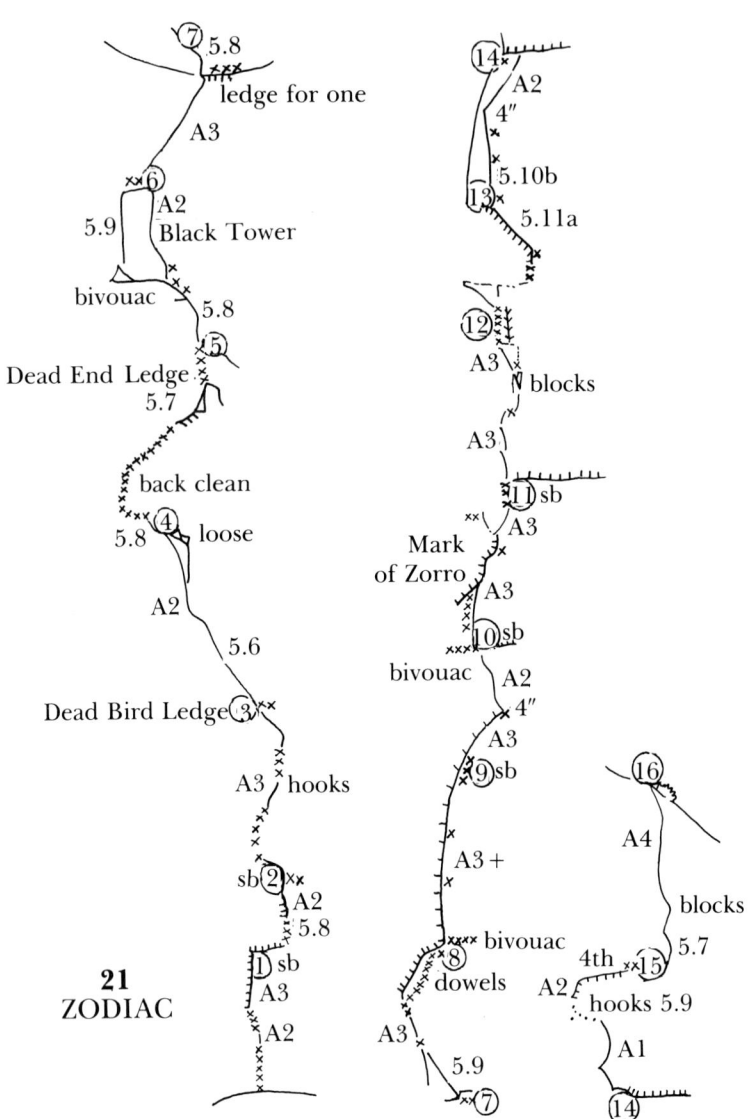

El Capitan

21 Zodiac VI 5.10-5.11a A4 Charlie Porter, 1972. One of the shortest and most beautiful aid routes on El Capitan. Pitons: 5 RURPS, 15 KB, 20 LA; angles: 5 ea. ½"-1½", 2 ea. 2", 1 ea. 2½", 3 ea. 3", 2 ea. 4"; ring angle claw, 10 keyhole hangers, extra small Friends.

Barney Sheafor on Texas Flake, Nose Route

Higher Cathedral Rock photo: National Park Service
22 Mary's Tears/ Crucifix 5.11c Mary's Tears: Bill Price and Mike Borris, 1980; Crucifix: Jim Bridwell and Kevin Worrall, 1973. Bring tiny nuts to 3½", and Friends.
23 Northeast Buttress IV 5.9 Dick Long, Ray D'Arcy and Terry Tarver, 1969. FFA: Frank Sacherer and Jeff Dozier, 1964. Bring a 3" nut.

YOSEMITE

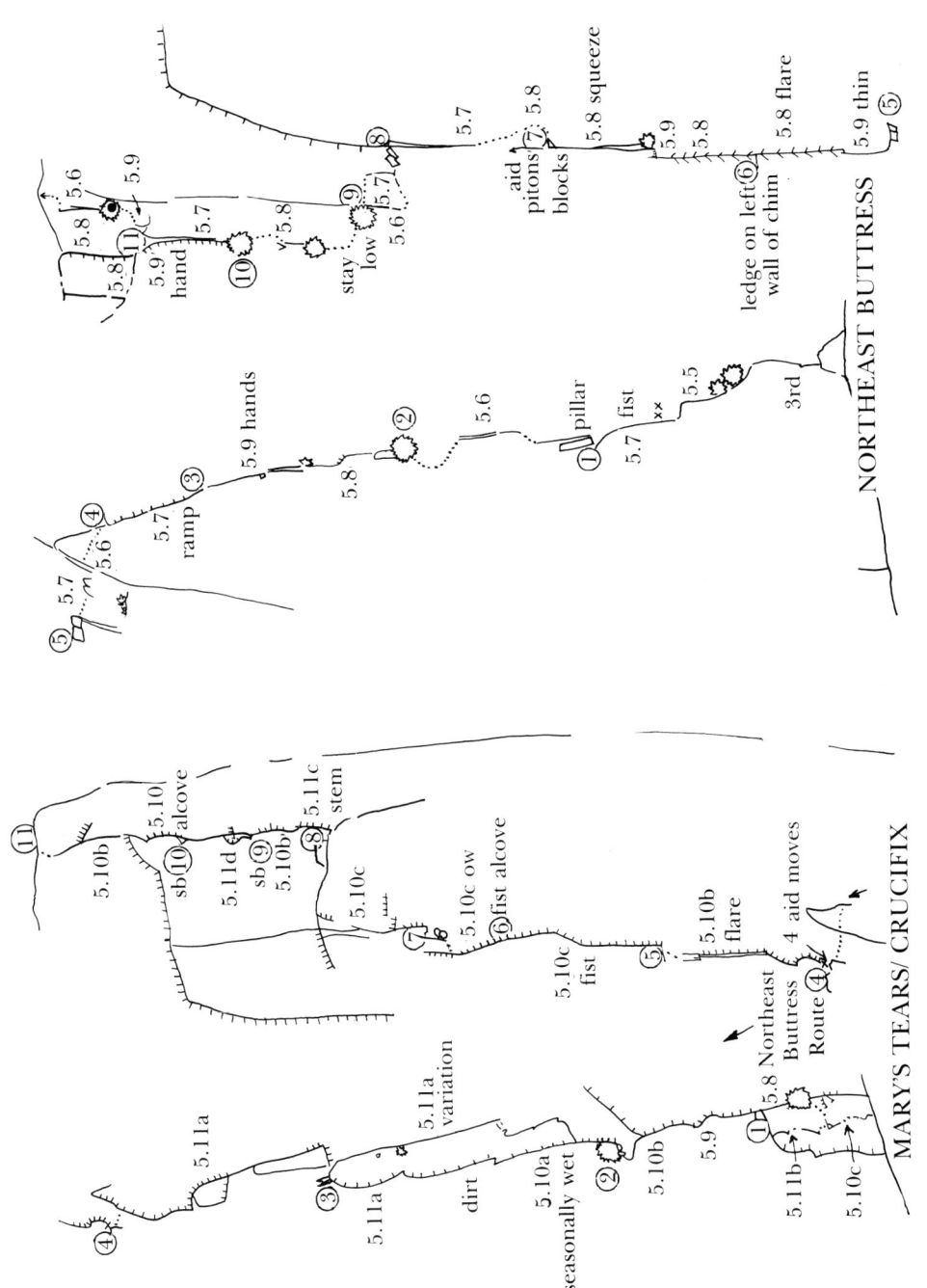

Middle Cathedral Rock

Descent: After unroping, scamble up 200 feet to the broken ledge system known as the Katwalk, then follow this left through heavy brush to Cathedral Chimney and down to the Valley floor. No roped climbing needs to be done.

24 East Buttress IV 5.10c (or 5.9 A0) Warren Harding, Jack Davis and Bob Swift, 1954. FFA: Frank Sacherer and Ed Leeper, 1965.

25 Bircheff-Williams Route III 5.11b Phil Bircheff and Steve Williams, 1969. FFA: Kevin Worrall and George Meyers, 1973. Bring 3″ nut and extra small nuts.

26 Central Pillar of Frenzy III 5.10a (or 5.9 for the more popular first 5 pitches) Jim Bridwell, Roger Breedlove and Ed Barry, 1973. The first 5 pitches can be very crowded.

27 Direct North Buttress V 5.10a Yvon Chouinard and Steve Roper, 1962. FFA: Frank Sacherer and Eric Beck, 1965. Bring 3″ nut and extra wires.

YOSEMITE

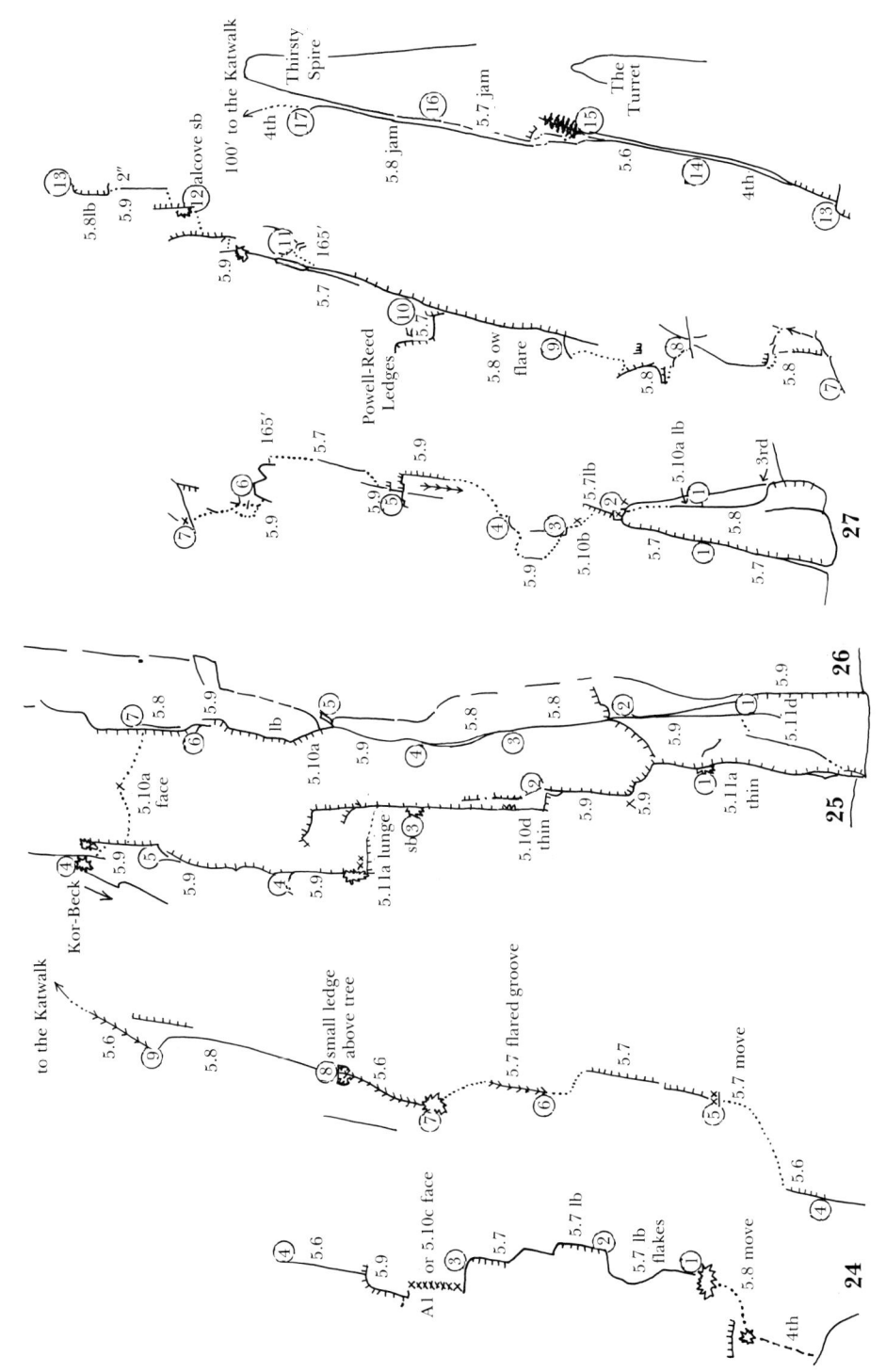

THE BROTHERS AREA
Manure Pile Buttress
28 **After Six** II 5.6 Yvon Chouinard and Ruth Schnieder, 1965.
29 **Nutcracker** III 5.8 Royal and Liz Robbins, 1967.

Rixon's Pinnacle
30 **West Face** II 5.10a Tom Frost and Bill Feuerer, 1959. FFA: Pat Ament and others, 1971. Bring a 3" nut.
31 **East Chimney** II 5.10a Don Goodrich and Dick McCracken, 1956. FFA: Royal Robbins and Dave Rearick, 1960.

The Folly
32 **Wild Thing** III 5.10c Ray Jardine and Ian Wade, 1973. FFA: Lou Dawson and Don Peterson, 1973. Bring nuts to 6", including several 2"-3½".
33 **Right Side** III 5.10d Warren Harding and Tom Fender, 1965. FFA: Dale Bard, Jim Bridwell and Kevin Worrall, 1973. Bring a 3" nut.

YOSEMITE

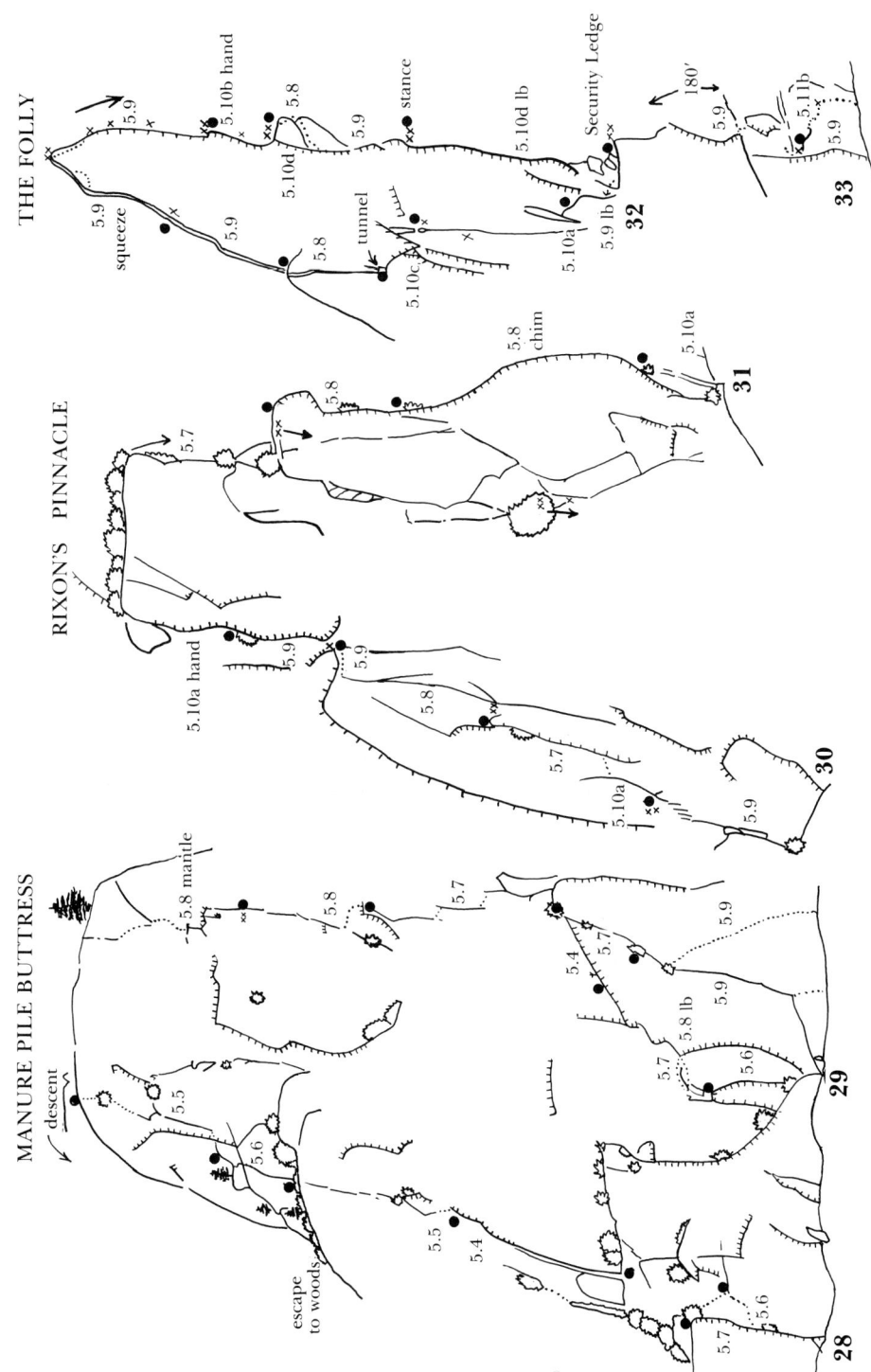

Sentinel Rock photo: George Meyers
Approach: Follow the Four Mile Trail for about a mile to the stream. Follow this up for several hundred feet, then ascend the prominent class 2 and 3 ramps diagonalling up and right.
Descent: From the top, work back to the gully to the east. Some tricky sections are encountered.
34 Chouinard-Herbert Route V 5.9 C2 or 5.11c Yvon Chouinard and TM Herbert, 1962. FFA: John Long and others, 1975. Pitons: Bring several LA and small angles for emergency use.
35 Steck-Salathé Route V 5.9 Allen Steck and John Salathé, 1950. Free variation: Steve Wunsch et al., 1972. One of the first wall climbs in Yosemite. Bring 3″ nut.
36 West Face V 5.11d C2 Yvon Chouinard and Tom Frost, 1960. Bring nuts to 4″.

YOSEMITE

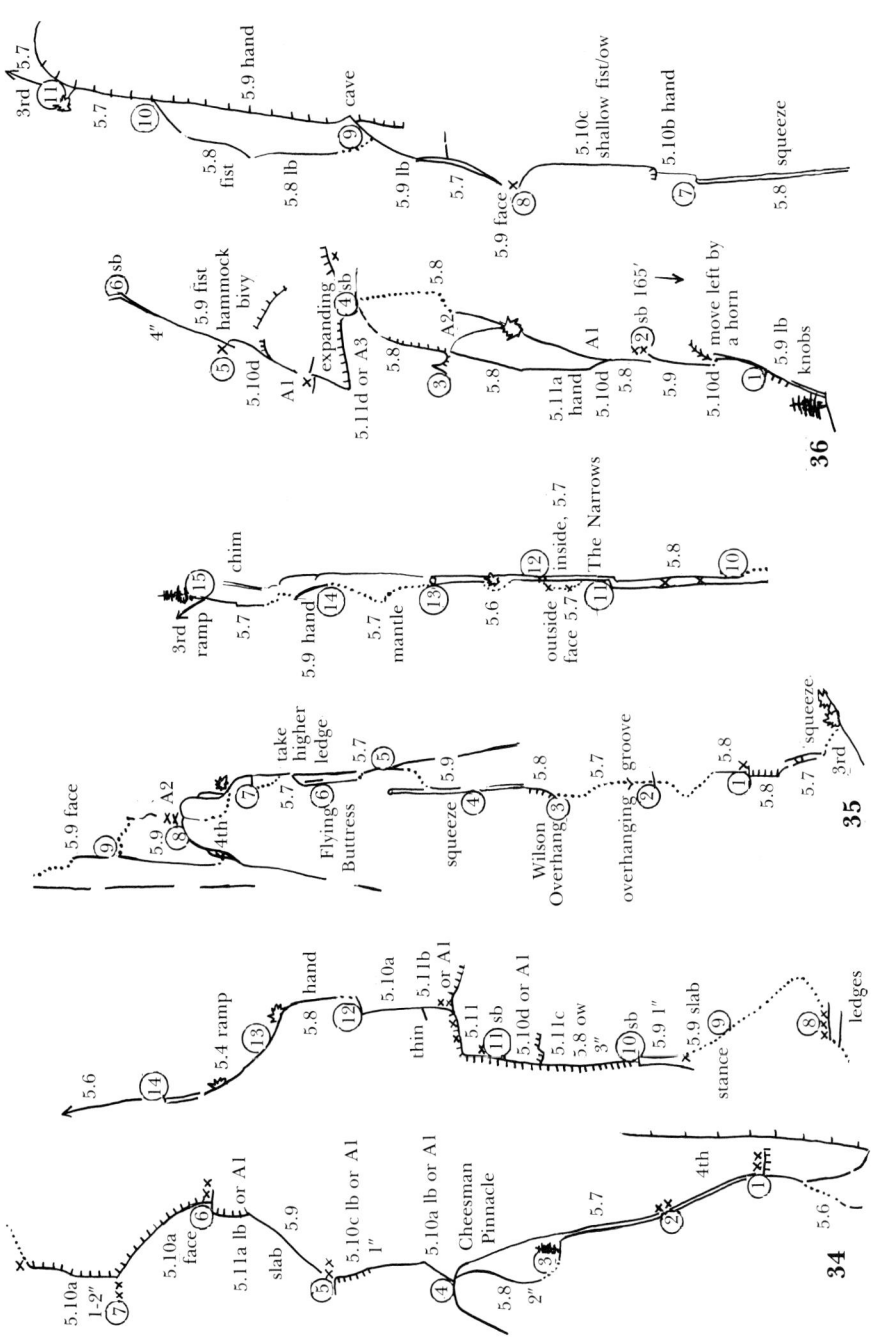

Sentinel Rock

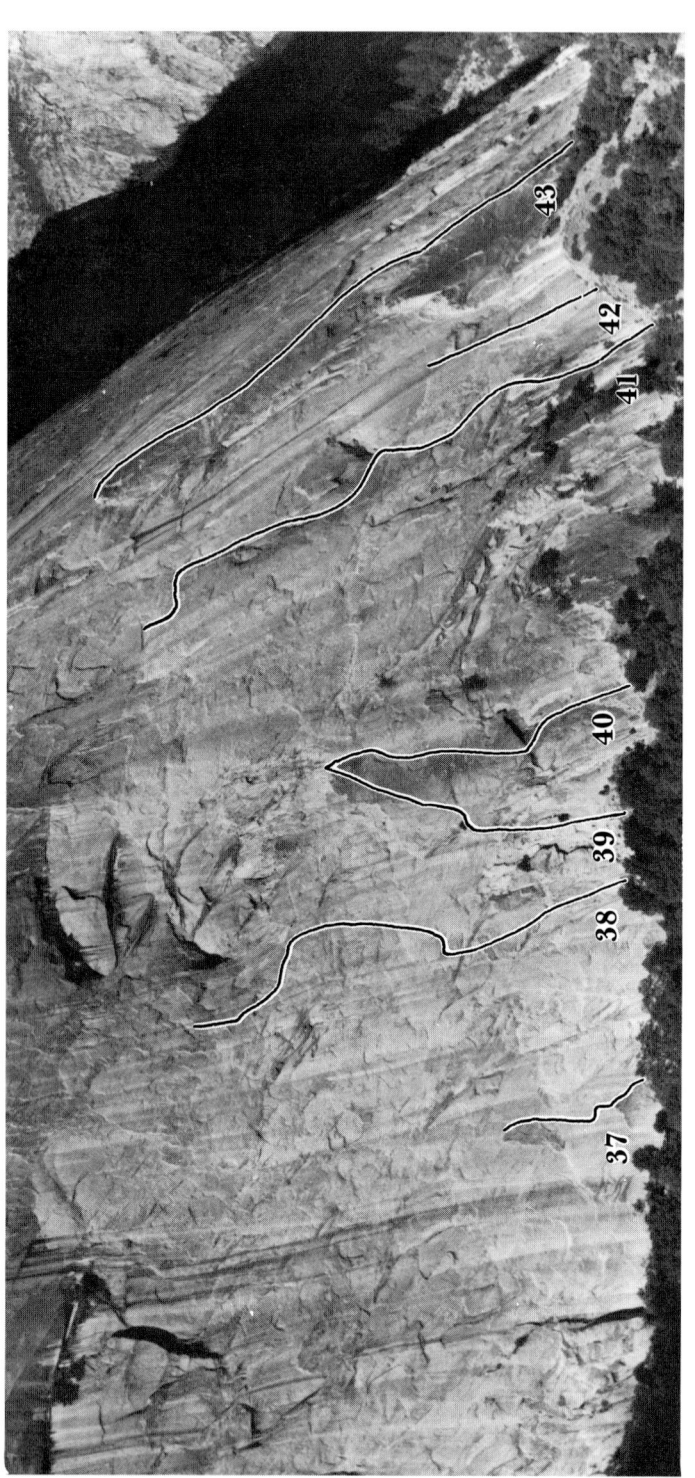

Glacier Point Apron photo: George Meyers
Descents are by rappel. Two 165' ropes are recommended.
37 The Calf 5.11b Joe McKeown and Jim Harper, 1963. FFA: John Long et al, 1974.
38 Hoppy's Favorite III 5.10b Dennis Oakeshott and Vern Clevenger, 1974.
39 The Grack, Center 5.6 Bill Sorenson and Jack Delk, 1967.
40 The Grack, Marginal 5.9 Ken Boche, Mary Bomba and Joe McKeown, 1970.
41 Regular Mouth 5.9 Bob Kamps and Tom Cochrane, 1964.
42 Misty Beethoven 5.10d Mark Wilfred et al, 1975.
43 Goodrich Pinnacle, Right 5.9 Royal Robbins, Liz Robbins and TM Herbert, 1964.

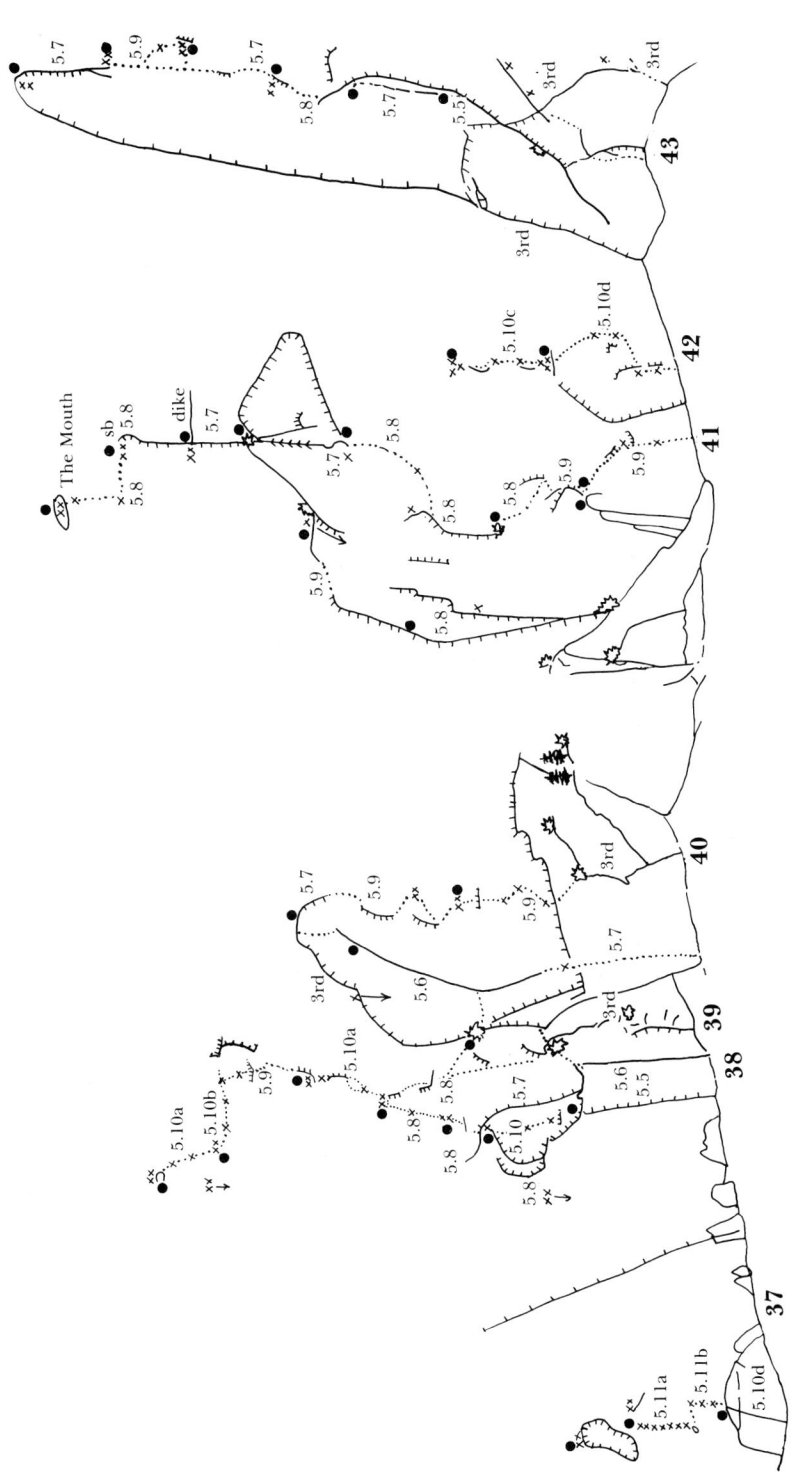

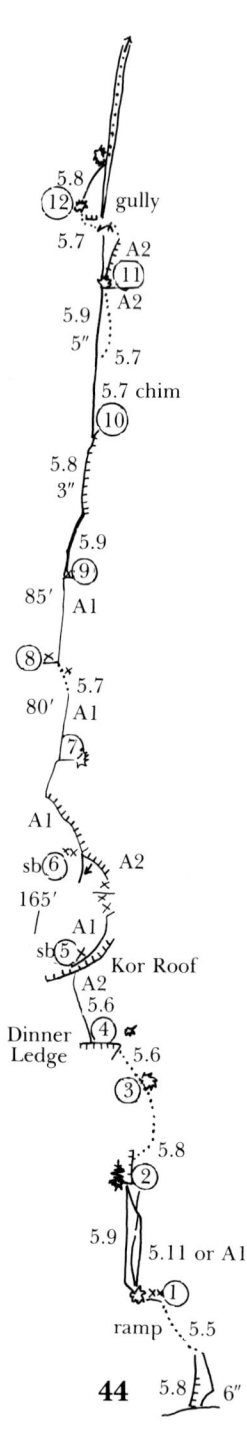

Washington Column photo: George Meyers
Descent: Hike east to the gully leading down to the Valley floor. If in doubt, keep high and continue east. No rappels should be attempted. A descent to avoid in the dark.

44 South Face V 5.9 C2 Layton Kor and Chris Fredericks, 1964. Bring a 3″ nut and extra nuts ⅛″ - 1½″.

YOSEMITE

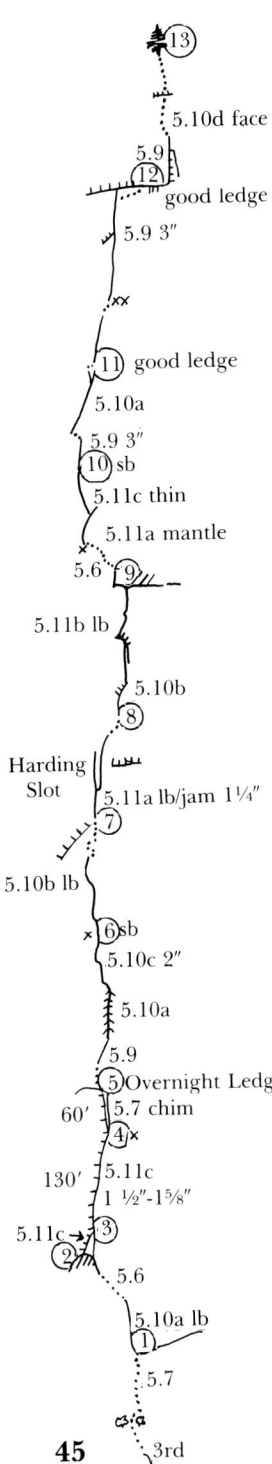

Washington Column photo: National Park Service
45 Astro Man V 5.11c Warren Harding, Glen Denny and Chuck Pratt, 1959. FFA: John Bachar, John Long and Ron Kauk, 1975. Bring nuts to 3½", including extra ¼"-2½".

photo: National Park Service

Half Dome - Northwest Face
Descent: A stairway climbs the north side of the Dome.

46 Northwest Face VI 5.9 A3 (or 5.12) Royal Robbins, Jerry Gallwas and Mike Sherrick, 1957. Free variations to 23rd pitch: Jim Erickson and Art Higbee, 1976. FFA: Leonard Coyne et al., 1980. The first Grade VI in Yosemite. Bring 3″ nut. Pitons: 1 KB and several LA for emergency use.

47 Direct Northwest Face VI 5.10 A3+ Royal Robbins and Dick McCracken, 1963. Bring nuts to 3½″. Pitons: 1 RURP, 3 KB, 8 LA; angles: 2 each ½″-1¼″, 1 2½″, large hooks.

YOSEMITE

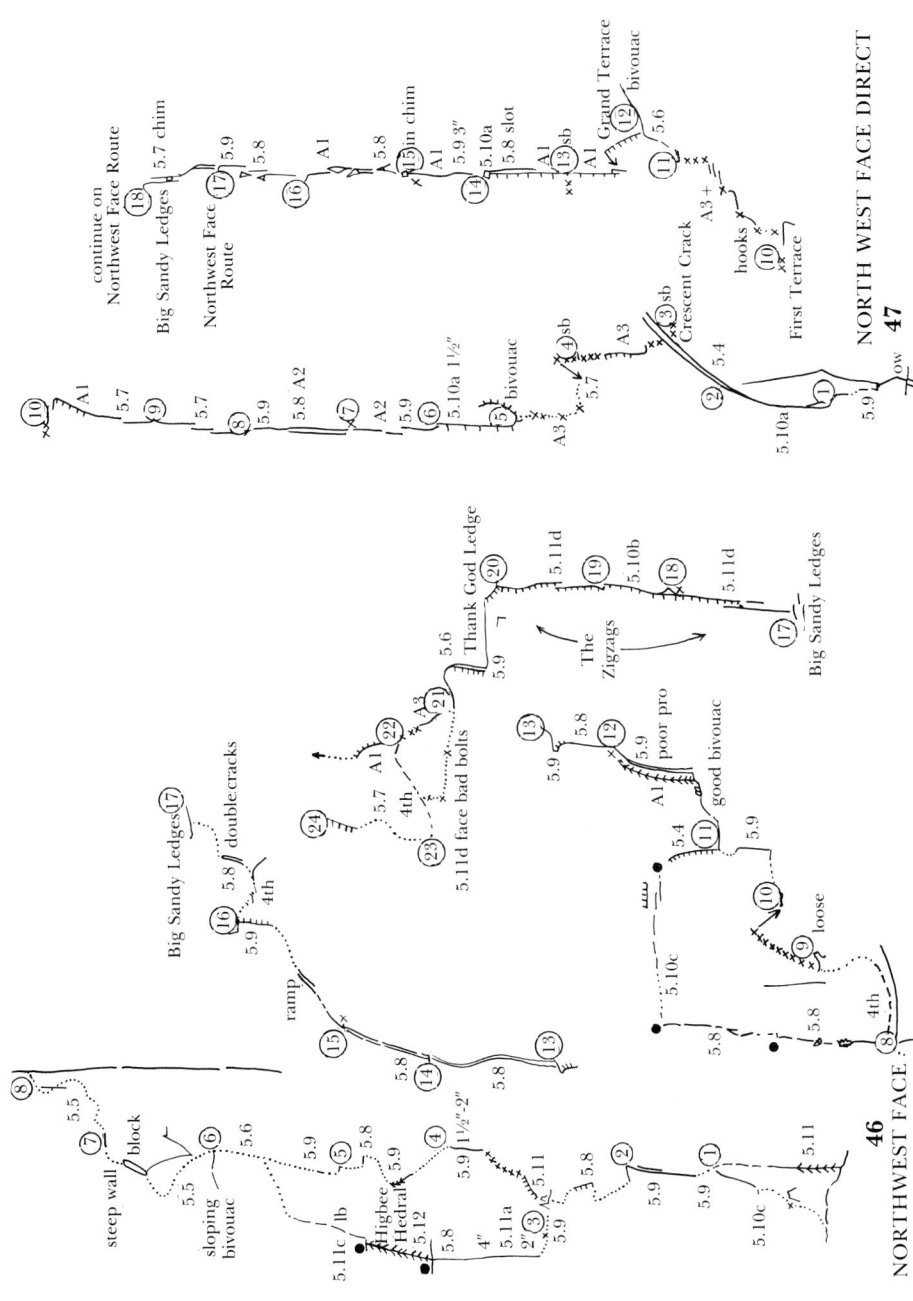

Bob Care on the Snake Dike photo: Tom Rogers

Half Dome - Southwest Face
48 Snake Dike 5.7 Eric Beck, Jim Bridwell and Chris Fredericks, 1965. A good full moon climb, this follows an incredible dike.

Half Dome from Glacier Point photo: Tom Rogers

Tenaya Lake and environs

TUOLUMNE MEADOWS

HIGHLIGHTS
Open spaces, clear blue skies and cool pine forests provide the setting for one of the "greatest proliferations of granite domes in the world." Rare indeed is the climber who is not moved by the gleaming white rock, warm sun and splendid scenery of Tuolumne Meadows. Though the widely scattered domes offer numerous crack and face climbing routes, it is the long runouts between bolts on blank walls that are most remembered. The tallest cliff is 900 feet, but most are much shorter. Because of the cooler weather, the Meadows become the summer home for climbers escaping the overcrowded oven of Yosemite Valley.

CLIMBING
Tuolumne domes come in all shapes and sizes: with both steep and low angle walls; with glassy smooth glacial polish and with rough, knobby rock; containing cracks, arches and roofs as well as smooth unbroken sheets of shining white granite. Nearby Cathedral Peak sports a pointed summit, but all of the domes tilt back to massive rounded tops. An important characteristic of many Tuolumne climbs is that even if the route begins with a crack, it is likely, at some point, to involve face climbing. Bolts are common for protection, although if the first ascen-

tionist was skilled enough to not need protection, they often didn't get put in. Thus a 5.10 climb is likely to have twenty to forty foot runouts on 5.8 and 5.9 ground. Widely spaced bolts can sometimes be very difficult to spot amid the knobs and shining feldspar crystals. Even on some routes protected mostly by bolts, a few wired nuts and Friends could prove useful. Since pitches are often long, a 165 foot rope is considered mandatory for reaching bolt belays. A belay seat can also increase one's belaying comfort significantly. The climbs of Tuolumne may seem somewhat harder than their ratings might suggest compared to Yosemite Valley, both technically and in the commitment involved.

ENVIRONMENT

If Yosemite Valley extended a few more miles eastward, it would cleave a chasm into Tuolumne Meadows. But 4,000 feet above the Valley's floor, the climate in Tuolumne remains comfortable while the midsummer weather in Yosemite roasts its visitors. Coming from the Valley, the visitor's first view of the Meadows is a panorama of the rich blue waters of Tenaya Lake, rimmed by glimmering white and grey domes. Where Yosemite impresses with power and grandeur, Tuolumne inspires with a lighter, elegant beauty. Most of the domes are within a few minutes' walk of the road that snakes through the Meadows on its way to Tioga Pass and the east side of the Sierras.

Numerous trails lead through the pine forests and onto the nearby tundra. A particularly spectacular hike climbs Cloud's Rest for a view that includes Half Dome and Yosemite Valley. Another follows Tenaya Creek to Yosemite Valley, passing along the foot of the Quarter Domes and Mt. Watkins and offering quiet, but cold, swimming holes.

CLIMBING HISTORY

In the 1950's and early 1960's, a few Yosemite "hardcores" trickled up to the Meadows for rest and relaxation. They climbed on a couple of the smaller domes and then put up the **Regular Route** on Fairview, the largest face in the Meadows. After a few seasons, people started taking the cliffs of Tuolumne more seriously. Yosemite Valley was still the place for truly "prestigious" climbing, but the smaller rocks of Tuolumne were developed with a unique face climbing style that included the use of bolts and an aversion to aid.

Through the sixties a small group of climbers was responsible for most of the routes, especially those on the open faces. The less initiated tended to stick to the more familiar cracks. By the 1970's, talented new climbers arrived on the scene with both fewer obvious lines to choose from and an evolving sense of climbing style that enabled the addition of many high quality routes. As Tuolumne became a climbing area of international stature, a frustration to visitors was that the only guide popularly available was the hopelessly incomplete *Climber's Guide to the High Sierra*. But in 1983, the situation was finally rectified with the publication of the first comprehensive guidebook.

CAMPING

There are two popular options for camping. The major campground (in fact, one of the largest in the National Park System) is located near the grocery store and the cafe, and has fairly modern facilities. Crowded on weekends, it is out of view of most of the domes, but is moderately priced (though the cost can be shared by up to six people per site). With a view of more climbs, and by the shores of a beautiful lake, the Tenaya Lake walk-in campground is free of charge. For those without a car, this campground has more convenient foot access to more climbs—though the big campground is far closer to Fairview Dome. Fourteen day limits are strictly enforced, especially at the main campground. Several Forest Service Campgrounds located just east of the National Park boundaries provide other camping options.

At the Tuolumne Meadows lodge, one mile east of the main campground, one can buy showers, restaurant meals and relatively luxurious quarters. Twenty miles further east (and 4,000 feet below) is the town of Lee Vining at the foot of the Sierra Nevada and the edge of the Nevada desert. Here more services can be found, including a laundromat. A pleasant day-long diversion includes a swim in the fabulous Hot Creek (a natural hot springs that is only open during the daylight hours), bouldering on the superb volcanic rock at Deadman's Summit, and maybe catching a movie in the ski town of Mammoth Lakes. Other attractions include the famous ghost town of Bodie and views of the high peaks of the Sawtooths and Mt. Conness.

SEASONS AND WEATHER

Approximate Months	Typical Temperatures High	Low	Likelihood of Precipitation	Frequency of Climbable Days
Nov-Apr	30's+	10's	med-high	low-med
May-Jun	50's+	20's+	med-high	medium
Jul-Aug	70's	40's−	low-med	high
Sep-Oct	60's	30's	med-low	med-high

Comments: The road is closed November through May because of snow. Afternoon thunderstorms are possible in the summer and wind is likely in the fall.

Bear-proof food bins

RESTRICTIONS AND WARNINGS

Bears are a problem here. Food must be well stashed by hoisting it between trees, using the bear-proof bins provided at certain sites, or locking it securely in a car trunk. These bears will break windows to reach food. Also be aware that human thieves sometimes prowl the area. Afternoon thunderstorms can be severe and have been known to precipitate accidents among the unprepared. In general, be ready for cold and wind to move in quickly.

GUIDEBOOKS
Rock Climbs of Tuolumne Meadows (1983) by Don Reid and Chris Falkenstein. Available from Chockstone Press, 526 Franklin Street, Denver, CO 80218 or from most climbing stores, the Tuolumne climbing school, and the ranger station of Tuolumne Meadows.

GUIDE SERVICES AND EQUIPMENT STORES
During the height of the summer season there is a guide service and equipment store near the main campground: The Yosemite Mountaineering School, Curry Village, Yosemite, CA 95389. Telephone (209) 372-1244 winter (Yosemite Valley) or (209) 372-1335 summer (Tuolumne).

EMERGENCY SERVICES
The nearest hospital is in Yosemite Village, Yosemite Valley. For rescues contact a ranger or call 911 in an emergency. The Park Service phone number is 372-4461.

GETTING THERE
Bus lines serve Yosemite from Merced and Fresno (both of which hold airports, though most people will bus there from San Francisco or Los Angeles). From Yosemite, buses serve Tuolumne. A more strenuous way to reach the Meadows would be to hike up either the Snow Creek or the John Muir trails. The Tioga Road (serving Tuolumne) is closed in winter.

Climbers on Daff Dome

TUOLUMNE

179

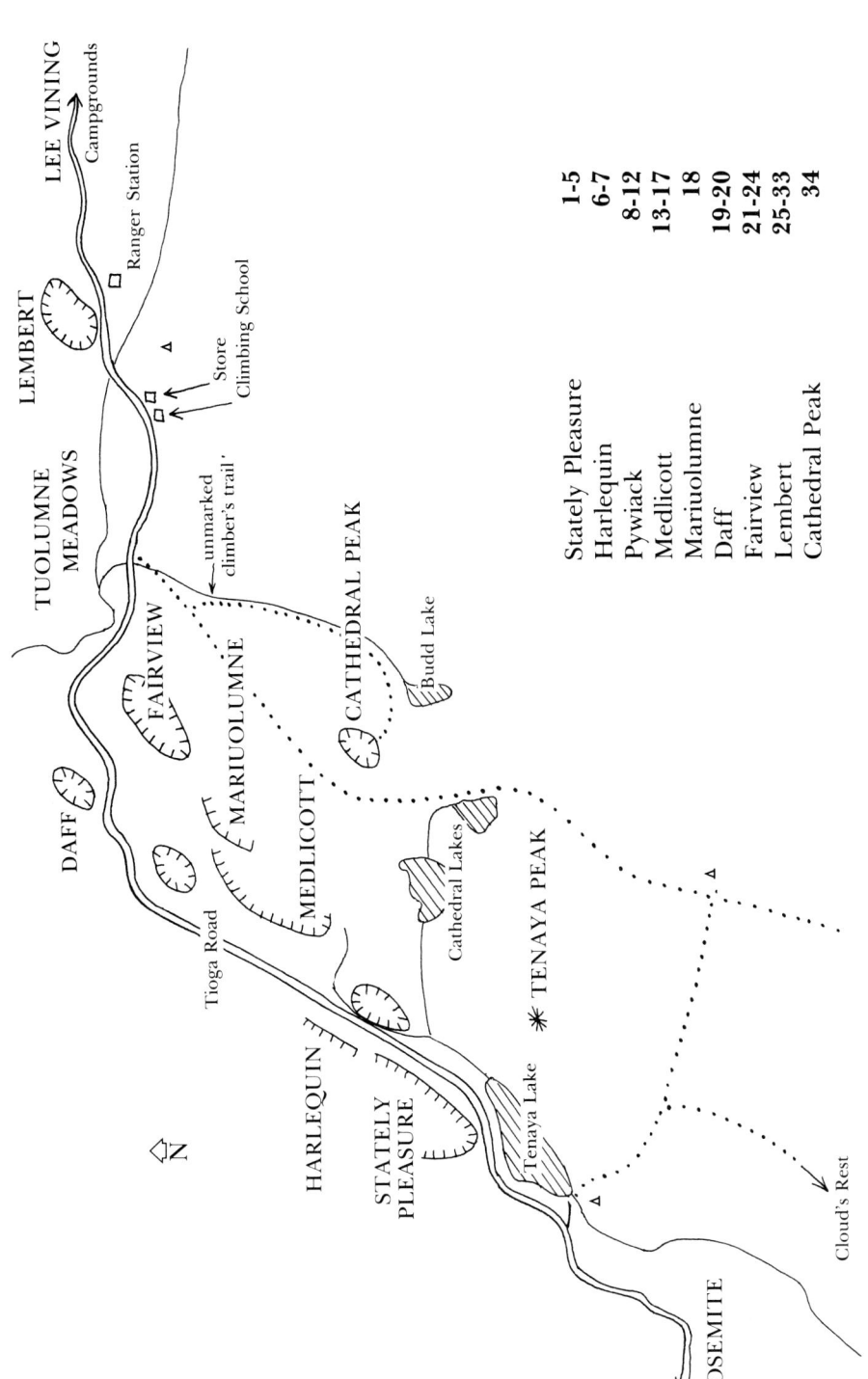

Stately Pleasure	1-5
Harlequin	6-7
Pywiack	8-12
Medlicott	13-17
Mariuolumne	18
Daff	19-20
Fairview	21-24
Lembert	25-33
Cathedral Peak	34

Tuolumne Meadows

Tenaya Lake and environs

Walt Shipley on Needle and Spoon, Pywiack Dome photo: Paul G. Gagner

Ralph Clark in the Left Water Crack, Lembert Dome

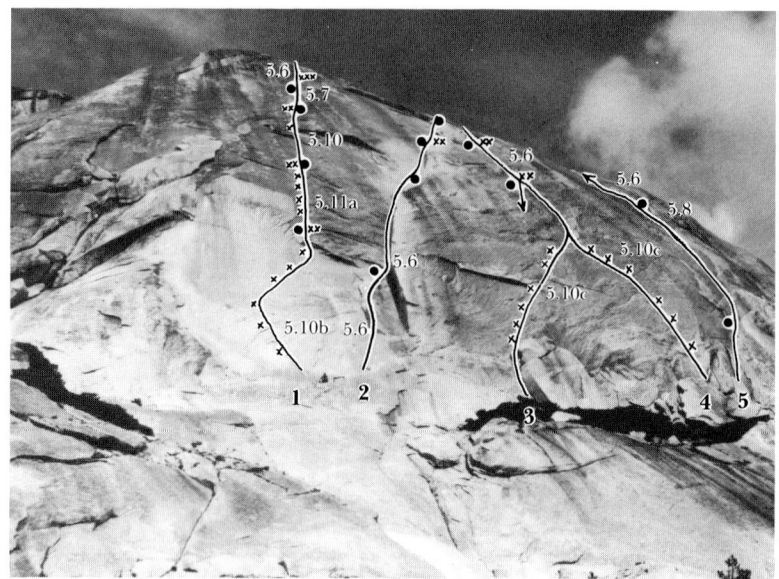

Stately Pleasure Dome

1 Table of Contents 5.11a First pitch: Dan Dingler and Steve Lesie, 1979; finish: Vern Clevenger and Claude Fiddler, 1981.

2 Great White Book 5.6 Hope Moorehouse, Jim Baldwin and Jeff Foott, 1962.

3 Get Slick 5.10c Vern Clevenger and Rob Frick, 1973.

4 Sweet Nothings 5.10c Vern Clevenger and Bill Nichols, 1974.

5 South Crack 5.8 Gordon Webster and Frank de Saussure, 1965. Very popular climb. Many smaller nuts.

TUOLUMNE

Stately Pleasure Dome

Harlequin Dome
6 Hoodwink 5.10a Jim Bridwell and Roger Breedlove, 1972.
7 The Sting 5.10b Vern Clevenger, D. Ferries and Bob Locke, 1975. Small wires.

Pywiack

8 Foott Route 5.10d or 5.11, depending on variation finish. Jeff Foott and Gary Colliver, 1968.

9 Fort Knox 5.11b Vern Clevenger and Bob Harrington, 1976. Well protected.

10 Golden Bars 5.11b Vern Clevenger, Bob Locke and Virginia Parker, 1975. Well protected.

11 Needle and Spoon 5.10a   Dennis Oakeshott, Bruce Morris and Peter Mayfield, 1975.

12 Dike Route 5.9 Tom Gerughty, Roger Evja and Dave Meeks, 1966.

Table of Contents, Stately Pleasure Dome

186 TUOLUMNE

Medlicott Dome

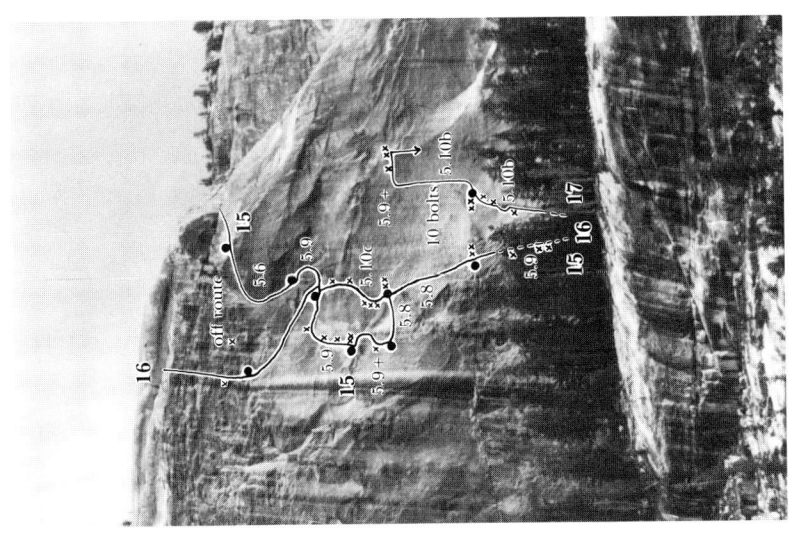

Medlicott Dome - East End

13 Scorpion 5.11a Dale Bard and Bob Locke, 1971.
14 The Yawn 5.9 TM Herbert and Gordon Webster, 1975. FFA: Phil Bircheff et al., 1969. Several large nuts to 4".

Medlicott Dome - West End

15 Sweet Jesus 5.9+ Tom Higgins and Chris Vandiver, 1972.
16 One Toke Over the Line 5.10c Vern Clevenger and John Yablonski, 1976.
17 Ciebola 5.10b Vern Clevenger, Bob Harrington and Alan Bartlett, 1977.

Mariuolumne Dome
18 Hobbit Book 5.7 Charlie Raymond and Gordon Webster, 1965.

TUOLUMNE

Daff Dome
19 West Crack 5.8 (one 5.9 move) Frank Sacherer and Wally Reed, 1963.

20 Crescent Arch 5.9+ Layton Kor and Fred Beckey, 1965. FFA: Bob Kamps and TM Herbert. Slightly runout.

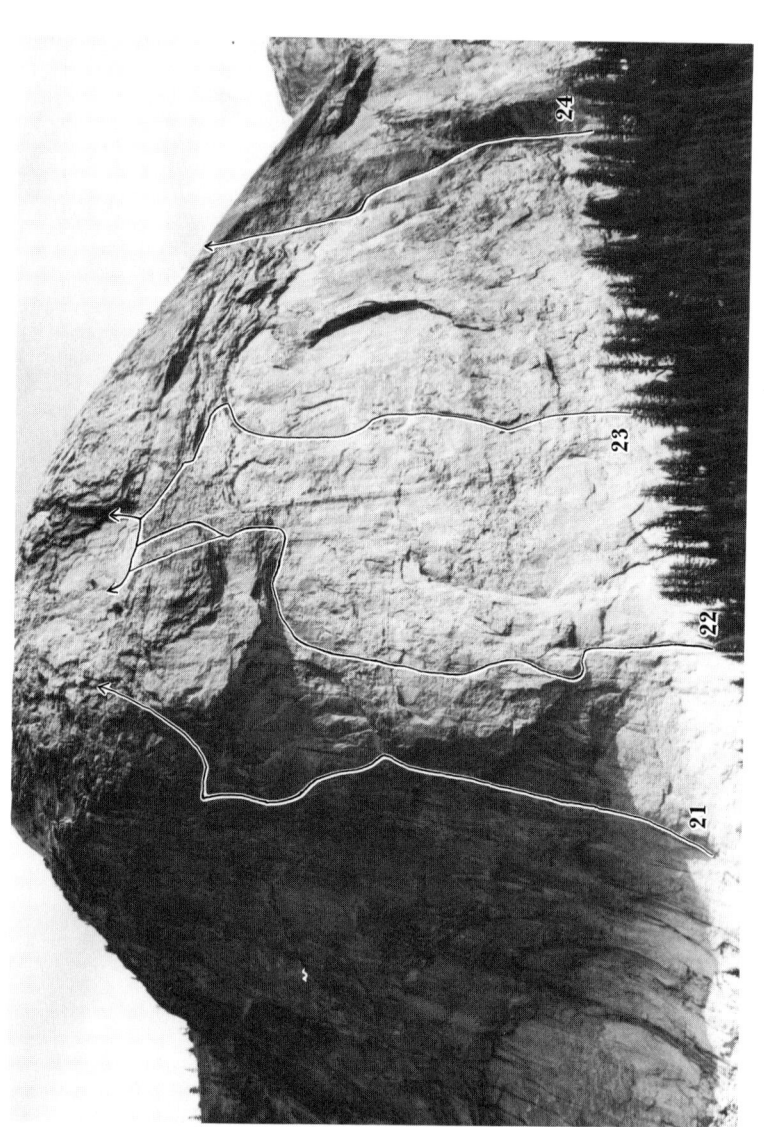

Fairview Dome

21 Regular Route IV 5.9 Chuck Pratt and Wally Reed, 1958. FFA: Steve Roper and Mark Powell, 1962. Twelve pitches if all are roped. One of the most popular routes in Tuolumne.
22 Fairest of All IV 5.10c Tom Higgins, Bob Kamps and Mike Erwin, 1973.
23 Pièce de Résistance V 5.11d Tom Higgins and Vern Clevenger, 1974.
24 Lucky Streaks IV 5.10 Bob Kamps and Tom Higgins, 1967.

TUOLUMNE

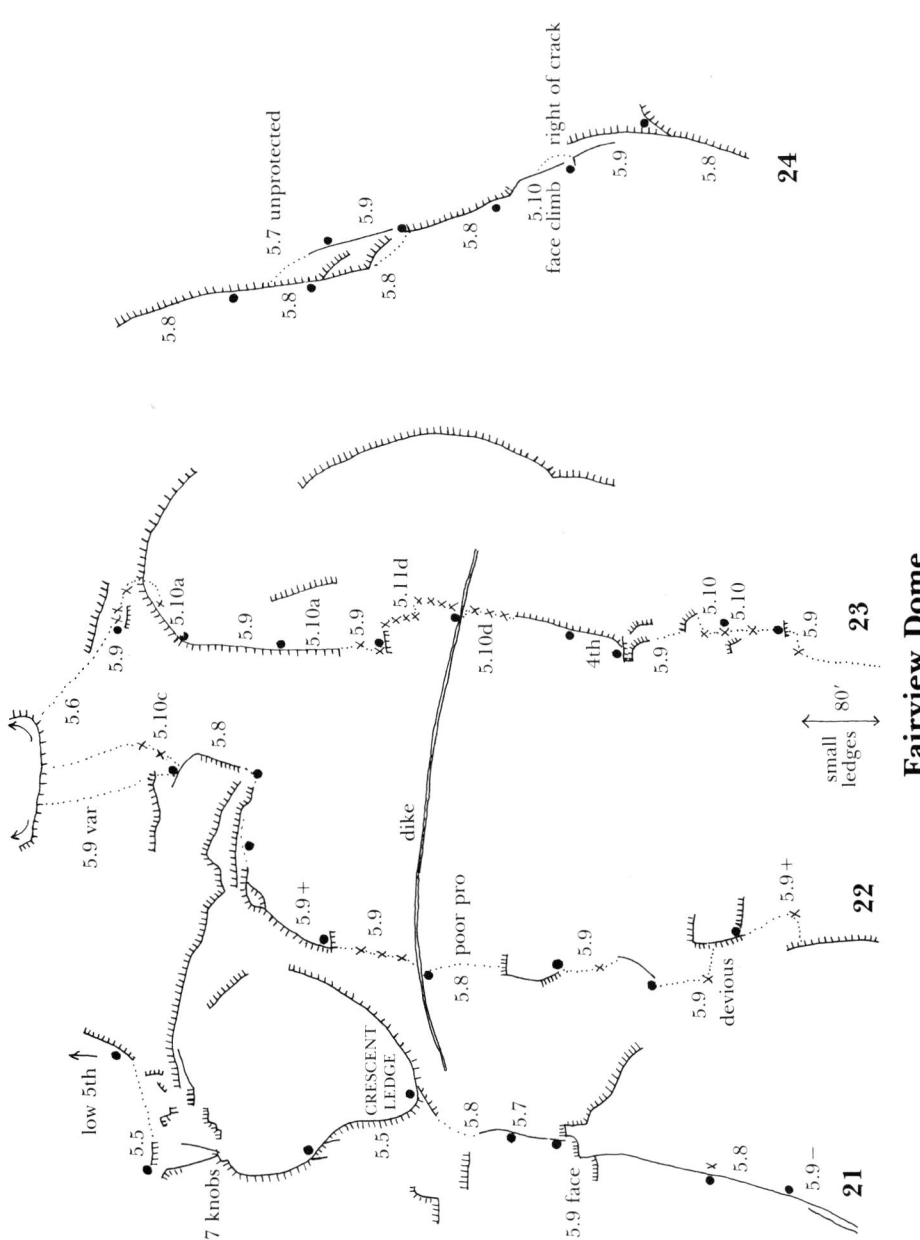

Fairview Dome

Descent from Fairview Dome

Lembert Dome

Lembert Dome

25 **Lunar Leap** 5.9 Mike Cohen, Ken Boche and Russ McClean, 1970. Spectacular leap and mantle move.
26 **Willie's Hand Jive** 5.11a Tim Harrison and Mike Breidenbach, 1973.
27 **Rawl Drive** 5.10a Bob Kamps and Tom Higgins, 1970.
28 **Truck n' Drive** 5.8 Dick Dorworth and Chris Vandiver, 1971.
29 **Left Water Crack** 5.7 Warren Harding, mid 1950's.
30 **Right Water Crack** 5.8 Warren Harding.
31 **Werner's Wiggle** 5.8 Werner Braun, 1971.

Lembert Dome - Northwest Face

32 Cry in Time Again 5.9 Bruce Morris et al. It's possible to escape before the final poorly protected pitch.
33 Big Boys Don't Cry 5.10c Kevin Leary, Rick Wheeler and Dennis Phillips, 1975. Escape is possible from the crux final pitch.
34 Direct Northwest Face 5.10b Russ Wayne, 1950's. FFA: Bob Kamps, Mark and Beverly Powell, 1962.

Cathedral Peak photo: Tom Rogers
35 Southeast Buttress 5.6   Chuck Wilts and Spencer Austin, mid 1940's.

Eichorn's Pinnacle - Cathedral Peak photo: Carl W. Smith

CALAVERAS DOME

Hammer Dome

Calaveras Dome

CALAVERAS DOME

HIGHLIGHTS
Many granite domes are scattered throughout the vast western slope of the Sierra. Although most are poorly known, word is spreading about Calaveras Dome and its 1,500 foot face of typically superb Sierran granite and convenient car access. Hammer Dome, adjacent to Calaveras, displays a less intimidating 400 foot cliff. Camping is free, though undeveloped. For those willing to drive a convoluted road, Calaveras will provide a sample of the incredible climbing that lies on the hidden domes of the Sierra.

CLIMBING
Calaveras is a typical dome, with a steep lower wall tapering upward to a lower angle. Because it faces north, occasional routes (notably the **Green Sponge**) can be mossy, but generally the granite is clean and smooth. Indeed, its north facing aspect is a major advantage in midsummer. Because of the rock's smoothness, routes on both Calaveras and Hammer either follow crack systems or are bolt-protected slab climbs. A number of short routes are available which climb Hammer or tackle just the lower reaches of Calaveras. Most complete ascents of Calaveras require a full day, or even two days of climbing. Though **Old Smokey** is 5.9, every other free route of length is at least 5.10, and aid routes range from 5.9 A3 to 5.10 A4. Indeed, 5.8 climbers will only have a few routes on Hammer Dome available to them and no routes of quality are at hand below that grade. Descents from Hammer Dome can be made

either by rappel or by a long walk off the back. From Calaveras, climbers will often rappel the entire route (two ropes are required).

ENVIRONMENT
At an elevation of only 4,000 feet, Calaveras is among the more temperate of the Sierran crags. The season is long and despite midsummer heat, climbing can be comfortable on the north faces. The Sierra Nevada receive plenty of precipitation in this area and the hillsides are densely covered with pine forests and the narrow valley floor holds numerous cedar trees. A whitewater stream flows on the valley floor, but its frigid temperature discourages swimming even on the hottest days. The large Salt Springs Reservoir located a mile up the valley holds some fish for those skilled enough to locate them. A trail runs along its north shore and eventually leads into the Mokelumne Wilderness.

CLIMBING HISTORY
The rock remained virgin until the early 1970's, although the road passing beneath the domes was built earlier. In 1972 one of the most aesthetic lines on Hammer Dome (also known as Low Cal Dome), the **Gemini Cracks**, was climbed by a skilled party who used the occasion to examine the massive Calaveras Dome across the valley. The next year they climbed the **Green Sponge** as a grade V, 5.8 A3. In the ensuing years a few, very skilled climbers took over development of the area, keeping track of the routes, but also being protective of this special place. The increasing number of people climbing here as an escape from the Yosemite madhouse are willing to share the beauties of Calaveras—but only with those who will similarly respect this treasured area.

CAMPING
White Azaleas, two miles from the domes, is the nearest official campground—though one can also camp closer to the domes by the side of the road. Campfire permits are required for this area. Water from the stream is probably safe, but as usual, it is wiser not to trust it. No services of any kind are available in the area.

SEASONS AND WEATHER

Approximate Months	Typical Temperatures High	Low	Likelihood of Precipitation	Frequency of Climbable Days
Nov-Mar	40's	30's	medium	med-low
Apr-June	70's	40's	medium	very high
Jul-Aug	90's+	50's	very low	medium
Sep-Oct	70's−	40's	med-low	high

Comments: The north-facing routes on Calaveras can be climbed in summer, but temperatures can be hot. South-facing Hammer Dome can be nice in winter. Snow falls occasionally in the winter, closing access to routes. In late winter, ice falling from the top of Calaveras can make the routes there excessively dangerous.

RESTRICTIONS AND WARNINGS
Watch out for vicious poison oak bushes and for rattlesnakes. Serious rescues would have to be performed by helicopter and would be extremely expensive.

GUIDEBOOKS
At press time, none were available to the public.

GUIDE SERVICES AND EQUIPMENT STORES
Climbing Unlimited, located in Meyers (near Lake Tahoe), is the nearest equipment store. They also guide at Calaveras Dome and can be reached at P.O. Box 11905 Tahoe Paradise, CA 95705; telephone: (916) 577-7750.

EMERGENCY SERVICES
The caretaker at the dam power plant has a phone that may be used only in the event of an emergency. For rescues call the Amador County Sheriff at 223-1131. The nearest hospital is the Amador Hospital in Jackson; telephone: 223-1120.

GETTING THERE
Though traffic is light (or non-existent), those cars that do pass by are likely to pick up a hitch-hiker. A word of warning: the last fifteen miles follow an incredibly winding, twenty mile-per-hour, paved but potholed road.

CALAVERAS DOME

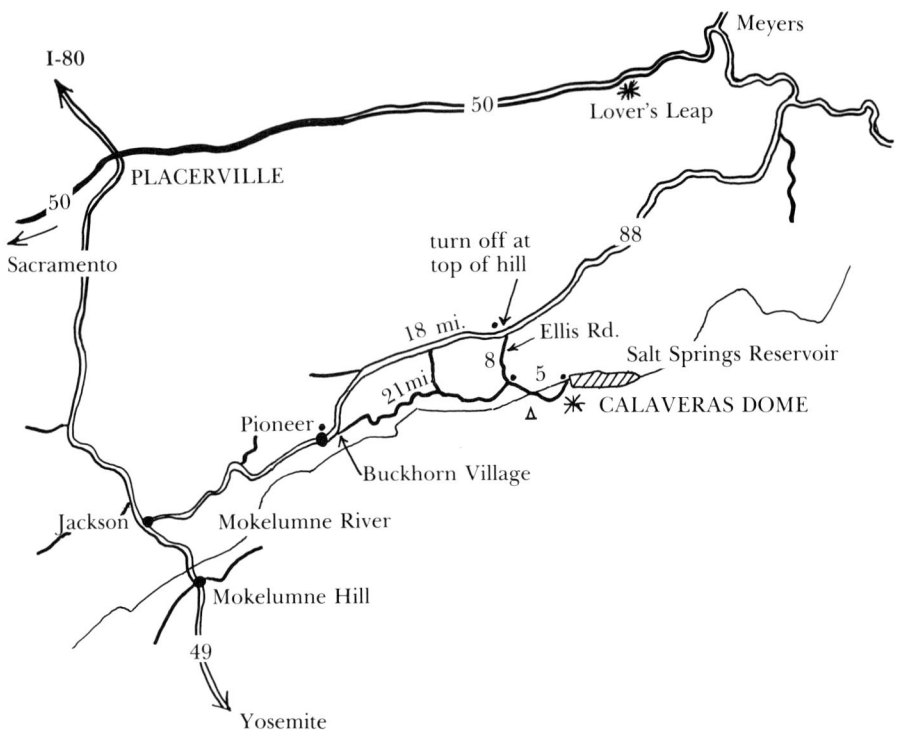

Calaveras Dome

When it is open, use the eastern access road. When this is closed due to snow, use one of the western access roads.

CALAVERAS DOME

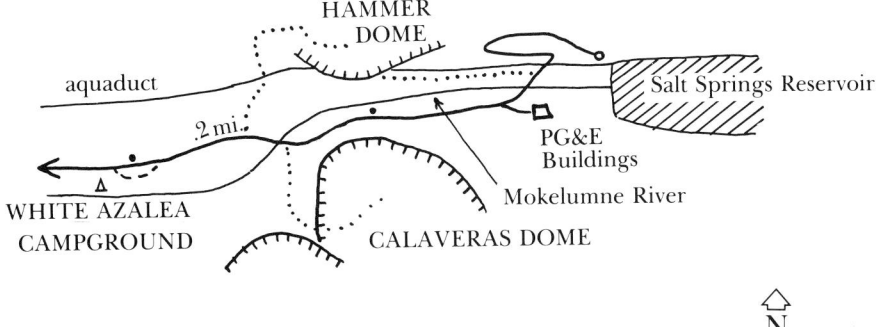

Calaveras Dome

CALAVERAS DOME

Hammer Dome

CALAVERAS DOME

Robert Boyd on Gemini Cracks

photo: Brock Wagstaff

Hammer Dome

Descent: Rappel the route or walk off either west (across slabs and down to aquaduct, along this for ¼ mile, then down to road at bridge—easiest but longer) or east towards reservoir (brushy). Most routes and rappels require a 165 foot rope.

1 Set the Controls for the Heart of the Sun 5.11 Paul Crawford and Karl McConachie, 1981. 3 pitches: 5.11, 5.10b, 5.8. Bolt protection and belays.

2 Stage Fright 5.9 Jay Smith and Jeff Altenburg, 1978. Second pitch is 165'. Poison oak bush at start of the route.

3 Corn Cob 5.8 FA: unknown. Vicious poison oak bush at start of the route.

4 Gemini Cracks 5.8 (or 5.9 var.) Greg Donaldson and Brian Cox, 1972.

5 Smoke Screen 5.10b or c Jay Smith and Paul Crawford, 1980.

6 Bad News 5.11a Jay Smith and Randy Grandstaff, 1980. 165+ feet. (Best belay at tree).

7 Red Eye Express 5.10a Jay Smith and Gary Anderson, 1980.

8 Too Bad 5.11a Jay Smith and Paul Crawford, 1982.

9 Wings and Stings 5.7 FA: unknown.

10 Sea of Holes 5.10a Jay Smith and Jeff Altenburg, 1978.

11 Itsy Bitsy Variation 5.10a Jeff Altenburg and Bob Pinkney.

CALAVERAS DOME

Calaveras Dome

Descent: Either rappel a route (War of the Walls is best), or better, walk off west between Calaveras Dome and the Hidden Wall.

12 Tsunami IV 5.11c or d Jay Smith and Paul Crawford, 1983. "Tsunami" means tidal wave.

13 War of the Walls IV 5.10c Jay Smith and Jeff Altenburg, 1978.

14 Beacons from Mars IV 5.10d Jay Smith, Jeff Altenburg and Brock Wagstaff, 1979.

15 Sole Sacrifice II 5.11a Jay Smith and Paul Crawford, 1980.

16 Thunderbolt II 5.10b Jay Smith and Jeff Altenburg, 1979.

17 Old Smokey III 5.9 Jeff Altenburg, Bob Pinkney, et al., 1977. The arch is somewhat decomposed.

CALAVERAS DOME

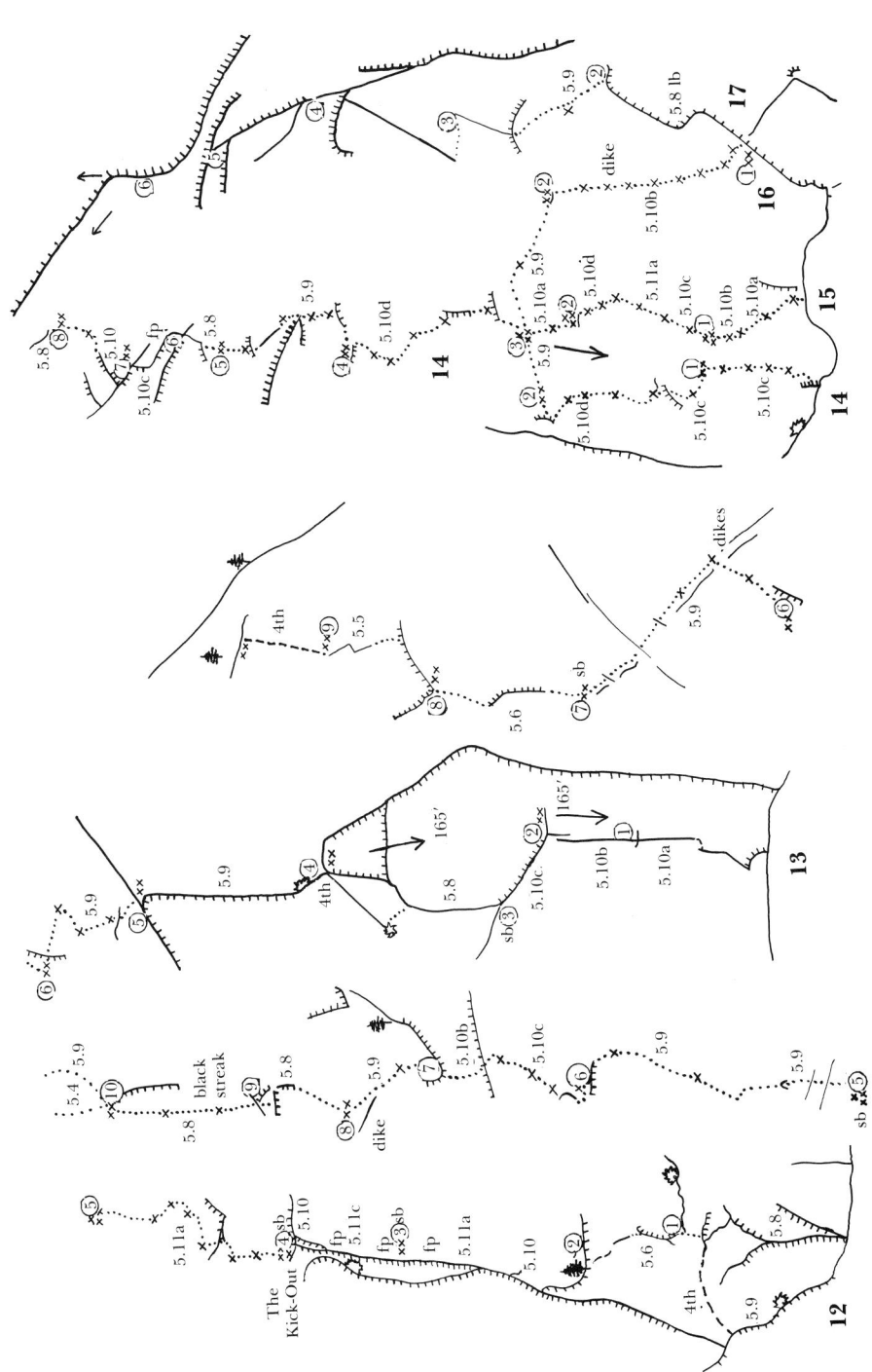

Paul Crawford follows the third pitch of Tsunami photo: Jay Smith

CALAVERAS DOME

Jay Smith on the first ascent of Beacons from Mars
photo: Brock Wagstaff

Lover's Leap - The Main Wall and Lower Buttress

LOVER'S LEAP

HIGHLIGHTS
Lover's Leap seems to inspire uniform affection among climbers who have visited the area. Offering a tremendous selection of diverse routes on a steep granite cliff 300-600 feet high, the Leap has the reward for the climber who likes steep and airy walls. Free camping is available at the head of the road—within a fifteen minute walk of some routes—and the northwest exposure makes midsummer climbing comfortable. In addition, the area is only three hours from San Francisco. Climbing here is excellent and so popular that on most summer weekends it is very crowded.

CLIMBING
The Leap is renowned for the horizontal bands of dikes that cross major sections of the granite face. Where particularly pronounced, these striations can make even the steepest wall amazingly easy. Indeed, the **Surrealistic Pillar** requires a long succession of identical mantle moves up a vertical staircase. Additionally, the Leap offers varied climbing of every sort, from thin face to large crack. The area is dominated by a major cliff almost 2,000 feet long which tapers from 600 to 300 feet high, but also includes the smaller Lower Buttress. There are over fifty routes from 5.5 to 5.11—with the majority in the comfortable middle range. Lover's Leap offers far more quality routes in the lower and middle grades than one can find in other Western rock climbing centers. Approaches to the climbs range from ten minutes to an easy half-hour,

and descents are walk-offs to the east that lead past a spring.

ENVIRONMENT

Looming just off the major road to South Lake Tahoe, the Leap impresses all who drive by. The residents of the small town located along the access to the rock have tried to block climbers, but thanks in part to the efforts of the American Alpine Club and a cooperative National Forest Service, public access has been maintained and a camping area installed. Even though the surrounding mountains and hills are densely forested and sport craggy outcrops, the proximity of the highway and community eliminates any sense of wilderness from the climbing experience. At a 7,000 foot summit elevation and lying in one of the heaviest snow deposit zones in the country, the weather is still mild enough for comfortable climbing from the early spring to late fall.

Offering an entertaining diversion to the climbing is a taste of the gaudy glitter of gambling in nearby Nevada. Closer to the hearts of most outdoor loving climbers, Lake Tahoe, the "Jewel of the Sierra," is considered one of the world's most beautiful large lakes.

CLIMBING HISTORY

Lover's Leap was discovered by the climbing community during the early 1950's. At a time when Yosemite was the overwhelmingly predominant challenge for climbers, little attention was paid to this "obscure" cliff to the north. In the 1960's, however, many people began to want an escape from Yosemite's midsummer heat, crowds, and intense competition.

The Leap soon became a regular haunt for many climbers. A 1969 guidebook-style write up in *Ascent* stimulated a burst of new route activity including the first 5.10 routes. In the ensuing years, new routes were put up by a diverse group of Yosemite climbers as well as an increasing number of resident climbers. During the mid-1970's free soloing became fashionable and a number of extremely bold and poorly protected routes were established. Though during this period locals played a role in most of the first ascents, Yosemite regulars established the first Lover's Leap 5.11 as well as 5.12 and even 5.13 routes on nearby Sugarloaf rock. A guidebook to the Lake Tahoe region, including Lover's Leap, was published in 1976, followed by another in 1980.

It is surprising that even though Lover's Leap is widely considered one of the finest climbing cliffs in the country and receives considerable traffic, it is still little known to the climbing world at large.

CAMPING

Camping for the Leap is conveniently located next to the car, just below the cliffs, and it is free. It can, however, be crowded and thefts have occured. Potable water is available, as is an outhouse, but all trash MUST be carried out and disposed of elsewhere. Because public access has been maintained only through intensive negotiation with local landowners, please be especially careful to maintain the condition of the campground.

Nearby South Lake Tahoe offers all the conveniences of a city, including a Recreation Complex with inexpensive showers, heated pool, weight room, and more (1180 Rufus Allen Boulevard, 541-4611). Various camping alternatives can also be found on the west shore of Lake Tahoe. While the gambling may not interest most climbers, all-you-can-eat buffets are available in many casinos at winning prices.

SEASONS AND WEATHER

Approximate Months	Typical Temperatures High	Low	Likelihood of Precipitation	Frequency of Climbable Days
Dec-Apr	40's	10's	medium	med-low
May-Jun	60's+	30's−	low-med	high
Jul-Sep	80's	40's	very low	very high
Oct-Nov	50's+	30's	low	med-high

Comments: Lover's Leap faces north.

RESTRICTIONS AND WARNINGS
Keep in mind that intense disputes have arisen between local landowners and the climbing community—discretion is strongly advised. Watch out for rattlesnakes.

GUIDEBOOKS
No guide books are currently in print or generally available. Visit Climbing Unlimited for more route information.

GUIDE SERVICES AND EQUIPMENT STORES
Climbing Unlimited provides instruction, guiding and equipment. They are headquartered in Meyers on Highway 50 and can be reached at P.O. Box 11905 Tahoe Paradise, CA 95705; telephone: (916) 577-7750.

EMERGENCY SERVICES
The nearest hospital is Barton Memorial Hospital on South Avenue and 4th; telephone: 541-3420. For rescues contact the El Dorado County Sheriff at 544-3464.

GETTING THERE
Greyhound Bus Lines serves South Lake Tahoe. With a polite request, the driver will stop at the small community of Strawberry, near the Leap.

LOVER'S LEAP

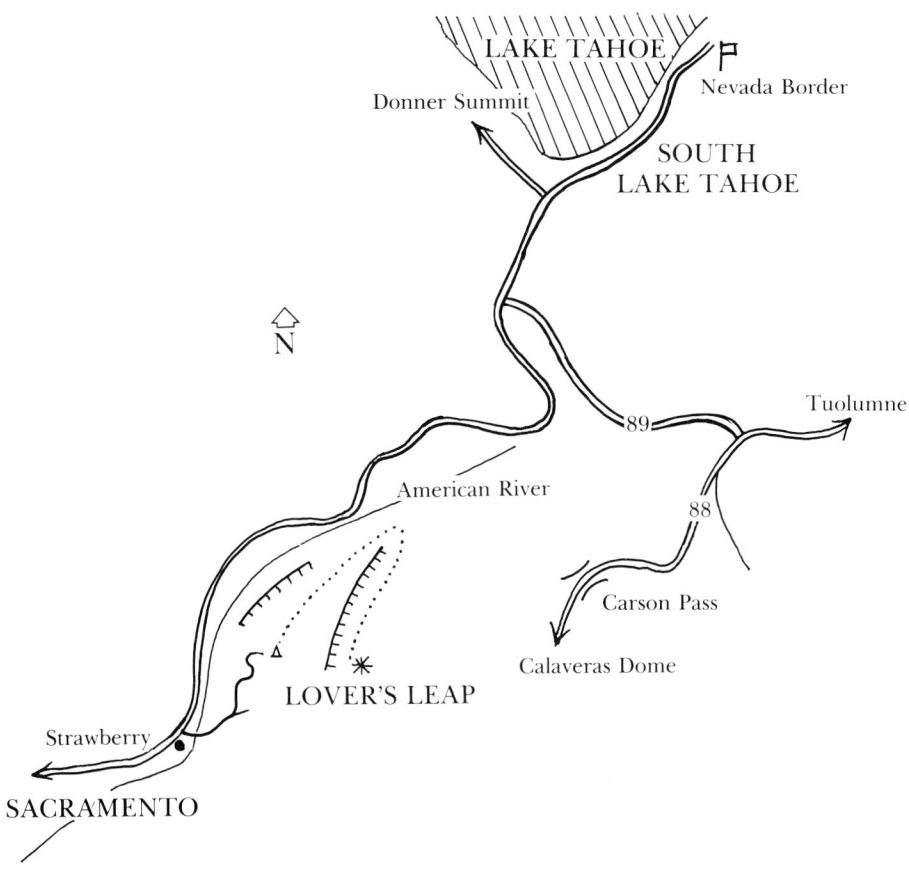

Lover's Leap

East Wall

1 Haystack 5.8 Ken Edsburg, TM Herbert and Jerry Sublette, 1965.

2 Fear No Evil 5.9 Norm Booth and Jay Smith, 1979.

3 Fantasia 5.8+ Royal Robbins and Ken Wilson, 1973. More bold than hard, this classic route is somewhat runout. Friends help to protect the first pitch traverse.

4 Scimitar 5.9 Michael Covington and Dick Erb. FFA: Jim Orey and Fred Van Overbeck, 1971.

5 East Crack 5.8 TM Herbert and Gordon Webster, 1966.

6 Bear's Reach 5.7 Phil Berry and Robin Linnett, 1956.

7 East Wall Route 5.6 Ken and Mike Edsburg and Jerry Sublette, 1964. Very popular, but not a beginner's route because of the unprotected traverse.

8 The Line 5.9 TM Herbert and Doug Tompkins, 1966. FFA: Tom Higgins and Frank Sarnquist, 1968. The name says it.

9 Bookmark 5.7 To Main Ledge: Steve Thompson and Gordon Webster, 1966; above Main Ledge: Phil Berry and Robin Linnett, 1954.

5.7 ow
5.7
5.7
9
5.7
5.8
fp
5.8
5.9
5.9
8
5.5
no pro
5.6
5.6
7
5.8
5.9
fp
5.7
5.8
fp
5.7
6
5.7
fp
5.9
5.9
fp
5.7
5
5.8+
5.9
fp
4
5.8+
5.8+
no pro
3
5.9
2 bolts
5.8
5.8
2
5.7
1

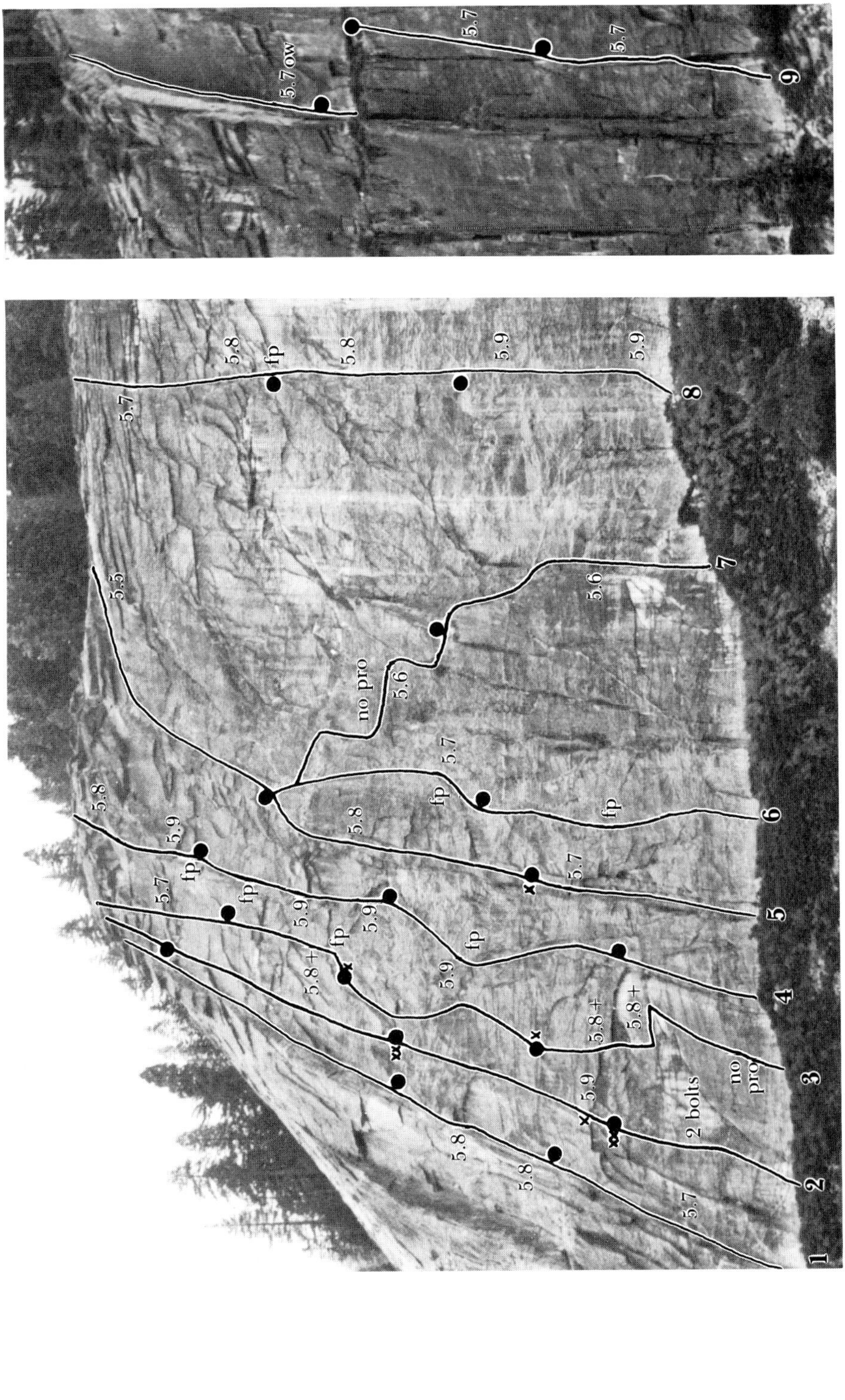

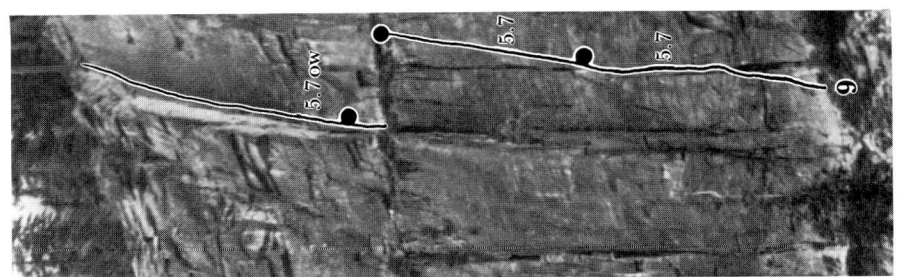

East Wall

Main Wall

10 Eagle Buttress Right Side 5.9 To Main Ledge: Phil Berry and Robin Linnett, 1956; above Main Ledge: TM Herbert and Gordon Webster, 1966. Take a 3" nut.

11 Eyeore's Ecstasy 5.7 To Main Ledge: Phil Berry and Robin Linnett, 1957; above Main Ledge: Frank DeSaussure and partner, 1953. FFA: Al McDonald and Steve Roper, 1959. 3" nut.

12 Eyeore's Enigma 5.9+ Warren Harding, TM Herbert and Galen Rowell, 1969. FFA: Jim Orey and partner, 1973. Bombay chimneys, roofs, and off-widths. Extra large nuts.

13 Traveler Buttress 5.9 To Main Ledge: Steve Roper, Steve Thompson and Gordon Webster, 1966. FFA above Main Ledge: Dick Long and Allen Steck, 1965. The classic among the many classics at Lover's Leap. 3" nut.

Main Wall
14 Corrugation Corner 5.7 Ken Edsburg et al., early 1950's.
15 Hospital Corner 5.10a Jay Smith and Rick Sumner, 1978. Continuous thin crack and bridging.
16 April Fools/ Dead Tree direct 5.8 To Slash: Gene Drake and J. Hicks, 1971. Above Slash: Bob Grow and John Harwood, 1971. 3" nut.
17 Mainline 5.11c Jay Smith and Bill Todd, 1976. FFA: John Bachar and Ron Kauk, 1978. Off-size fingers.

Janet Tornow on the Bookmark photo: Tom Rogers

Traveler's Buttress photo: Jay Smith

Lower Buttress
18 Surrealistic Pillar 5.7 Ken and M. Edsburg and Jerry Sublette, 1963. Bring a 3" nut. **Direct Start 5.10a** (or 5.10b taking thin crack through overhang) Jeff Lowe and Jean Vives, 1969.
19 The Groove 5.7 First ascent unknown.

Direct start to the Surrealistic Pillar photo: Tom Rogers

The Black Wall

DONNER SUMMIT

HIGHLIGHTS
Though the Donner Summit area holds a number of fine small crags, it is by no means worth a long trip in itself. Nevertheless, its major cliffs, the Black Wall and Snowshed Wall, are well worth a stopover day while entering or leaving California on Interstate 80. The climbing has been described as "typical California crack climbing"—which is to say superb, and on equally good granite. Because the Black Wall faces south, on a sunny winter's day its multi-pitch routes may well be climbable, despite the 7,000 foot elevation. The north facing Snowshed Wall is popular on hot summer days. Because its routes are short and extremely difficult, top-roping is popular at this cliff.

CLIMBING
Sporting cracks of all sizes and with face climbing as well, the Black and Snowshed Walls are compact masses of excellent granite climbing. About 300 feet high by almost twice that in width, the Black Wall is convoluted into several sections of cliff, some smooth and steep, others terraced and more broken. Though a few routes exist in the 5.7-5.8 range, most of the Black Wall climbs involve harder moves. Snowshed Wall's routes are shorter, but involve strenuous and difficult crack or face climbing.

ENVIRONMENT
High on an open ridge, Donner Summit features both panoramic views

and extremely convenient access. In the winter, Donner is buried in snow, though it is often still warm enough to climb if one has a means of traversing the snow-covered approach. One of the nation's largest downhill ski resorts, Squaw Valley, is within a few miles of the Summit. In the summer, the nearby north shore of Lake Tahoe is one of the premier outdoor vacation areas in California. Numerous river rafting companies abound in the region, and windsurfing on the lake can be excellent.

CLIMBING HISTORY

The Snowshed Wall gets its name from the avalanche shelter that was built over the railroad tracks that pass near the cliffs. Undoubtedly many laborers were forced to climb the rocks as they built the railway. But recorded recreational climbing at Donner Summit began in 1969 with a single route on the Black Wall. By 1973 the region was already extensively developed (mostly by a small group of Lake Tahoe area residents) and a climber's guide was published. Later in the 1970's an increasing number of "hard core" climbers took up residence in this scenic area and quite a few routes in the 5.11 and 5.12 grades were established. Because of its reputation for short hard routes, Donner is now a stopover point for many well-travelled rock climbers.

DONNER SUMMIT

CAMPING

The most famous camping expedition to Donner summit involved the 1846 wintering of the Donner Party. The story of their attempted crossing of the Sierras, starvation, and cannibalism is well known. Few climbers will choose to camp here in the winter.

A number of campgrounds can be found in the area, including the nearby Donner State Park, and all the usual services can be found in nearby Truckee or on the shores of the lake.

SEASONS AND WEATHER

Approximate Months	Typical Temperatures		Likelihood of Precipitation	Frequency of Climbable Days
	High	Low		
Nov-Apr	40's	10's	medium	low
May-Jun	60's	30's−	low-med	med-high
Jul-Aug	90's−	40's+	very low	high
Sep-Oct	70's	30's	low	high

Comments: The Black Wall faces south and can be an oven in the summer. The Snowshed Wall faces north and can be comfortable in the summer, but it is usually windy and cold in the fall.

GUIDEBOOKS

Donner Rock (1982) by Gene Drake. A looseleaf topo guide, it is sold "under the counter" at Alpenglow Sports in Truckee or may be obtained from Gene Drake, P.O. Box 3469, Truckee, CA 95734—if it stays in print long enough.

GUIDE SERVICES AND EQUIPMENT STORES

Alpenglow Sports sells some equipment in Truckee, as does the Basecamp in Tahoe City.

EMERGENCY SERVICES

The nearest hospital is the Tahoe Forest Hospital in Truckee; telephone: 587-6011. For rescues contact the Nevada County Sheriff at 587-4611.

GETTING THERE

Truckee is served by Greyhound Bus Lines, along I-80.

Max Jones on Manic Depression photo: Hoffman collection

DONNER SUMMIT

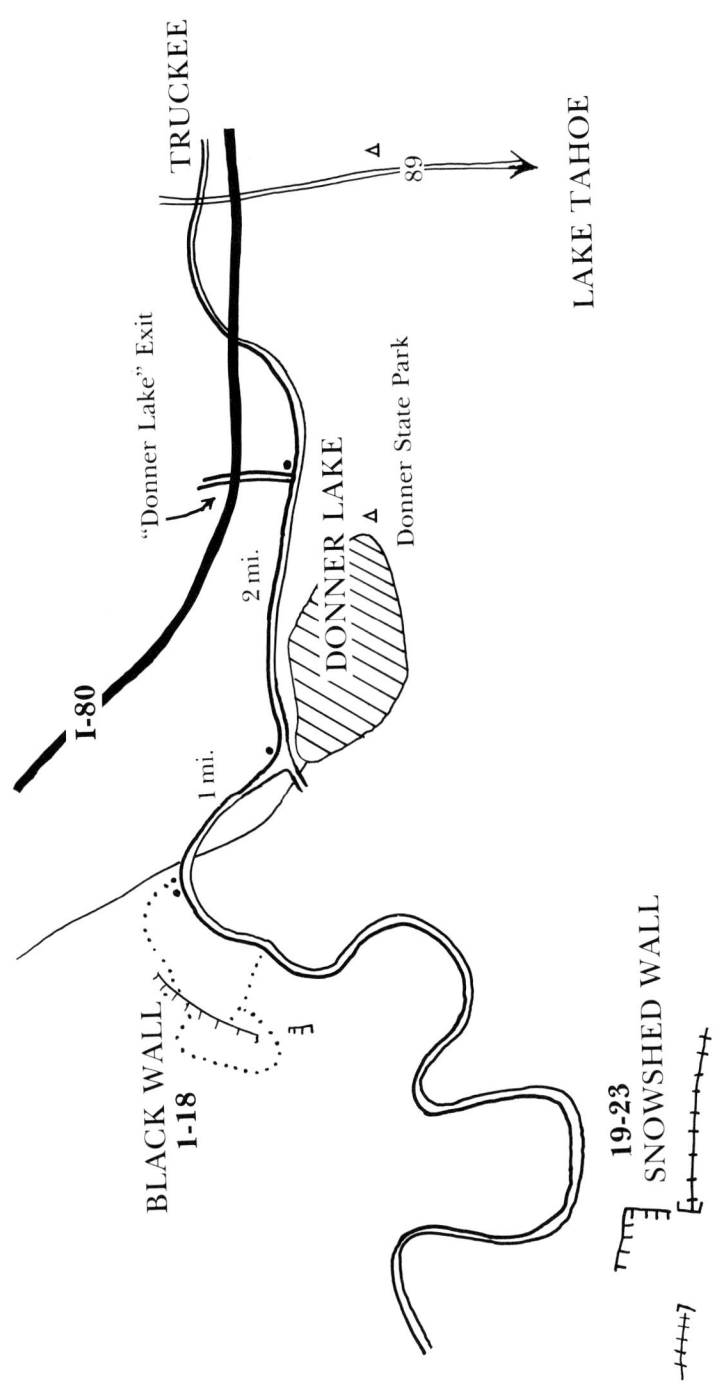

Donner Summit

228 DONNER SUMMIT

The Black Wall

The Black Wall
1 Cannibal Gully 5.7
2 Empty Overgo 5.10a
3 Touch and Go 5.9
4 One Hand Clapping 5.9
5 Skywalker 5.10a
6 Bliss 5.10d
7 Fascination 5.10c
8 Firecracker 5.10b
9 New Moon 5.10d
10 Full Moon 5.11d
11 On Ramp 5.8
12 Imaginary Voyage 5.11c

The Black Wall
13 Mr. Clean 5.10c/d
14 Inside Out 5.8
15 Lightning Bolt Roof 5.11a (or 5.12)
16 Black September 5.9+
17 Rated X 5.8 (or 5.9)
18 Fingerlicker 5.10d

Snowshed Wall photo: Eric Barrett
19 Manic Depression 5.12a
20 Monkey Paws 5.12a
21 Bottomless-Topless 5.10a
22 Panic in Detroit 5.12c
23 Peter Principle 5.11

Main area as seen from the picnic area

Asterisk Pass   photo: Tom Rogers

SMITH ROCK

HIGHLIGHTS
Smith Rock is a special place. Lying in the desert of Central Oregon, the complex of towers and cliffs commands an exquisite view of nearby snow-covered volcanic peaks. On the better routes, the volcanic rock (welded tuff) is soft, but solid nonetheless. Camping is pleasant among the open juniper scrub. With an extremely diverse collection of routes from one to six pitches in length and of every free difficulty, in addition to aid climbs, Smith Rock has something for everyone. But what truly sets it apart from other Northwest climbing areas is the predictably good weather. Most of the ten or so inches of rain that does fall comes down in early winter—leaving the rest of the year for uninterrupted climbing.

CLIMBING
Soft volcanic rock is not normally sought out for climbing. Even though the rock at Smith Rock has been likened to hardened peanut butter, both crack and face routes can still be of superb quality. Many of the clean corners provide unsurpassed stemming problems. The area is comprised of numerous distinct bluffs, some of which rise to summits, while others are simply cliffs protruding from the hillside. Most routes are between one and four pitches long, though the spectacular Monkey Face hosts routes up to six pitches in length. This pinnacle has both free and mixed routes—though doing all six pitches free involves considerable 5.11 climbing. Standards tend to be at the upper limits at Smith Rock and those seeking difficulty will be amply rewarded. There are, however,

a number of fine routes down to 5.6, and anyone should be able to enjoy the climbing. To finish off the day, any number of easily located boulders will provide problems of all difficulties. Approach walks vary from fifteen minutes to forty-five minutes in length, but the pleasantness of walking along the river bank makes them seem even shorter.

ENVIRONMENT

About three hours southeast of Portland (and some six hours from Seattle), Smith Rock lies in the rain shadow of Oregon's Cascade Mountains. The juniper scrub and sagebrush desert belies the usual stereotype of the Northwest, but it is a welcome change. Indeed, the colorful rock, the expansive vistas (due to a lack of trees), and the tremendous views of Mt. Washington, Jefferson and other snow-clad volcanoes make Smith Rock a scenic delight. An Oregon State Park, it received its status as a tourist attraction, not as a climbing area. Attesting to its popularity is a large collection of picnic tables at the end of the road, with modern restrooms and manicured lawns. Still, climbers on cliffs are far enough away from the tourists that a pleasantly isolated feeling can generally be experienced. The small town of Terrebonne is just six miles away, while the amenities of a small city can be had in Redmond, just six miles further south.

A CLIMBING HISTORY

A few Oregon mountaineers visited Smith Rock before World War II, but little is known about that period. Though some climbers attempted "everything with a summit" in the late 1940's, it wasn't until the 1960's that climbing came of age at Smith Rock. The 1960 first ascent of **Monkey Face** may have been a bolting extravaganza, but it was the first time that modern aid techniques were used in Oregon. The 1961 guidebook stimulated a burst of aid route exploration. Aid climbing was not only the passion of the times, but was further encouraged by the nature of the rock—the higher quality rock here usually demands more difficult climbing.

With only occasional exceptions, the 5.9 and 5.10 standards waited until 1972 before coming to Smith Rock. At that time climbers started applying techniques learned in Yosemite, so that by 1976, 5.10 was solidly established. Standards continued to skyrocket, and in 1977, 5.11 became common, while 1979 saw the first 5.12. By the early 1980's, considerable climbing near the top standards of the day was being done.

CAMPING

Smith Rock campsites are in an open juniper forest, perched on a bluff and with views of the cliffs across the river. Technically, it is considered "bivouacking" by the State Park and is not widely advertised to the public. A small per person fee is charged. Breakfast can be cooked on the picnic tables near the parking lot, where fresh water is plentiful and something of a climber's scene takes place. The nearest motels and laundromat are in Redmond, thirteen miles south, and public showers and excellent swimming are found at the Cove-Palisades State Park, twenty-five miles north. The tiny town of Terrebonne (three miles from Smith Rock) has a saloon, market and restaurants. Another alternative is Bend, twenty miles south of Smith. Besides a greater number of food and entertainment spots (and excellent bouldering), Bend has the Juniper Aquatic Center with its pools, showers and gyms. Wonderful swimming in a beautiful mountain setting can be found at Suttle Lake, an hour west from the summer heat at Smith Rock.

SEASONS AND WEATHER

Approximate Months	Typical Temperatures High	Low	Likelihood of Precipitation	Frequency of Climbable Days
Nov-Feb	40's	20's	medium	medium
Mar-Apr	50's	20's	low	high
May-Jun	70's−	30's+	low	very high
Jul-Aug	90's+	40's	very low	very high
Sep-Oct	70's−	30's	very low	very high

Comments: Climbing can be comfortable the year round, though spring and fall are obviously best. Despite the mid-summer heat, one can keep in the shade most of the day and climb without roasting.

RESTRICTIONS AND WARNINGS

The fragile nature of the desert terrain requires the use of established trails because of significant erosion that has taken place due to careless climber-travel. Be sure to respect neighboring private property and do not camp in the Crooked River valley. Note that the river is polluted and not recommended for swimming.

GUIDEBOOKS

Oregon Rock, A Climber's Guide (1983) by Jeff Thomas. This is the definitive guide. Available locally from the Juniper Junction store (near the entrance to Smith Rock State Park), found in many Northwest climbing stores, or obtainable from The Mountaineers Books, 715 Pike Street, Seattle, WA 98101. *A Climbing Guide to Oregon* (1976) by Nicholas A. Dodge. Available from mountaineering stores or from The Touchstone Press, P.O. Box 81, Beaverton, OR 97005.

GUIDE SERVICES AND EQUIPMENT STORES

Timberline Guides, providing classes and guided climbs at Smith Rock, can be visited in Juniper Junction, or reached at P.O. Box 464, Terrebonne, OR 97760; telephone: 548-1888. The Juniper Junction store stocks some climbing equipment, and another limited selection can be found in Bend, but the nearest major suppliers are in Portland.

EMERGENCY SERVICES

In an emergency, contact the ranger in the mobile home near the Juniper Junction store. If he is not in, the store may coordinate emergency services, but responsibility for rescues lies with the Deschutes County Sheriff: telephone 388-6655. The nearest hospital is in Redmond, thirteen miles south of Smith Rock (Central Oregon District Hospital, 1253 N. Canal Boulevard; telephone: 548-8131).

GETTING THERE

Public transportation by bus is available to Terrebonne on Greyhound Bus Lines from either Portland or Redmond (ask the driver to stop at Terrebonne). Regularly scheduled small airline flights serve Redmond, from which a car can be rented. Hitch-hiking will also serve well to reach Smith Rock. For those driving up from California, Highway 97 provides the most scenic route.

Bill Ramsey on Karate Crack photo: Alan Kearney

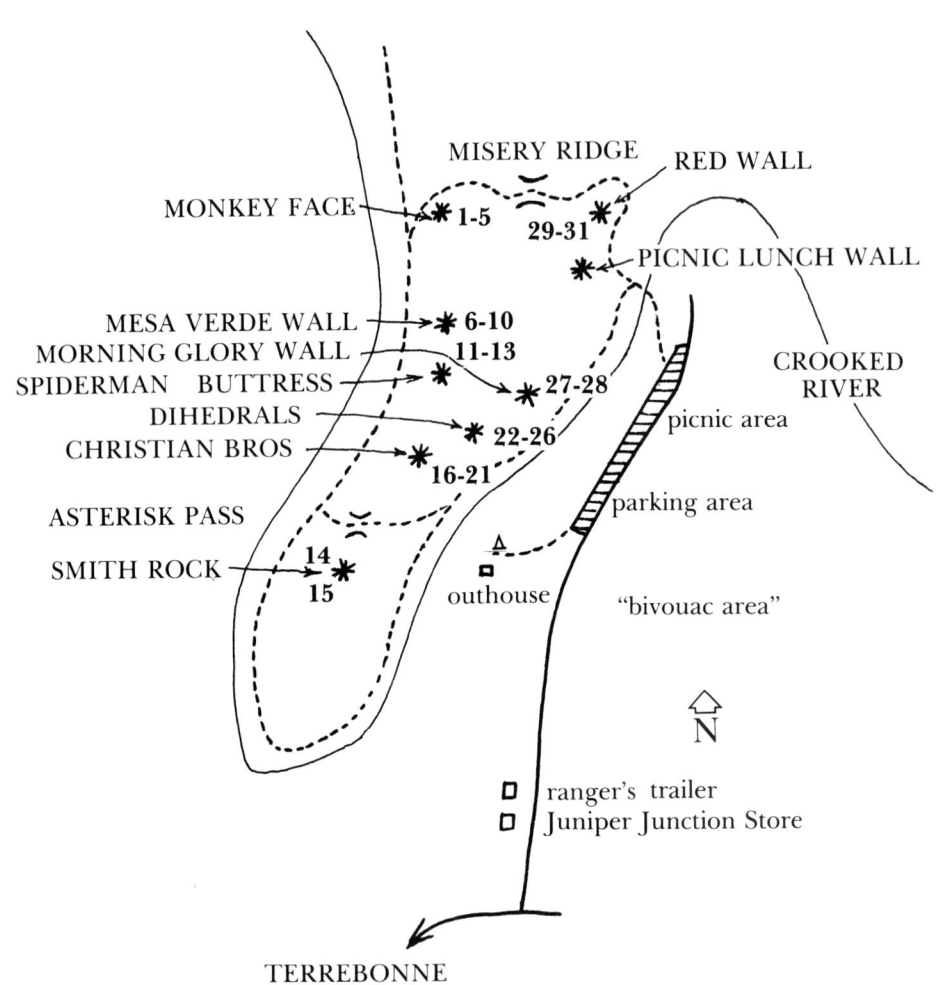

Smith Rock

Smith Rock

Monkey Face
Descent: a double rope rappel leads from bolts located on a large boulder on the east side of the summit.
1 Southwest Corner III 5.6 C4 Tom Bauman, 1970.
2 Astro Monkey III 5.11c (free variation of Southwest Corner) Different pitches freed by Mike Seely, Jeff Thomas, Mike Smelsar, Alan Watts, Bob McGown, 1972-1980.
3 Monkey Space II 5.11b Bob McGown and partner, 1978. FFA: Chris Jones and Bill Ramsey, 1979. Spectacular face climbing.
4 Pioneer Route II 5.7 C1 Dave Bohn, Jim Frazer, Vivian Staender, 1960. Bolt ladder. Exiting the cave is called the "Panic Point"—for good reason.
5 West Face Variation II 5.8 Tom Bauman and Bob Ashworth, 1965. FFA: same party, 1967.

Alan Lester on Astro Monkey photo: Alan Kearney

Mesa Verde Wall

Descent: Ledges to the north.

6 Trezlar I 5.10a Tom Rogers, Clay Cox and Bob Johnson, 1972. FFA: Jeff Thomas and Jim Davies, 1976. Descend ledges to the left.

7 Minas Morgul II 5.11d Wayne Arrington, 1972.FFA: Alan Watts, 1981. Thin cracks and a roof.

8 Down Syndrome I 5.10a First complete ascent by Chuck Buzzard, 1980.

9 Tale of Two . . . II 5.10a First complete ascent by Jeff Thomas, Chris Jones and Mike Hartley, 1978.

10 Chimney De Chelly II 5.10a Jeff Thomas and Ken Currens, 1977. Desolation Row Variation 5.11 – FFA: Alan Watts and Pat Carr, 1981. Original route is somewhat loose.

SMITH ROCK

Mesa Verde Wall

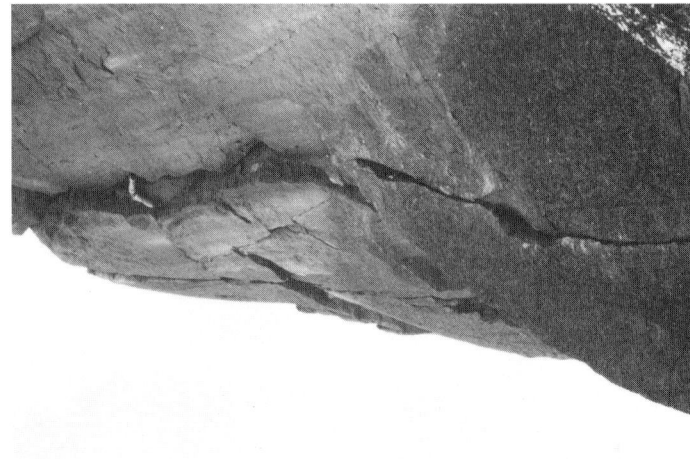

Spiderman photo: Tom Rogers

Spiderman Buttress

11 In Harm's Way I 5.7 Bob Johnson and Doug Phillips, 1975. Small nuts only.

12 Explosive Energy Child I 5.10c Mike Smelsar, Bob McGown and John Tyreman, 1976-1977. Tiny nuts only.

13 Spiderman I 5.7 Steve Strauch and Danny Gates, 1969.

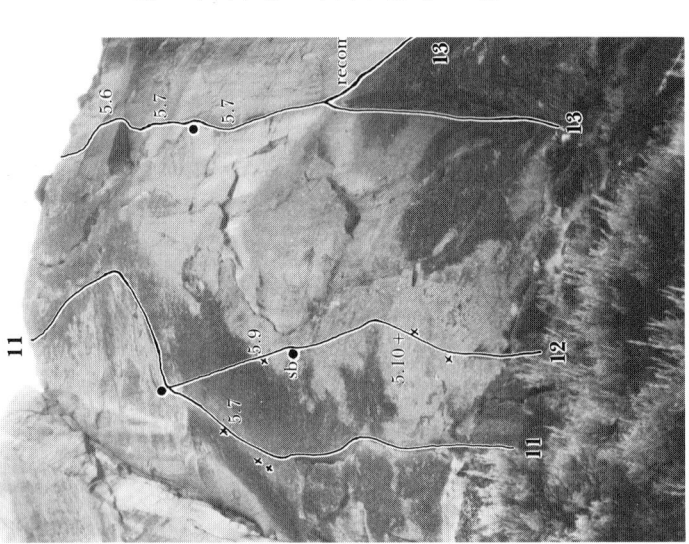

Spiderman Buttress

SMITH ROCK

The Awl
14 Inside Corner I 5.10c Jim Ramsey, 1961. FFA: unknown. Short but sweet.

Smith Rock
15 White Satin II 5.8 Jeff Thomas and Doug Phillips, 1974.

The Christian Brothers
16 Dancer (first pitch) **I 5.7** Tim Carpenter and John Tyreman, 1976. Bolt protection.
17 Hesitation Blues I 5.10b Alan Watts and Kent Benesch, 1980.
18 Revelations I 5.9 Tim Carpenter and John Tyreman, 1975. Bolt protection.
19 New Testament I 5.9 or 5.10a Dean Fry and Larry Kemp, 1973.
20 Temptation I 5.10a Alan Watts and Wayne Kamara, 1981.
21 Golgotha I 5.11a to 5.11c Alan Watts and Mel Johnson, 1981. Crux is a long reach.

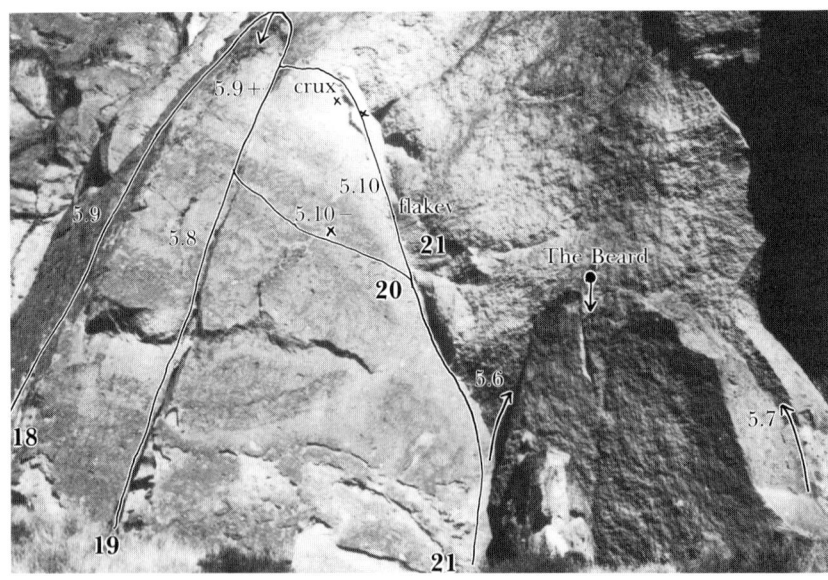

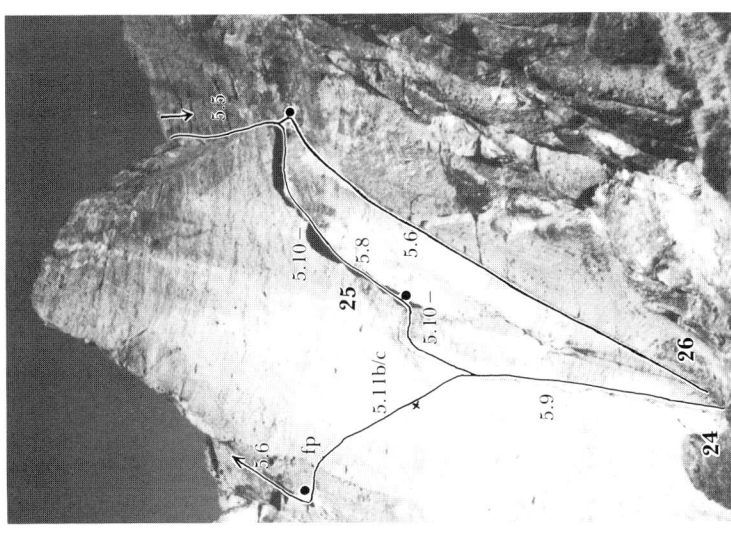

The Dihedrals

Descent: Rappel Cinnamon Slab.

22 Moonshine Dihedral I 5.9 First complete ascent unknown. Rotten rock on the second pitch.

23 Sunshine Dihedral I 5.12a First complete ascent by Tom Rogers, Dan Muir and Jack Barrar, 1971. FFA: Alan Watts and Alan Lester, 1981. Good protection, intricate stemming.

24 Karot Tots I 5.11c Dave Jensen and George Cummings, 1970. FFA: Alan Watts and Mark Cartier, 1980. Very fingery.

25 Karate Crack to the Peapod I 5.10a Dean Caldwell and Bryan Babcock, 1966. FFA: Dean Fry and Steve Lyford. A local classic.

26 Cinnamon Slab I 5.6 First complete ascent by Wayne Haack and Phil Dean, 1969. Popular favorite.

Dave Mahler on Super Slab photo: Tom Rogers

Morning Glory Wall

27 Zebra II 5.10a Bob Martin and Ray Snyder, 1970. FFA: unknown.

28 Lion's Chair III 5.11a Phil Dean, Steve Hiem and George Selfridge, 1968. FFA: Jeff Thomas and Ted Johnson, 1977.

SMITH ROCK

Red Wall
Descend Misery Ridge

29 Super Slab II 5.7 Danny Gates, 1969. FFA: Danny Gates and Neal Olson, 1970. A classic.

30 Peking II 5.8 Tom Bauman and Osa Thatcher, 1969.

31 Moscow II 5.6 Pat Callis and Mickey Schurr, 1965. Often crowded.

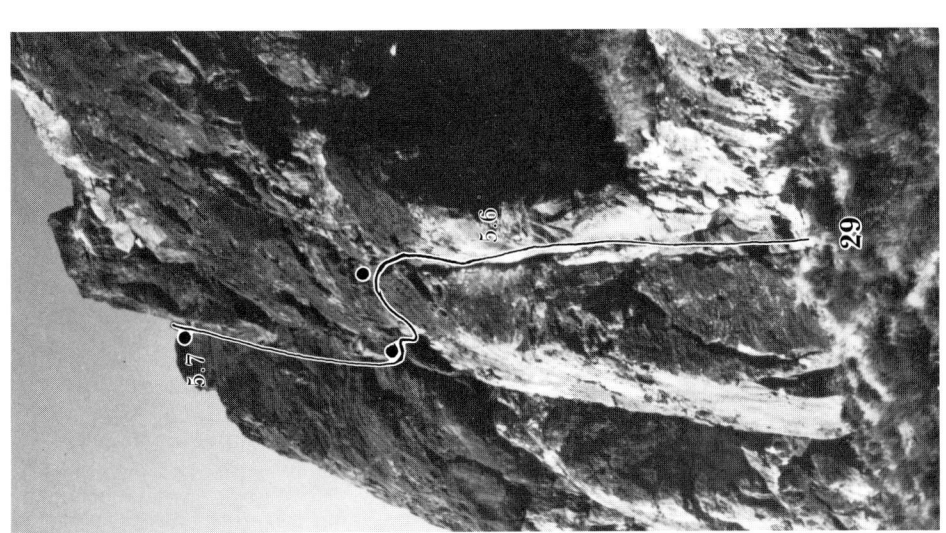

Beacon Rock and the Columbia River photo: Tom Rogers

BEACON ROCK

HIGHLIGHTS
Beacon Rock is a small crag with a number of difficult free climbs on excellent volcanic rock. Because of its small size and remoteness from other rock climbing centers, Beacon is not a destination climbing area. It is climbed principally by residents of northern Oregon and southern Washington, and it offers an excellent stop-over for climbers travelling between Smith Rock and the Washington mountains or rock climbing centers.

CLIMBING
Beacon Rock climbing takes place on a single cliff about 500 feet long by 400 feet high. The routes are almost exclusively stemming and crack climbs on very solid basalt (andesite). Almost all the routes are very steep, and few can be free climbed at less than 5.9 (though a couple of excellent 5.7 and 5.8 routes do exist). Since protection is usually good and plentiful, this is an excellent crag to push one's ability by risking falls. Routes either continue to the top of the cliff and are descended by a hiking trail, or they are rappelled after one to three pitches of climbing on the lower section of the wall.

ENVIRONMENT
Beacon Rock is located in the gorge of the Columbia River—the largest river in the Northwest. It is considered the second largest monolith in

the world (after Gibraltar) and is the eroded core of an ancient volcano. The surrounding countryside is forested rolling hills, with Mt. Hood, one of the Northwest's most spectacular volcanoes, nearby. Beacon Rock was noted by the Indians who travelled down the Columbia and was named by the explorers Lewis and Clark in 1805. Later river travellers knew this rock as indication that the last of the rapids had been negotiated and smooth water stretched to the Pacific Ocean, 150 miles away.

CLIMBING HISTORY

The first ascent of Beacon Rock was made in 1901 as a result of rivalry between two steamboat companies. Though a trail was built to the summit in 1916, rock climbing did not arrive until the **Southeast Face Route** was climbed in 1954 by a Yosemite-trained leader. This route, at 5.7, is the easiest on the cliff, but is still considered one of the best routes of its grade in the Oregon area. The **Dod's Jam** route involves a 5.9 offwidth that was led free in 1961 during an early attempt. This standard was well ahead of its time in Oregon and indeed the entire route was not freed until 1972 (5.10b) when other 5.10's were also being climbed. Climbing at Beacon Rock was restricted to the local Mazama Mountain Club members until 1969 when the American Alpine Club managed to open the area to all climbers. Now, Beacon Rock sees considerable climbing activity, principally by Portland residents.

CAMPING

Beacon Rock State Park has a moderately priced campground with kitchens, shelters, restrooms, and hot showers. Only one vehicle is allowed per campsite, with a seven day camping limit imposed. The campground can easily fill on a nice weekend, but sites are usually available during the week. Free camping is difficult to find nearby and is not legal. Laundry facilities are available one-half mile west of the park at the Beacon Rock Trailer Park (private). A small grocery store can be found further west about a mile.

SEASONS AND WEATHER

Approximate Months	Typical Temperatures High	Low	Likelihood of Precipitation	Frequency of Climbable Days
Nov-Mar	40's	30's-	very high	very low
Apr-Jul	60's+	40's	medium	medium
Jul-Aug	80's+	50's	very low	very high
Sep-Oct	60's+	40's	high	medium

Comments: High winds are possible any season. In the summer it can get very hot and humid but the sun leaves the face by mid afternoon.

BEACON ROCK

RESTRICTIONS AND WARNINGS
Beacon Rock is part of the Washington State Park system. Climbers must register before climbing and sign back in after climbing. This is done near the bulletin board located at the east end of the roadside rest area. Climbing is restricted to the south (river side) face of Beacon Rock because of rockfall hazard to the hiking trail. VIOLATIONS COULD JEOPARDIZE CLIMBING AT BEACON ROCK! Poison Oak is very common along the base of the cliff. Wearing long pants and washing after climbing is recommended. Rock fall is also possible, especially near the **Dod's Jam** area, because of the hiking trail above. Wearing a hard hat when climbing near here is a good idea. All climbing routes are difficult and climbing here should be done only by capable and experienced people.

GUIDEBOOKS
Oregon Rock (1983) by Jeff Thomas. Available from the Mountaineers Books, 715 Pike Street, Seattle, WA 98101, or locally from Portland mountaineering stores. *A Climbing Guide to Oregon* (1976) by Nicholas A. Dodge. Available from mountaineering stores or from The Touchstone Press, P.O.Box 81, Beaverton, OR 97005.

GUIDE SERVICES AND EQUIPMENT STORES
The nearest equipment stores are in Portland, Oregon.

EMERGENCY SERVICES
In case of emergency, contact the park ranger; the Park Service coordinates rescues and ambulances. The nearest hospitals are in Vancouver, about thirty-five miles away: St. Joseph's Community Hospital, 600 NE 92nd; telephone: 256-2000; Vancouver Memorial, 3400 Main; telephone: 696-5000.

GETTING THERE
No public transportation is available. Airplanes, trains, and buses serve Portland, Oregon, from which a Greyhound bus can be taken to Stevenson, Washington, about twelve miles east of Beacon Rock. Hitchhiking will get you there.

BEACON ROCK

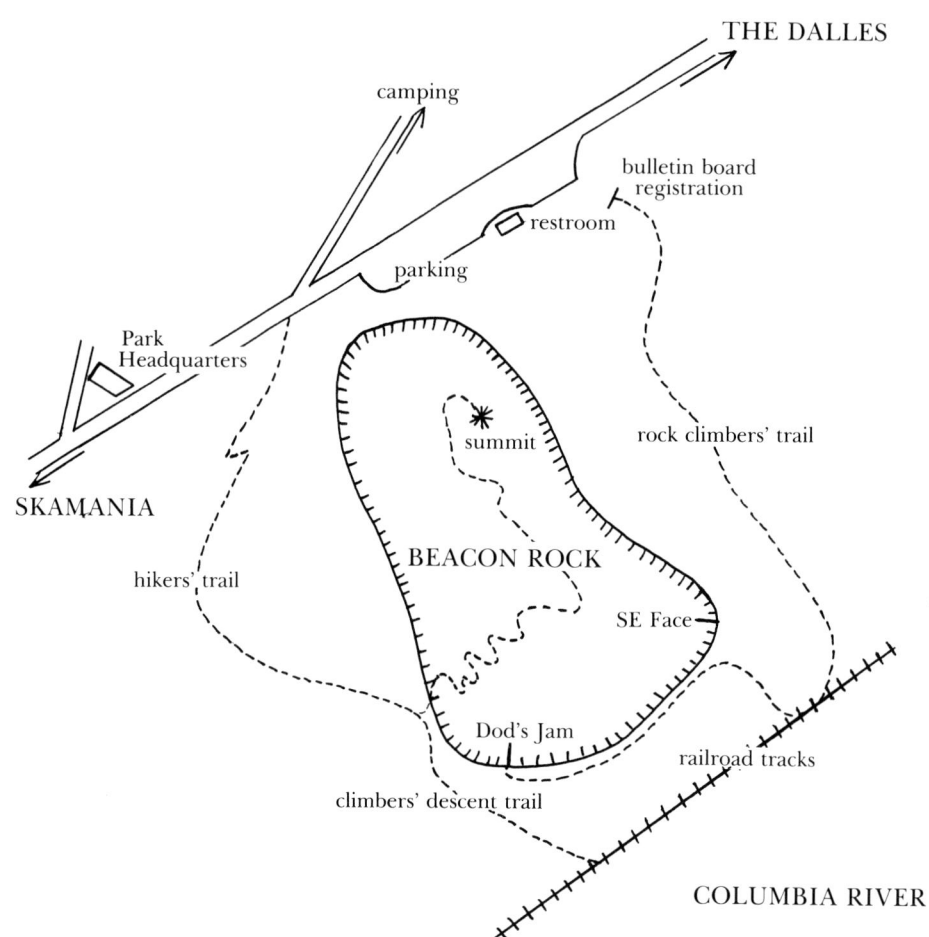

Beacon Rock

Beacon Rock – River Face

Free For All

Beacon Rock - River Face
1 **Free For Some I 5.11a** Henry Barber, 1978. Painful.
2 **Free For All I 5.8** Dean Fry and Steve Lyford, 1973. Rappel, or continue on Dod's Jam (with the crux above).
3 **Dod's Jam III 5.10b** Eugene Dod, Bob Martin and Earl Levin, 1961. FFA: Wayne Arrington and Jack Barrar, 1972. The upper cracks are 5.9, but many people rappel off.
4 **Steppenwolf to Big Ledge II 5.10c** Les Nugent, Bill Herman and Bill Nickle, 1971. FFA: Bob McGown, Levi Grey and Mike Smelsar, 1977. Pitch above Big Ledge 5.12 – FFA: Alan Lester, 1983.

BEACON ROCK

Beacon Rock - River Face

Dod's Jam

Beacon Rock - River Face

5 Blownout II 5.10a Steve Strauch and Danny Gates, 1969. FFA: Jeff Thomas and Ken Currens, 1976.

6 Second Wind variation to Blownout II 5.11d Ted Johnson and Bill Strayer, 1981.

7 Bluebird II 5.10a or b Jeff Elphinston and Dave Mention, 1972. FFA: Jeff Thomas, Monty Mayko and Ed Newville, 1976.

8 Bluebird Variation #3 I 5.9 Jeff Elphinston and Dave Mention, 1972.

9 Left Gull III 5.10a or 5.8 A0 Dean Caldwell and Chuck Erwin, 1965. FFA: Jeff Thomas and Steve Lyford, 1973.

10 Right Gull III 5.10a or 5.7 A0 Dean Caldwell and Chuck Erwin, 1965. FFA: Dean Fry, 1972.

11 Southeast Face III 5.7 John Ohrenschall and Gene Todd, 1954. Easiest route, but a classic.

BEACON ROCK

Beacon Rock - River Face

Snow Creek Wall is the smooth sunlit face

Photo from Icicle Canyon by Tom Rogers

LEAVENWORTH

HIGHLIGHTS
Leavenworth is Washington's traditional crag climbing area. Of primary importance to most climbers is the fact that Leavenworth is far drier than any other climbing area in the state. Besides its climate, the area offers both diverse granite climbs and the only sandstone climbing in the Northwest. Thus, Leavenworth provides a smorgasbord of friction, face and crack climbs from one to seven pitches in length. Camping is both excellent and convenient, and the town of Leavenworth is a suprisingly attractive, fake Bavarian village.

CLIMBING
The Leavenworth area can be divided into four distinct sub areas. Castle Rock is the original and most popular of the crags. Situated next to the main road, its steep rough granite walls hold excellent two pitch routes from 5.5 to 5.11.

Peshastin Pinnacles is perhaps the second most popular area and is unique in the Northwest. Its soft white sandstone has occasional protruding pebbles that provide diverse friction and face climbing, as well as cracks. All levels of difficulty are well represented here. While most routes are one pitch, there are several two pitch climbs as well. Most routes have the added appeal of climbing to summits. Peshastin is one of the driest places in the state of Washington and in mild years climbing is possible the year round (except late summer and fall when the rocks are closed because of apple harvesting in the nearby orchard). The approach to the Pinnacles involves a minimal walk through the orchard and some desert scrub.

Snow Creek Wall is by far the largest crag in the Leavenworth area. At the end of an hour long uphill hike along an excellent trail, the spectacular granite wall presents a multitude of seven pitch routes, all 5.8 or harder. The rock is rough, steep and solid, and its crack climbs are oftentimes combined with a unique knobby face climbing.

Icicle Creek Canyon is where most people camp and its many boulders offer excellent climbing, roped and unroped. Except for some of the Peshastin Pinnacles, rappels are not needed to descend from climbs in the Leavenworth area.

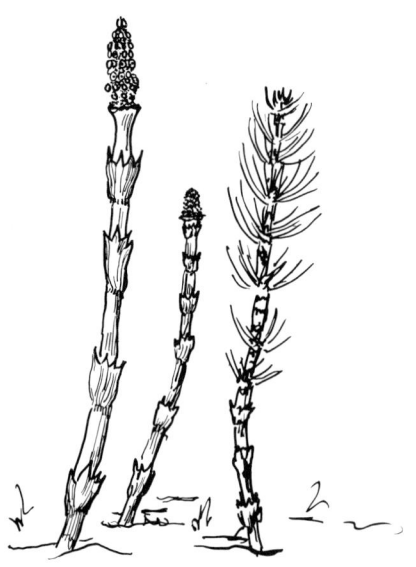

ENVIRONMENT

On the eastern slope of the Cascades, Leavenworth lies in a rain shadow. Though well forested with coniferous trees, the fir, hemlock and spruce trees of the western side give way to pine forests on the eastern slope. One notices immediately the lessened undergrowth and dustier air of the east side. Peshastin, ten miles further east, is out of the foothills entirely (at the start of the eastern Washington plains) and is desert. The orchards lining the valley floor must be continually irrigated. But these orchards provide summer climbers with a fruit feast that is unsurpassed anywhere in the world. The town of Leavenworth, a "Bavarian" village, is packed with tourists in summer months. Away from the town and the fruit stands, the rivers can provide good fishing and the numerous trails some pleasant hikes into the spectacular mountains of the Alpine Lakes Wilderness Area. Several rafting companies will be happy to provide further diversion.

CLIMBING HISTORY

Midway, a 5.5 on Castle Rock, was one of the pioneering rock climbs in Washington. Until then, climbers did only the minimum rock climbing necessary to reach a desired summit. The first ascent of **Midway** involved aid, fixed ropes, and multiple attempts before its completion in the late 1940's. By 1957 people were taking rock climbing more seriously and the number of Leavenworth area routes shot up to over a hundred. But the crags were still used almost exclusively as training for the mountains and Washington rock climbing lagged well behind other crag areas in America. By the mid 1960's, some pure rock enthusiasts began plumbing the area's true potential. In 1965, after the first visit to Yosemite by locals, the new(!) technique of "jamming" in cracks was introduced. During the 1970's climbing suffered a doldrums stage, but with the coming of the 1980's climbers discovered a new willingness to clean grungy rocks in quest of first ascents, allowing a boom in route production.

CAMPING

Icicle Creek Canyon holds a wealth of Forest Service pay campgrounds and completely free tenting near the road. Shown on the map are some of the campgrounds and the unofficial "climber's campground"— which is free. Water from the nearby stream is definitely not potable. Icicle Canyon is aptly named, for if the temperature elsewhere near Leavenworth is pleasantly warm, it could still be time for pile jackets in the Canyon. Another option for climbers principally interested in Snow Creek Wall is to pack in near the base of the wall, next to the creek. Many hotels are available in Leavenworth, and showers can be obtained at "The Court House," a health and fitness facility located at 3 Titus Road. The nearest laundromat is several miles away in the town of Peshastin. The KOA campground offers a more expensive alternative for cleaning up.

SEASONS AND WEATHER

Approximate Months	Typical Temperatures		Likelihood of Precipitation	Frequency of Climbable Days
	High	Low		
Nov-Mar	30's+	20's−	medium	med-low
Apr-Jun	60's−	40's−	low	med-high
Jul-Sep	70's+	40's+	very low	very high
Oct	50's	30's	med-high	low-med

Comments: These predictions would apply best at Castle Rock. For Snow Creek Wall decrease the temperature perhaps ten degrees and increase the likelihood of precipitation slightly. For Peshastin Pinnacles, increase the temperature ten degrees and reduce the precipitation, except in October when miserable drizzles are likely, but climbing is usually off limits anyway.

RESTRICTIONS AND WARNINGS

No Leavenworth crag requires signing out, but the Peshastin Pinnacles are on private land and must be carefully respected to ensure continued access. The Pinnacles have been closed before and could be closed again if climbers are not careful! During the fall apple harvesting season, the area is likely to be off limits (approximately September and October). Always enter through gates and DO NOT BLOCK ACCESS ROADS. The rock near Eight Mile Campground is also on private land and cars are prohibited. For your own sake, watch out for poison oak and rattlesnakes. Another warning: When parking along side the road near Peshastin or in Icicle Canyon, be sure to stay off the white line at the road's edge— a ticket is likely otherwise.

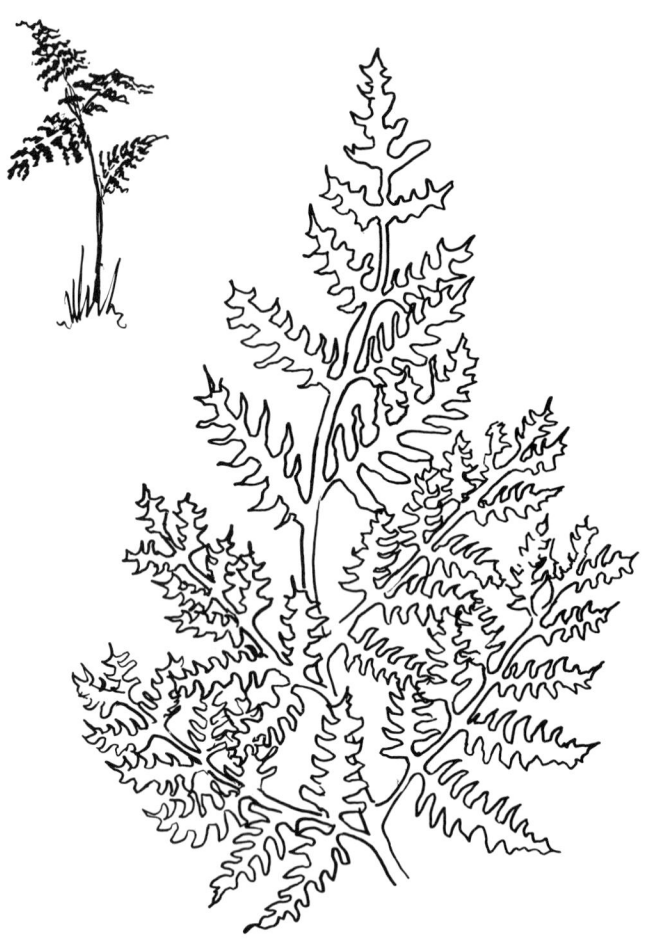

GUIDEBOOKS

A Climber's Guide to Washington Rock (1982) by Don Brooks, is available from The Mountaineers Books, 715 Pike Street, Seattle, WA 98101 or from Northwest area mountaineering stores. An extremely valuable further reference is *Rock Climbing Leavenworth and Index, a guide*, (1976) by Rich Carlstad and Don Brooks. Though it is out of print and hard to find, it has excellent photographs.

GUIDE SERVICES AND EQUIPMENT STORES

Leavenworth Alpine Guides is available at 106 211th Place NE, Redmond, WA 98053. This is a relatively large outfit, offering diverse classes and guiding. Climbing and backpacking equipment is available at The Alpinist, 894 Hwy 2, Leavenworth. Also based out of Leavenworth are the North American Alpine Guides at Eight Mile Creek, Leavenworth, 98826; telephone: (509) 548-4140. While they specialize in big alpine climbs, they also offer local routes and courses—and they have a basecamp near Leavenworth.

EMERGENCY SERVICES

The hospital in Leavenworth is the Cascade Hospital and Clinic at 817 Commercial Street; telephone: 548-5815. For rescues, contact the Shellan County Sheriff at 911 emergency, or 548-7931 non-emergency.

GETTING THERE

Public transportation from Seattle is available by Greyhound Bus Lines. The nearest airport with scheduled service is in Wenatchee, twenty-five miles east. Hitch-hiking works reasonably well for getting to Leavenworth and to the climbs.

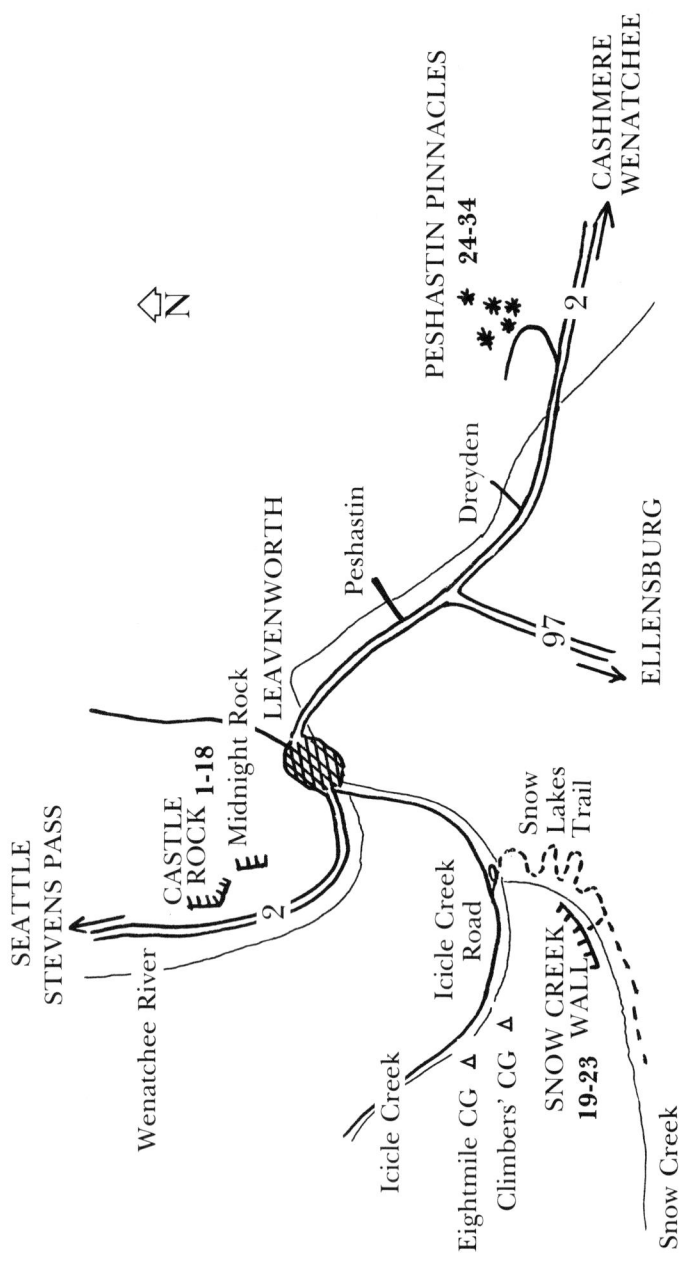

LEAVENWORTH

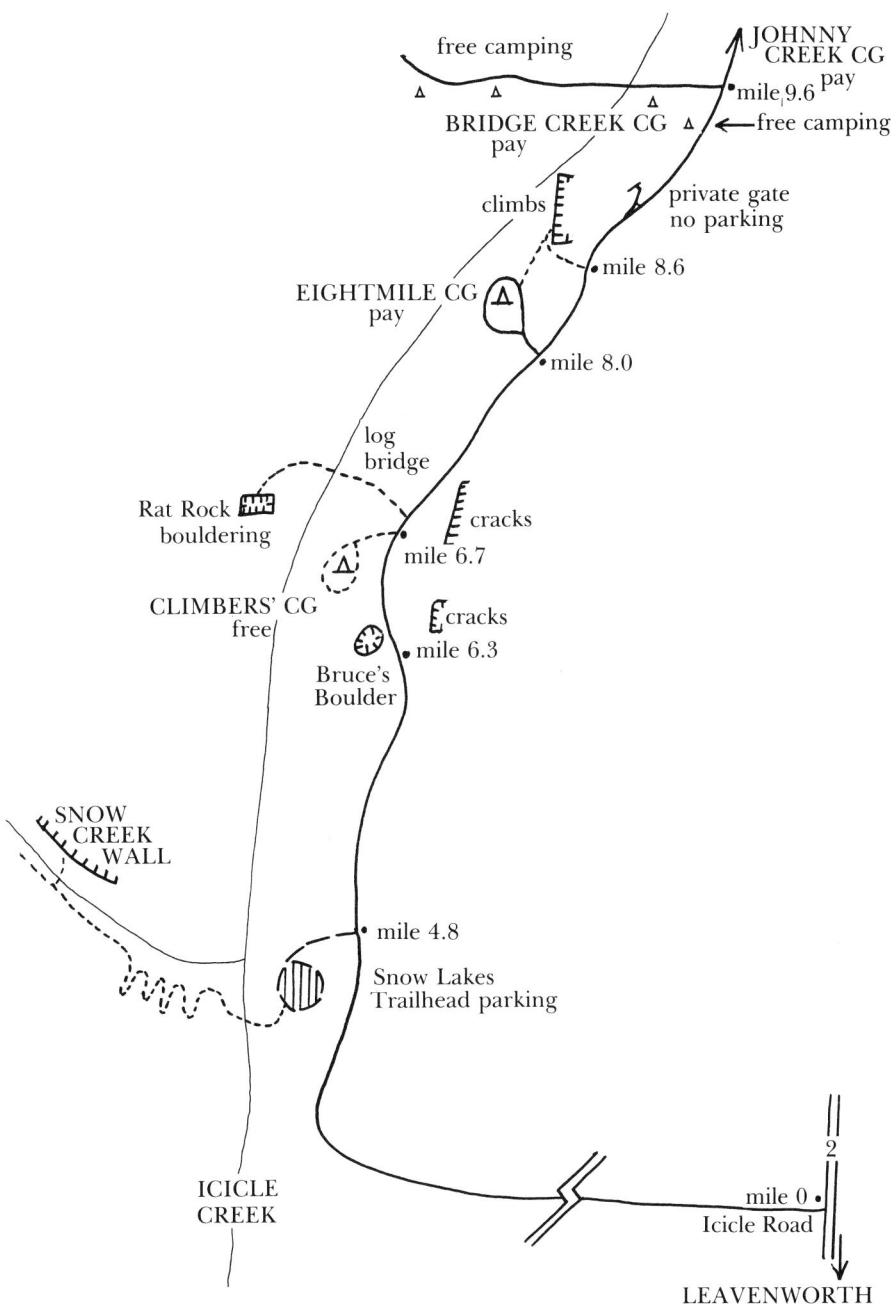

Icicle Creek - Snow Creek Wall

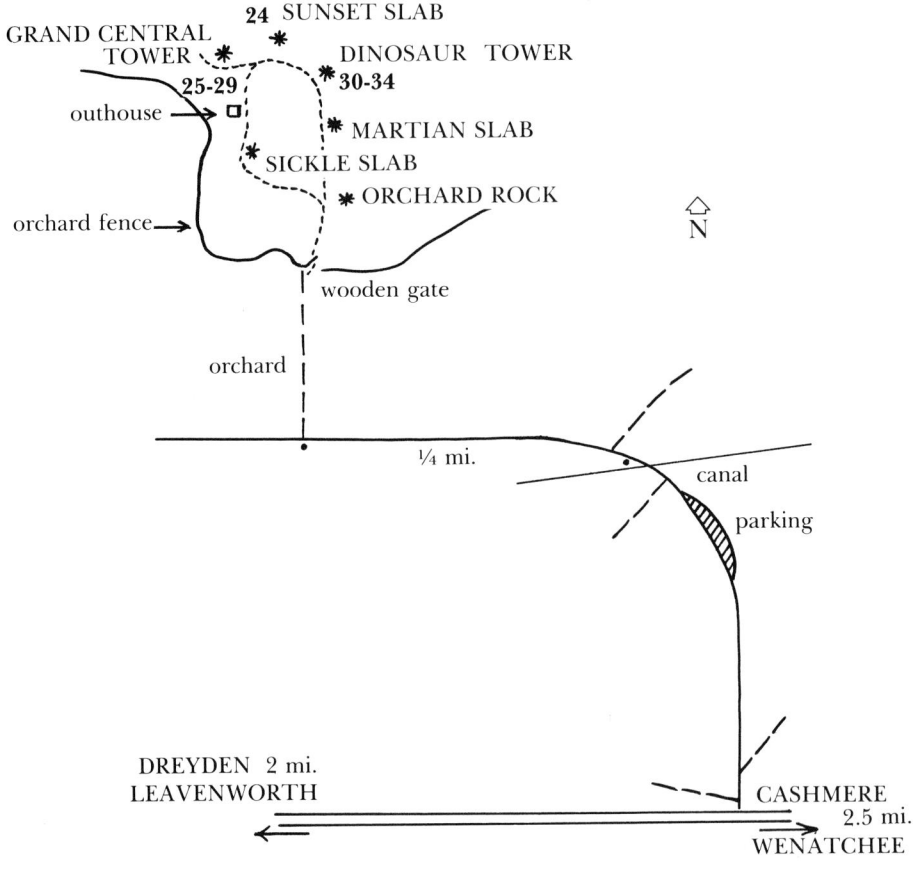

Peshastin Pinnacles

Scary Canary - Castle Rock photo: Karl Schneider collection

Castle Rock from the highway

Lower Castle Rock
  1 **Brass Balls I 5.10a** Jim Yoder and Paul Christensen, 1979.
  2 **Fault-Catapult II 5.8** Jane Stuart and P.D. Nelson, 1963.
  3 **The Bone I 5.9** Eric Bjornstad and Dave Hiser, 1964. FFA: Jim Yoder and Paul Christensen, 1979.
  4 **J.J. Overhang I 5.10d** Jim Yoder and Jim Donini, 1980. A tester.

LEAVENWORTH

Lower Castle Rock

Upper Castle Rock

5 Rainbow Connection I 5.11a

6 Saints-Rainshadow II 5.9 Fred Beckey, Eric Bjornstad and Jim Stuart. FFA: unknown.

7 Saints II 5.8 Fred Beckey, John Rupley and Klindt Vielbig, 1957. FFA: Steve Marts and Pat Callis.

8 Damnation I 5.9 John Rupley, 1957. FFA: TM Herbert and Ed Cooper, 1960.

LEAVENWORTH

Upper Castle Rock

9 M.F. Overhang I 5.10c Fred Beckey and Don Wilde, 1950. FFA: unknown.
10 Heavenly Traverse I 5.7
11 Midway Direct I 5.6 Slightly runout.
12 Midway I 5.6 Fred Beckey, Wes Grande and Jack Schwabland, 1948. This classic route was the first climbed in Leavenworth.
13 Devil's Fright I 5.10b Ed Cooper and TM Herbert, 1960. FFA: Jim Madsen, about 1966.
14 Devil's Delight I 5.10d Fred Beckey, Pete Schoening and Wes Grande, 1951. FFA: Jim Madsen, about 1966.
15 Crack of Doom I 5.9
16 Canary II 5.8 Fred Beckey, Dave Collins and Don Gordon. FFA: Henry Madher and John Rupley.
17 Hangdog I 5.11a
18 Sabre I 5.4 Pete Schoening and Dick Widria, 1949.

Lee Cunningham on Rainbow Connection, Castle Rock photo: Mark Handley

Classic Crack, 8 Mile Campground

Outer Space, Snow Creek Wall photo: Karl Schneider

Snow Creek Wall

Descent: Scramble left (south) and down around the Snow Creek Wall. On reaching the base of the cliff, the easiest descent route continues high, eventually making a short rappel. Be sure to leave plenty of daylight for this tricky descent.

19 Orbit III 5.8+ Fred Beckey and Dan Davis, 1962. FFA: unknown. Everyone gets lost. Clue: on the third pitch, at the roof, don't go to obvious pins to the left. Instead, go right.

20 Mary Jane Dihedral III 5.9 First ascent included Don McPherson.

LEAVENWORTH

Snow Creek Wall
21 Iconoclast III 5.10c or 5.11 C2 (with last pitch). For the final pitch, bring brass nuts and a skyhook (or traverse to Outer Space). Mead Hargis and Tom Hargis, about 1967. Last pitch: Jim Yoder and Dan McNerthney, 1983. Excellent route.

22 Hyperspace III 5.10d Jim Yoder, Neil Cannon and Kevin Busemeier, 1982. Most overhanging, exposed, and continuously difficult climb in Leavenworth.

23 Outer Space, with Remorse start III 5.8+ or 5.9 Fred Beckey and Ron Niccoli, 1960. FFA: Fred Beckey and Steve Marts, about 1964. The classic Leavenworth route. Incredible crack and knob climbing.

Peshastin Pinnacles

LEAVENWORTH

Sunset Slab
24 **5.3-5.7** Wander anywhere on the face, using bolts as desired.

LEAVENWORTH

Grand Central Tower

Peshastin Pinnacles
Grand Central Tower, Back Side
Descent: One rope rappel down the east side.
25 **Bomb Shelter** I **5.11a** Fred Beckey, Eric Bjornstad, Henry Mather and Dan Davis, 1962. FFA: unknown. Washington's first 5.11.
26 **Vertigo** I **5.8** Ed Cooper, Dan Gorden and Galen McBee, 1960. FFA: Fred Beckey and Charley Bell.

Grand Central Tower
27 **Lightning Crack** II **5.8+** Fred Beckey and Dick McGowan, 1960. FFA: unknown. A Pinnacles classic.
28 **West Face, first pitch** I **5.8** Dave Collins and Tom Miller, 1959. FFA: Fred Beckey, solo.
29 **West Face, Direct** I **5.10d** Jim Madsen, mid '60's. Usually done with a top rope.

Dinosaur Tower
Descent: West, one two-rope rappel; east, two one-rope rappels.
30 **Cro Magnum** I **5.8**
31 **Dr. Leakey** I **5.10b** (by traversing in)**5.11** (direct start)
32 **Pebbles** I **5.10b**
33 **Washboards 5.10c / Primate 5.10d** Longest hard route in the Pinnacles.
34 **Potholes** I **5.7+**

The North Cascades as seen from Liberty Bell

The Liberty Bell massif from the Washington Pass overlook

LIBERTY BELL

HIGHLIGHTS
Liberty Bell is a spectacular granite massif located next to a major road, state highway 20. Convenience combines with relatively sound rock and large cliffs. Rising to 7,720 feet from a 5,500 foot pass, the peak has Grade V routes that can be affected by severe mountain weather if luck is against the climber. Liberty Bell sits on the eastern edge of the North Cascades and commands tremendous views of rugged peaks. With convenient camping to top it off, this is truly one of the finer rock climbing situations in North America.

CLIMBING
The Liberty Bell Massif consists of several separate rock towers, from the Early Winter Spires north to the Liberty Bell itself. The unpolished alpine granite that forms these peaks is of excellent quality, and drops in clean sweeps directly from the summits to the talus fields below. The largest walls (up to 1,200 feet) face east, while shorter routes lie on the west side of the massif. Routes on the east side are mostly Grade III to V, depending on both the style of the ascent and route choice. Difficulties range from 5.8 A1 to 5.11 and 5.9 A4. Climbing at the Liberty Bell is a classic alpine blend of cracks and face climbing. The west side provides the easiest route up Liberty Bell at Grade II 5.5—this, the **Beckey Route,** is the most popular climb in the area. The west side of North Early Winter Spire holds a couple of fine Grade III routes in the 5.7 A1 and 5.9 range. The approach to the east face of Liberty Bell is the shortest

in the area—less than an hour of moderate uphill hiking. West side approaches take closer to an hour and a half; the last part is a fairly grueling uphill slog, especially for the **Beckey Route**. All descents involve route finding and rappelling.

ENVIRONMENT

A long drive from any other rock climbing center (and approximately four hours from Seattle), Liberty Bell lies at the fringe of some of the most spectacular mountains in the Continental U.S.: The North Cascades. The nearby highway accomodates thousands of tourists who come to visit North Cascades National Park and its environs. But Liberty Bell is just outside the Park boundaries, sitting on the easternmost divide before the mountains taper off towards the foothills of eastern Washington. This location means that it escapes much of the moisture that endows the North Cascades with its tremendous glaciers. Climbers are far more likely to have good weather here than on most of the peaks in the region. Liberty Bell rises out of a subalpine forest, and the climber is treated to expansive views of other mountains and forested valleys. Camping is reasonably close, but the nearest store or gas station is a half hour away. A rafting company exists there and they will happily splash cold water on climbers weary of hard rock. Fishing and hiking are also superb in the area.

CLIMBING HISTORY

Confusing placement of the words "Liberty Bell" on the early topographic maps lead the first mountaineers to believe that they were climbing the Bell when they first scrambled up the Southeast Couloir on South Early Winter Spire (the highest point of the massif) in 1937. Liberty Bell itself was not ascended until 1947; the resulting **Beckey Route** remains extremely popular because of its accessibility to most mountaineers. A few new routes were climbed in the 1950's, but it was not until the mid 1960's that a burst of route exploration was done. Between 1964 and 1968 most of the current routes were established, including the major climbs on the East Face of Liberty Bell. The **Liberty Crack** (5.8 to 5.11, A3) was the first route to pierce the East Face; it was climbed over a several day period, though now it is often done in a single day with some pitches fixed. Parties using a significant amount of aid still opt for spending a night on route. The **Thin Red Line** (5.9 A4) is the only quality climb that still normally requires a bivouac. A few new routes were added in the 1970's, but the most important trend through the early 1980's was the freeing of many established routes. **Liberty Crack** now goes free, except for the Lithuanian Roof, low on the route. With its inclusion in *Fifty Classic Climbs of North America,* this route has come to see a considerable amount of traffic.

LIBERTY BELL

CAMPING

Many climbers prefer to camp right next to the road on the hairpin below the East Face. This spot, however, is not legal and a tent should not be set up. People also park on the west side of the pass and camp in the woods. A small free campground at Cutthroat Trailhead is located a few miles east of the pass and one and one half miles north up a side road. This site has a single night limit, however. The Lone Fir Campground is a Forest Service area located seven miles east of Liberty Bell. Moderately priced, it is near a stream. While this campground can be full on weekends, others exist further east. The nearest public showers are at the Mazama Country Inn (home of the Liberty Bell Alpine Tours guide service), approximately twenty-five miles east of Liberty Bell. A laundromat, restaurants and motels are located twelve miles further east in Winthrop.

SEASONS AND WEATHER

Approximate Months	Typical Temperatures High	Low	Likelihood of Precipitation	Frequency of Climbable Days
Nov-Apr	Highway closed—no car access			
May-Jun	60's	30's+	med-high	medium
Jul-Aug	70's	40's	med-low	high
Sep	60's	40's	medium	med-high
Oct-Nov	50's	30's	med-high	med-low

Comments: The road over Washington Pass opens for the season in early May. The exact closing date varies, but usually occurs in late November. Be prepared for rain and snow, even during the summer.

RESTRICTIONS AND WARNINGS
Because rescues would be unusually difficult for a rock climbing area, Liberty Bell climbing should be treated with extra respect. Hard hats would be an especially good idea here because of both the remoteness and the occasional loose rock.

GUIDEBOOKS
Cascade Alpine Guide, Rainy Pass to Fraser River (1981) by Fred Beckey is available from Northwest climbing stores or from The Mountaineers Books, 719 Pike Street, Seattle, WA 98101. For **Liberty Crack** see *Fifty Classic Climbs of North America* (1979) by Steve Roper and Allan Steck. This Sierra Club book is available from most mountaineering stores.

GUIDE SERVICES AND EQUIPMENT STORES
Liberty Bell Alpine Tours is the locally based guide service. Originally just a climbing guide service, they now also do wind surfing, rafting, and helicopter skiing. Liberty Bell Alpine Tours, Mazama, WA 98833; telephone: (509) 996-2250. There are no local equipment stores.

EMERGENCY SERVICES
The nearest hospital is in Twisp, almost fifty miles east (Twisp Medical Center, 997-2011). Rescues are handled by Aero Methow Rescue Service, also at 997-2011.

GETTING THERE
Once weekly, between June and September, a Grey Lines Tour Bus travels from Seattle, through the North Cascades, to Washington Pass (Liberty Bell). Otherwise, hitchhiking is practial.

LIBERTY BELL

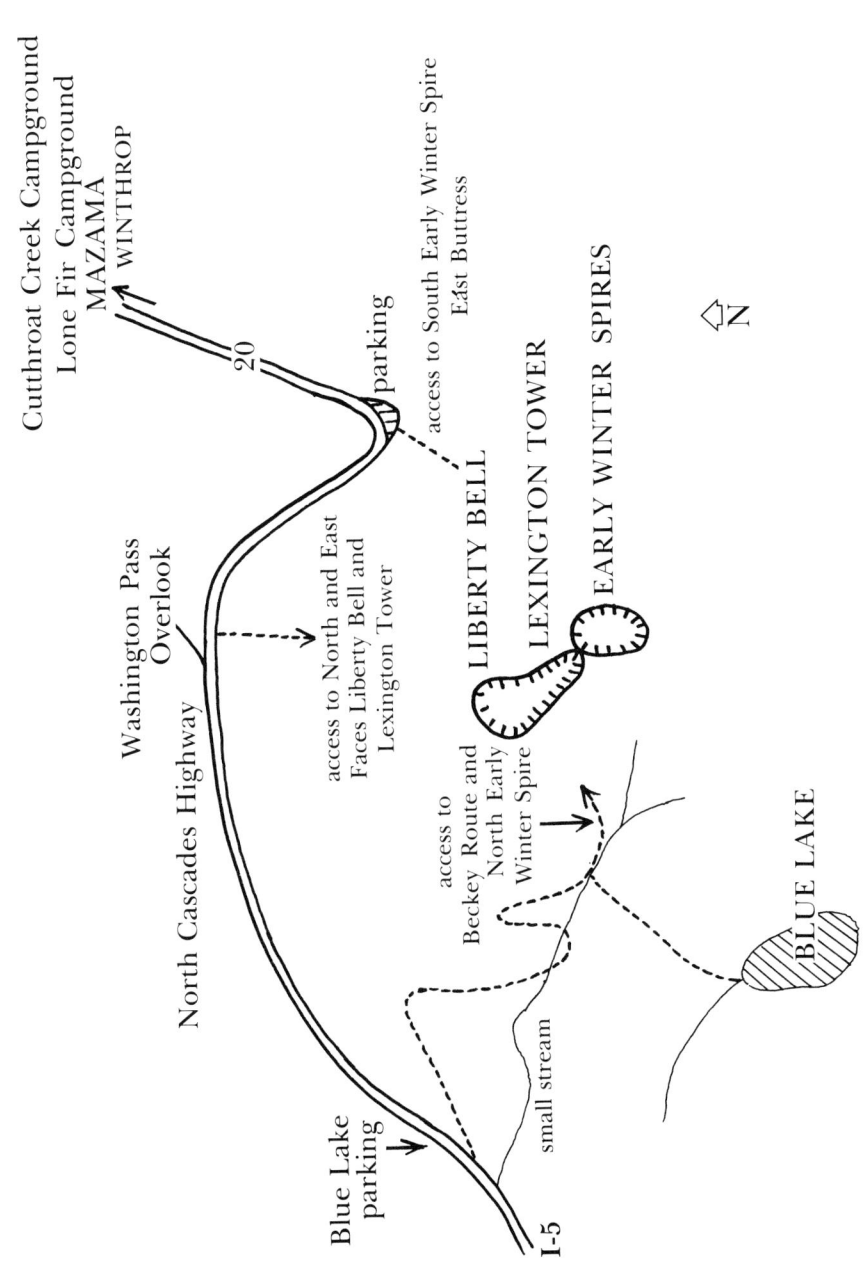

Liberty Bell

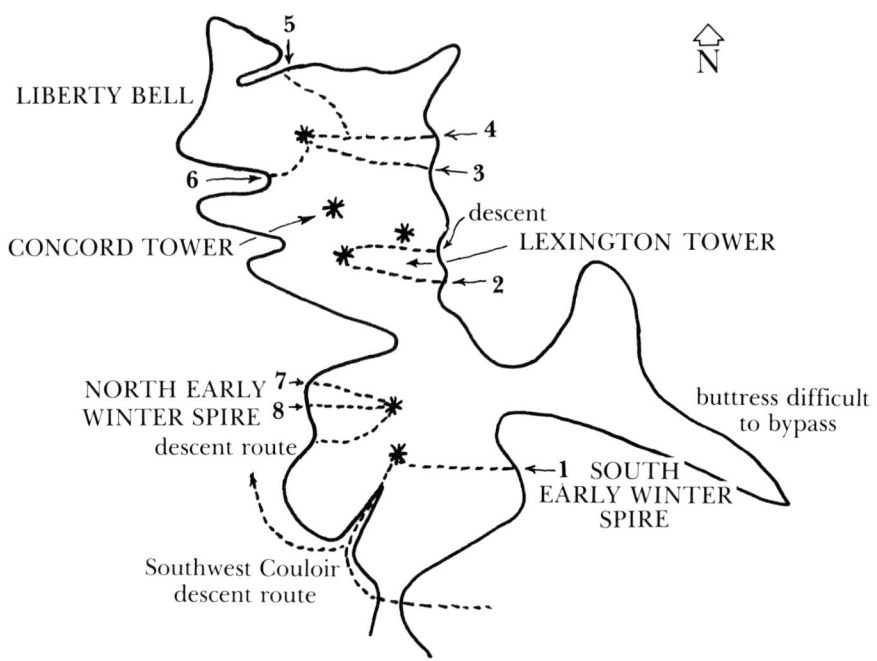

Liberty Bell

Northeast view of the Liberty Bell massif

South Early Winter Spire

LIBERTY BELL

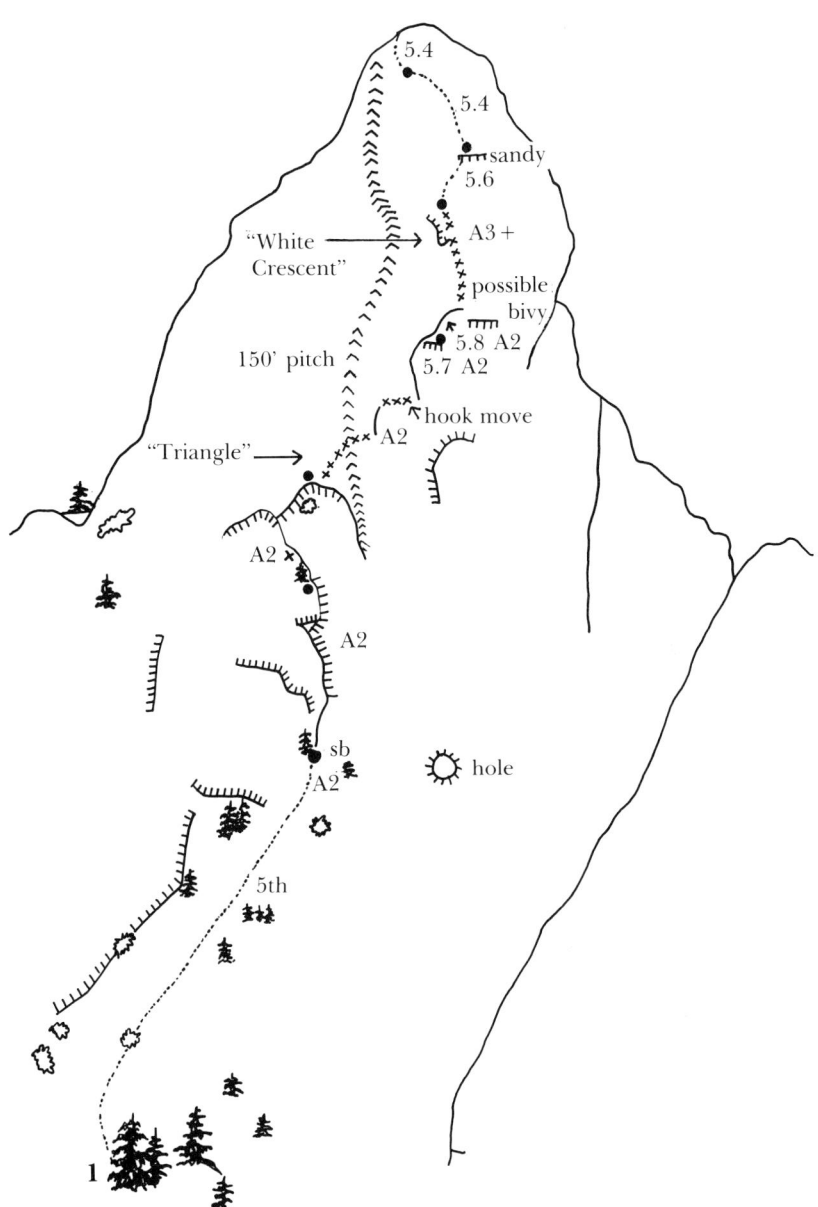

South Early Winter Spire

1 East Buttress Direct IV 5.8 A3 (or 5.10+) Doug Leen and Fred Beckey, 1969. Even with aid, this spectacular route goes mostly free. Bring large nuts and skyhooks.

Lexington Tower

2 East Face III 5.9 Steve Marts and Don McPherson, 1966. Sustained climbing. In early summer, the cracks might be wet.

East and North Faces, Liberty Bell

East Face, Liberty Bell

3 Liberty Crack V 5.9 A3 or 5.10 A3 (or 5.11 A1, but poorly protected) Steve Marts, Don McPherson and Fred Stanley, 1965. Pushed to 5.11 by Mark Hudon and Eric Sanford, late 1970's. Bring a few smaller pitons for emergency use. Other routes in the area are considered to pale in comparison with this one, and consequently, it is very popular. Logistics are simpler if one climbs the route in one day. With a long run out on 5.11 face, the climb will go free except for the huge Lithuanian Roof. If aid is used on only the pitch above the roof, the route goes free at 5.10.

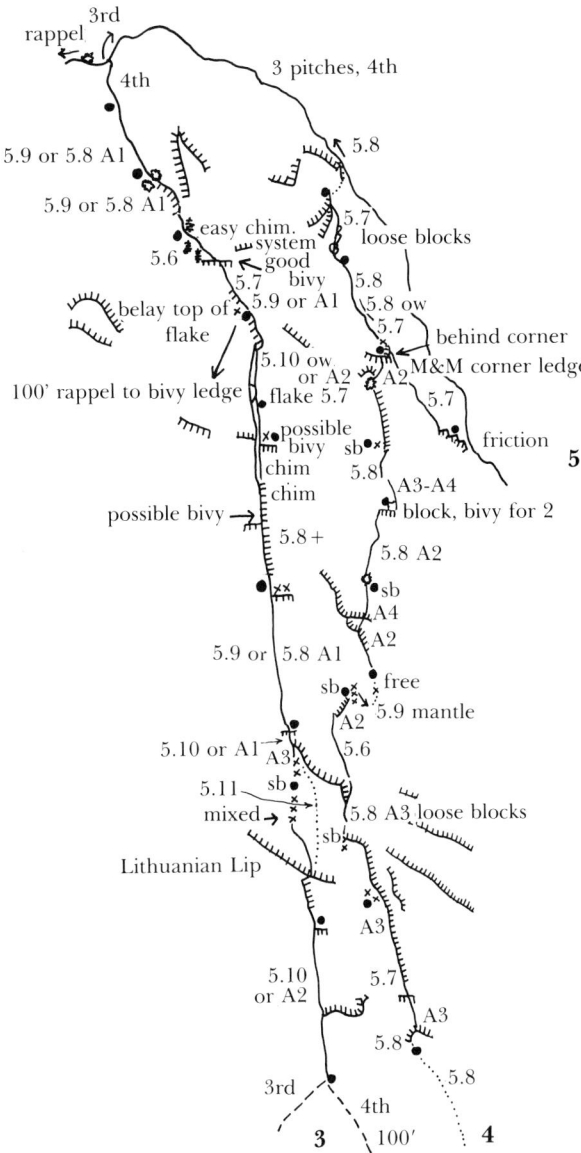

East Face, Liberty Bell

4 Thin Red Line V 5.9 A4 Jim Madsen and Kim Schmitz, 1967. Pitons: 2 KB, 12 LA, 2½", 1 ea. ¾" to 1" skyhooks and a large nut rack. Good aid route with some loose sections.

5 Barber Pole III 5.8 A1 or 5.9 Sandy Bill, Cindy Wade Burgner and Frank Tarver, 1966. The first ascent was made by mistake—the climbers intended to climb the North Face Route, to the right.

West view of Liberty Bell, showing descent route

LIBERTY BELL

Beckey Route photo: Karl Schneider

Liberty Bell

6 Beckey Route (Southwest Face) II 5.5 Fred Beckey, Jerry O'Neil and Charles Welsh, 1946. The most popular route up Liberty Bell and often third classed. A more difficult variation (High Exposure, 5.7) involves steep, good climbing.

North Early Winter Spire
7 Northwest Corner III 5.9 Paul Boving and Steve Pollock, 1976. Very sustained 5.7 to 5.9 climbing.

8 West Face III 5.7 A1 Fred Beckey and Dave McPherson, 1966. A long, enjoyable fairly low angle crack high on a wall.

North Early Winter Spire, northwest view

LIBERTY BELL

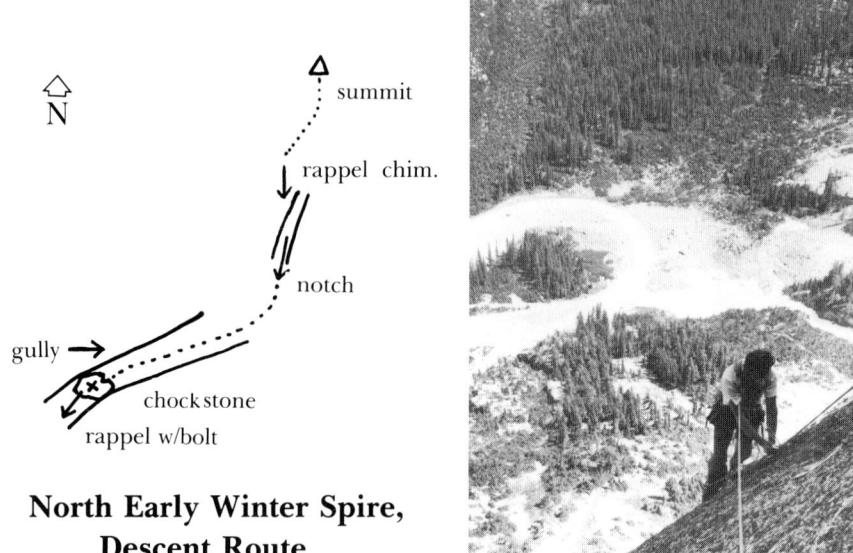

North Early Winter Spire, Descent Route

Fred Beckey, East Buttress Direct
photo: Doug Leen

Fred Beckey on the summit of South Early Winter Spire

photo: Doug Leen

Climber with haul sack beneath the Lithuanian Roof

Upper Town Wall and the Skykomish River

INDEX TOWN WALLS

HIGHLIGHTS
Index is the closest rock climbing area to metropolitan Seattle and offers superb aid and free climbing routes up to 600 feet in length. Climbs on sound, vertical granite are within minutes of the car, while the longest routes are never further than an hour away. Camping is available nearby. Index, however, suffers from the rainy weather indigenous to western Washington; it has been referred to as the "Sponge of the World." But when the weather is favorable, it offers excellent climbing.

CLIMBING
Because of its steep and smooth nature, Index has long been popular for practicing aid climbing. Now, many of these old routes—often clean, sharp edged cracks—have been free climbed. Two cliffs are most often climbed. The smaller of the two, but most popular, is the Lower Town Wall, which sits within a few minutes' walk of the parking lot. It offers a dense concentration of vertical cracks that provide routes from one to four pitches in length. The clean, unpolished granite is still considered by many to be a fine aid climbing practice ground.

Located forty-five minutes straight up a steep hill is the Upper Town Wall. Climbs here are longer and fairly hard—the six pitch routes put 600 feet of vertical rock under one's feet. The wall can be scaled either entirely free or with mixed climbing and provides a full day's outing. Descents from both the Upper and Lower Walls involve some rappelling with two ropes.

ENVIRONMENT

The "Town Walls" were named because of their proximity to the small town of Index, located an hour from Seattle on a major road. The cliffs are nestled into the dense and beautiful Northwest coniferous forest. Of particular attraction are the towering (but horribly loose) granite walls of Mt. Index, across the valley and within full view from the Index Town Walls. Lying at the foot of the western slope of the Cascades, the area inevitably gets soaked by plenty of rain. But this water supplies the Skykomish River that flows through the valley, and fishing the river could easily occupy a rainy day.

INDEX TOWN WALLS

CLIMBING HISTORY

As a Washington rock climbing area (frequented principally by Seattle area residents) Index has traditionally taken second place to Leavenworth, just a couple hours further down the road. Once rock climbing started getting popular in the 1950's, the Town Walls were still passed over in favor of the crumbly mountaineering walls of nearby Mt. Index. While Northwesterners sometimes crag climbed, they were still primarily mountaineers. The Upper Town Wall was not opened until 1965 when the **Davis-Holland Route** was climbed (then 5.8 A2, now 5.10b). Soon, both the Upper and the Lower Town Walls gained recognition and many routes were "gardened" out of the sometimes vegetated rock. Originally the Index Town Walls were thought of principally in terms of their superb aid climbing routes, but now the area also sees considerable free climbing, often at a very high standard.

CAMPING

The woods below the Lower Town Wall hold a number of campsites. Though dark, they are a short walk from the car. Another option is the Forest Service pay campground located ten miles east on the highway. This is Money Creek Campground, located on the Skykomish River, with piped water and picnic tables. No local laundries or pay showers exist, but Index does have a small general store, a hotel, restaurant, and a good tavern.

SEASONS AND WEATHER

Approximate Months	Typical Temperatures High	Low	Likelihood of Precipitation	Frequency of Climbable Days
Oct-Mar	40's	20's	very high	very low
Apr-Jun	60's−	30's+	med-high	medium
Jul-Aug	70's+	40's	low-med	med-high
Sep	60's	40's	medium	med-low

Comments: Even in summer, rain can last for days. Carrying a rain jacket on Upper Wall routes may prove important.

RESTRICTIONS AND WARNINGS

Speedy rescues, especially from the Upper Wall, would be difficult to obtain.

GUIDEBOOKS

A Climber's Guide to Washington Rock (1982) by Don Brooks. *Darrington and Index Rock Climbing Guide* (1976) by Fred Beckey. Both are available from The Mountaineers Books, 715 Pike Street, Seattle, WA 98101 or from Northwest mountaineering stores.

EMERGENCY SERVICES
The nearest hospital is in Monroe, twenty-five miles west of Index (Valley General Hospital, 14701 179th Ave. SE; telephone: 794-7497). For rescues contact the Snohomish County Sheriff dispatch at 911 in an emergency, 258-2484 non-emergency.

GETTING THERE
Public transportation is available by Transit bus from Everett. Hitchhiking to Index also works.

INDEX TOWN WALLS 307

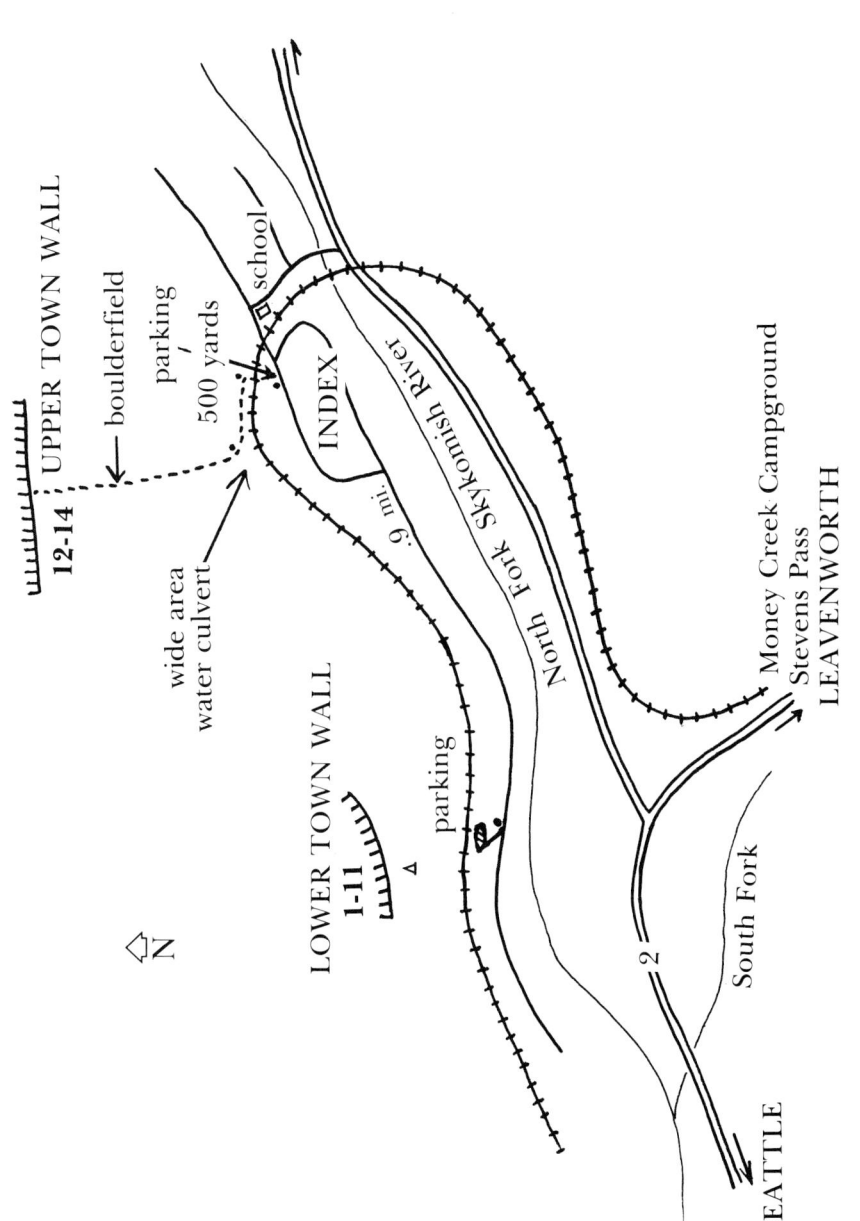

Index Town Walls

Lower Town Wall - Slab Area

1 Archies I 5.6 First ascent unknown.

2 The Great Northern Route I 5.6 Paul Guimarin and Phillip Leatherman, 1965.

3 Pisces I 5.10a Mike Berman and Mark Weigelt, 1969.

4 Taurus I 5.8

5 Aries I 5.8 Ron Burgner and Thom Nephew, 1970.

INDEX TOWN WALLS

Lower Town Wall - Main Wall photo: Dennis Brooks
  6 **City Park I C1** Roger Johnson and Richard Mathies, 1966.
  7 **Godzilla II 5.10a** Don Harder and Donn Heller, about 1973.
  8 **Slow Children I 5.10c** First ascent unknown.
  9 **Narrow Arrow Overhang III 5.7 C3** Greg Donaldson and Richard Mathies, 1968.
10 **Thin Fingers I 5.11a** Bob Crawford and Pat Cruver, 1975.
11 **Free at Last III 5.10b** Ron Burgner and Mark Weigelt, 1970. FFA: Mead Hargis and Jim Langdon.

Index Town Walls

Pisces, on the Lower Town Wall photo: David Ek

312 INDEX TOWN WALLS

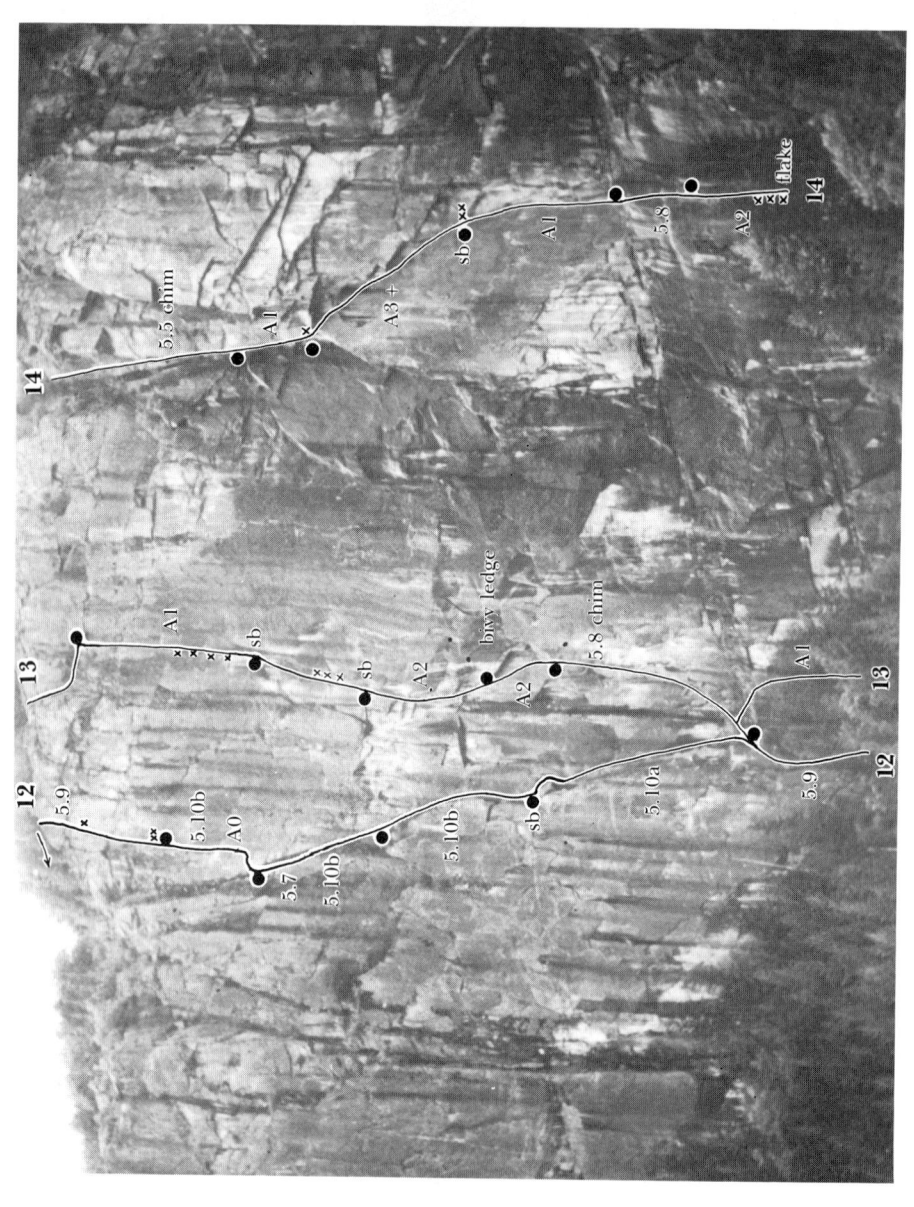

Upper Town Wall

Upper Town Wall

12 Davis-Holland to Lovin' Arms III 5.10b A0 First three pitches: Dan Davis and John Holland, 1964. FFA: Pete Doorish and Mead Hargis, 1970. Lovin' Arms: Don Brooks, 1980. The classic area free route. Some parties rappel after three pitches.

13 The Town Crier IV 5.8 A2 Fred Beckey and Dave Beckstead, 1966. This is the classic area aid route. Pitons: 2 KB, 10 LA, 3 ea. ½" to 2", 1 ea. 2½" and 3".

14 The Golden Arch IV 5.7 A3 Ron Burgner and Jim Madsen, 1967. Pitons: rurp, 20 KB and LA, miscellaneous to 2½". Use nuts and skyhooks on the upper arch to save the delicate flakes.

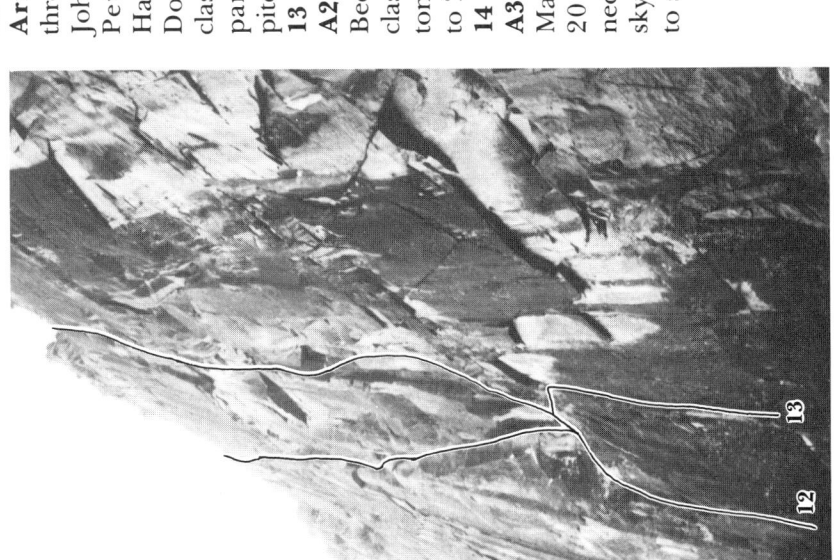

Upper Town Wall - Route Starts

Dave Lane climbing, with the Squamish Chief and Mt. Garibaldi in the background photo: John Howe

SQUAMISH CHIEF

HIGHLIGHTS
Squamish Chief is often compared with Yosemite; clean granite walls rise to 1,500 feet. The area offers hundreds of routes, from short free climbs to long free and multi-day aid routes. Approach walks are short, camping is free, a town is nearby, and the scenery—of mountains and a large fjord—is spectacular. Unfortunately, rain can hamper a climbing vacation, and the nearby pulp mill can poison the atmosphere with its smoke. Still, despite the unpredictable weather, Squamish can provide some of the finest rock climbing in North America.

CLIMBING
The climbing at Squamish involves crack climbs from one to seventeen pitches in length, high angle slab routes up to seven pitches in length, and two day aid climbs. Whatever the choice, the medium is superbly sound and smooth granite (granodiorite). All of the popular routes are relatively free of vegetation, but this is in large measure due to diligent effort by the first ascentionists.

The Squamish area holds a number of small cliffs in addition to the massive Chief itself. On the assumption that most first time visitors will be drawn to the larger cliffs, portions of only two of these smaller areas are included in this book: the Little Smoke House Bluffs and the Malamute. From the Chief, two areas are included: the Grand Wall—home of the finest and longest Squamish free and aid routes—and the Apron—lower angle than most of the Chief and home of difficult slab routes. Descents are accomplished either by multiple rappels or by walk-off, depending on the route climbed.

ENVIRONMENT
Forty miles north of Vancouver, the town of Squamish sits at the head of Howe Sound, a deep water fjord in the extensive coastal waterways of British Columbia. The small town's principal industry is logging, and watching the logs being pushed around the inlet and loaded onto ships is an entertaining diversion. But the smoke billowing out of the pulp mill across the Sound can sometimes be irritating—as can the frequent rains that permit so many trees to grow. A mild climate makes temperatures rarely a problem on climbs, even though nearby 8,787 foot Mt. Garibaldi displays huge glaciers to the town. Squamish Chief overlooks the town and Howe Sound, offering magnificent views.

CLIMBING HISTORY
Early climbing at Squamish was sporadic because the few climbers active at the time were preoccupied doing summit routes in the mountains. Nevertheless, a few gully routes were ascended in the mid 1950's. By the late 1950's a few technical routes appeared, but it was 1961 before the all-weather highway was built and the first serious route was established. This, **The Grand Wall,** involved a month-long siege, with 136 bolts (most unnecessary by today's standards), and considerable financial and moral support from the town. The climber-watching tourist influx was a tremendous boon to the town's economy—up to 2,000 spectators gathered, blocking traffic for twelve miles.

Other technical routes were rapidly established, as was the notorious habit of grading routes two decimal points lower than they would be in the States. This was not officially corrected until the 1975 guidebook. Through the 1960's, various "groups" led development, including Washingtonians, University of British Columbia students, and the self-named "Hard Cores" who climbed as much in Yosemite as they did at home. In the early 1970's development slowed, but from the mid-seventies up to the present, extremely difficult free climbs were established on both slabs and cracks. With the discovery of the Smoke Bluffs and with crowds increasing on the Apron, many climbers shifted their emphasis away from the slabs and more to the outlying crags.

Squamish now sports most of the hardest climbing in Canada and indeed has become a world-class climbing area with many resident climbers keeping the standards at the top level.

CAMPING
A private campground (Klahannie) exists just south of Squamish near Shannon Creek, while seven miles north is Alice Lake, a Provincial Park

pay campground. Most climbers will prefer staying at the free camping sites alongside the Stawamus River at the north end of the Chief. Another free possibility is in the woods near the southern base of the Chief. The water of Oleson Creek near the latter site is considered safe, but that of the Stawamus should be treated. Pay showers and a laundromat are available at Klahannie. Another laundromat and motels are available in town. Other than the Smoke Bluffs parking lot, the best place to meet climbers is in Vancouver; every Wednesday night a group gathers at the Ivanhoe Pub on Main Street, 1000 Block. Most local climbers would be happy to show visiting climbers around. There is good swimming at Browning Lake in Murrin Park, as well as at Brohm Lake, north of Squamish. For those so inclined, the Cliffside Pub (within walking distance of the Smoke Bluffs) is a trendy rainy-day hang-out.

SEASONS AND WEATHER

Approximate Months	Typical Temperatures		Likelihood of Precipitation	Frequency of Climbable Days
	High	Low		
Oct-Feb	40's	30's	very high	very low
Mar-Jun	60's	40's	medium	medium
Jul-Aug	70's+	50's	low-med	high-med
Sep	60's	40's	medium	med-high

Comments: Even in summer, rain can last for days.

RESTRICTIONS AND WARNINGS
When driving to the Little Smoke Bluffs, please go slowly through the residential area—otherwise access privileges may be denied. When approaching the Malamute, do not drive through the lumber company's private property or otherwise act conspicuously. Instead, park at the Apron parking area.

GUIDEBOOKS
Squamish: The New Free Climbs (1984) by Kevin McLane. Available from Kevin McLane, P.O.Box 5181, Squamish, B.C. VON 3GO. *Squamish Rock Climbs (1985)* by Jim Campbell. Available from Northwest mountaineering stores, or from Jim Campbell, 2066 W.8th Ave., North Vancouver, B.C., V6J IW5, Canada. *A Climber's Guide to the Squamish Chief* (1980) by Anders Ourom. Available from the B.C. Mountaineering Club, P.O. Box 2674, Vancouver, B.C., V6B 3W8, Canada, but considerably out of date for the harder routes.

GUIDE SERVICES AND EQUIPMENT STORES
No services are available locally. In Vancouver, the Mountain Equipment Co-op at 428 West 8th Ave., and Carlton Cycle, at 3201 Kingsway, carry climbing equipment.

EMERGENCY SERVICES
The location of the local hospital is shown on the area map (Squamish General Hospital, Clarke Drive, 892-5211). For rescue services contact the RCMP (Royal Canadian Mounted Police) at 911 in an emergency, or 898-9611 non-emergency.

GETTING THERE
The most practical public transportation from the major city of Vancouver, B.C. is by bus; SMT Coachlines serves the area. Hitch-hiking works quite well—it is best to take a local bus through Vancouver to the main highway north (Hwy. 1).

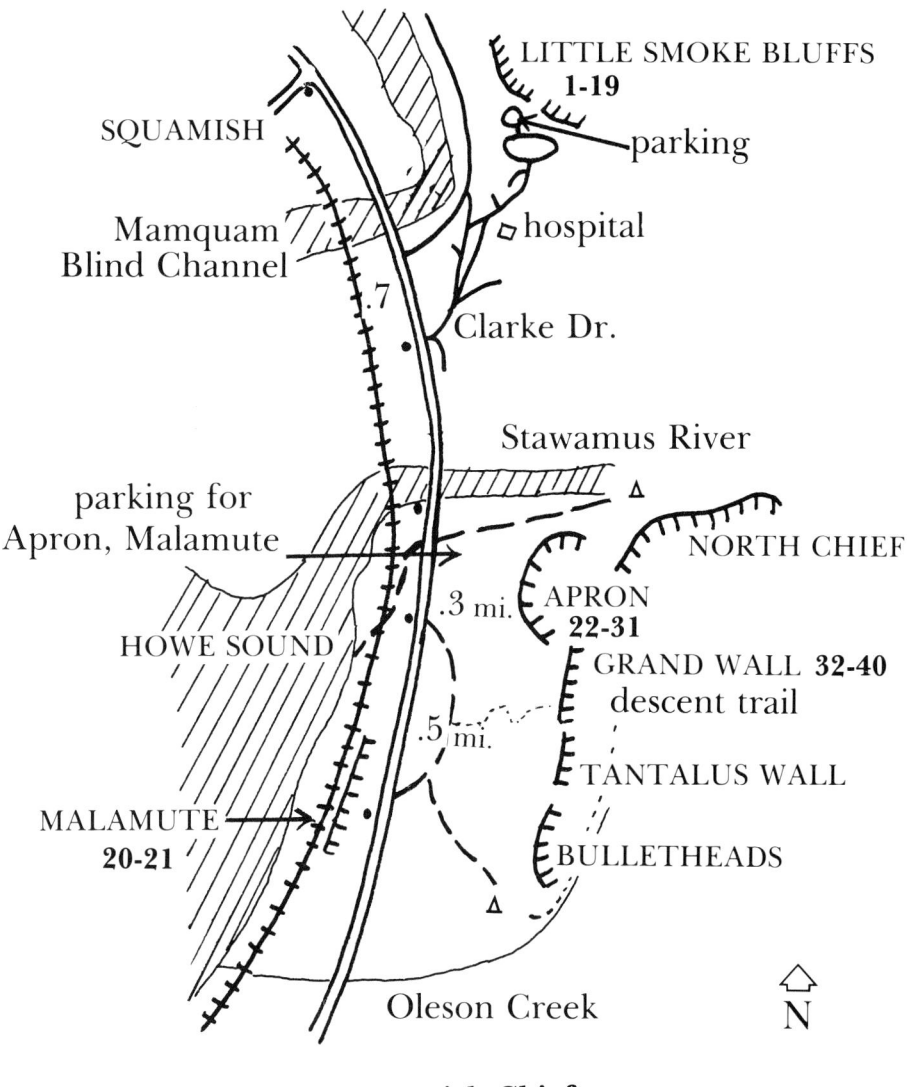

Squamish Chief

The Squamish highway will undergo a major widening and upgrading over the next eight years that might affect access to some areas.

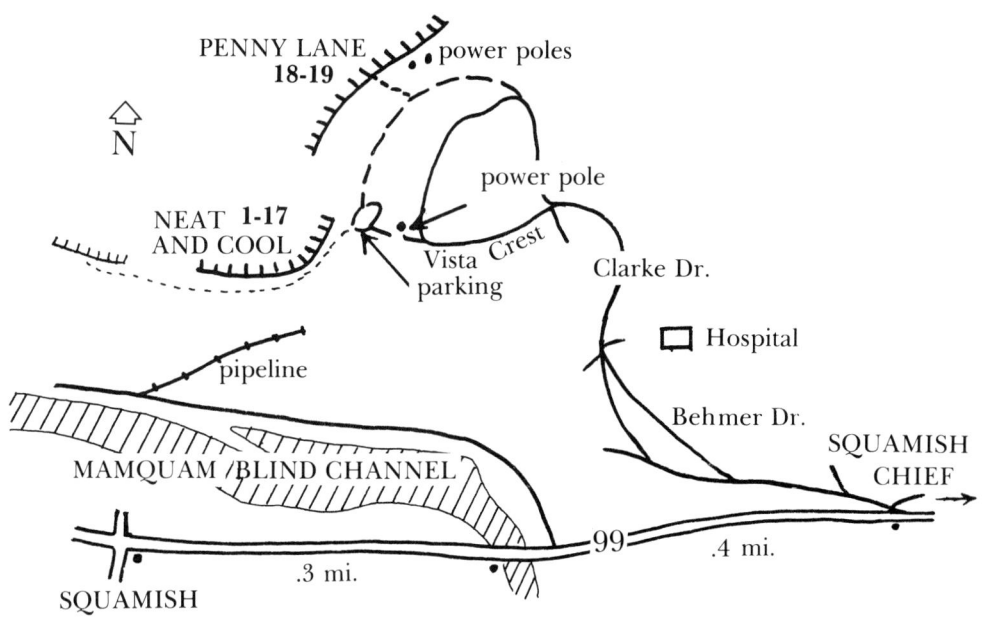

Squamish Chief - Little Smoke Bluffs

SQUAMISH CHIEF

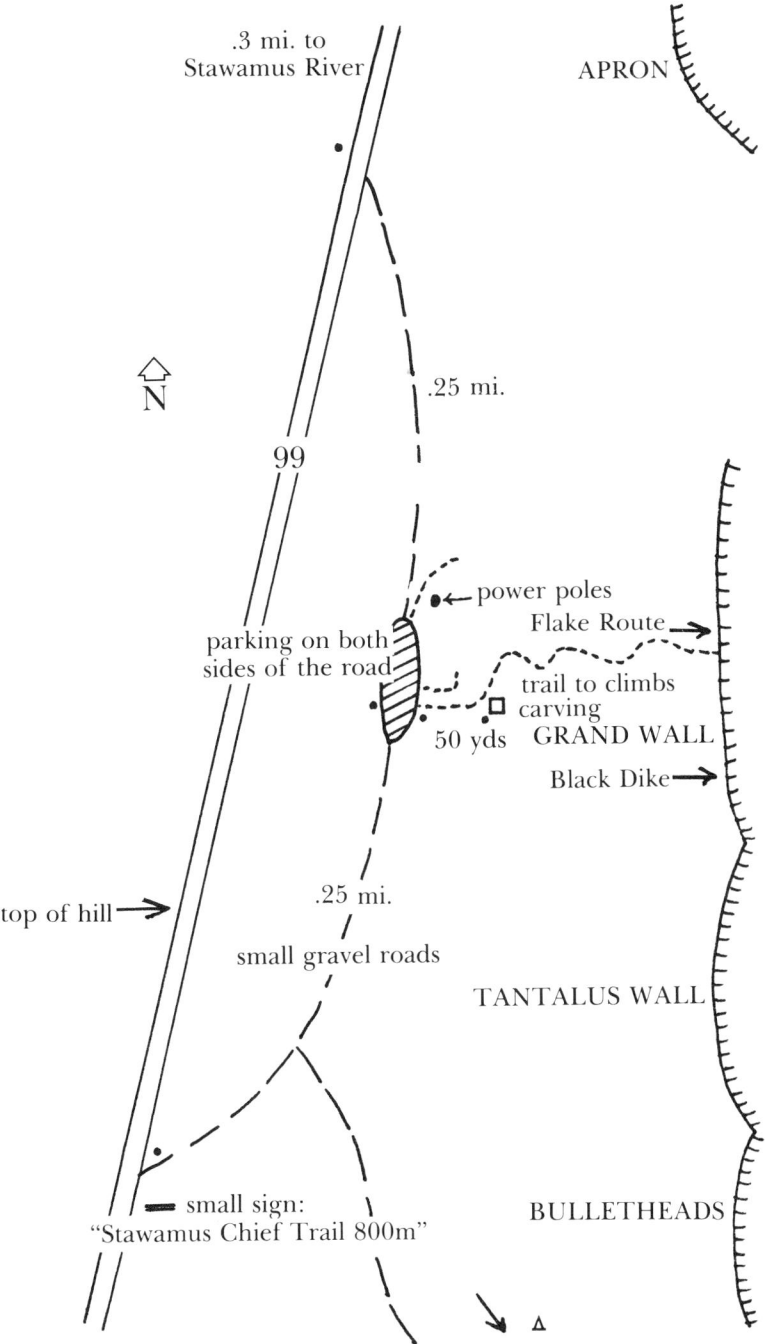

Squamish Chief - Grand Wall

The Little Smoke Bluffs and Mt. Garibaldi

Squamish Chief and The Malamute

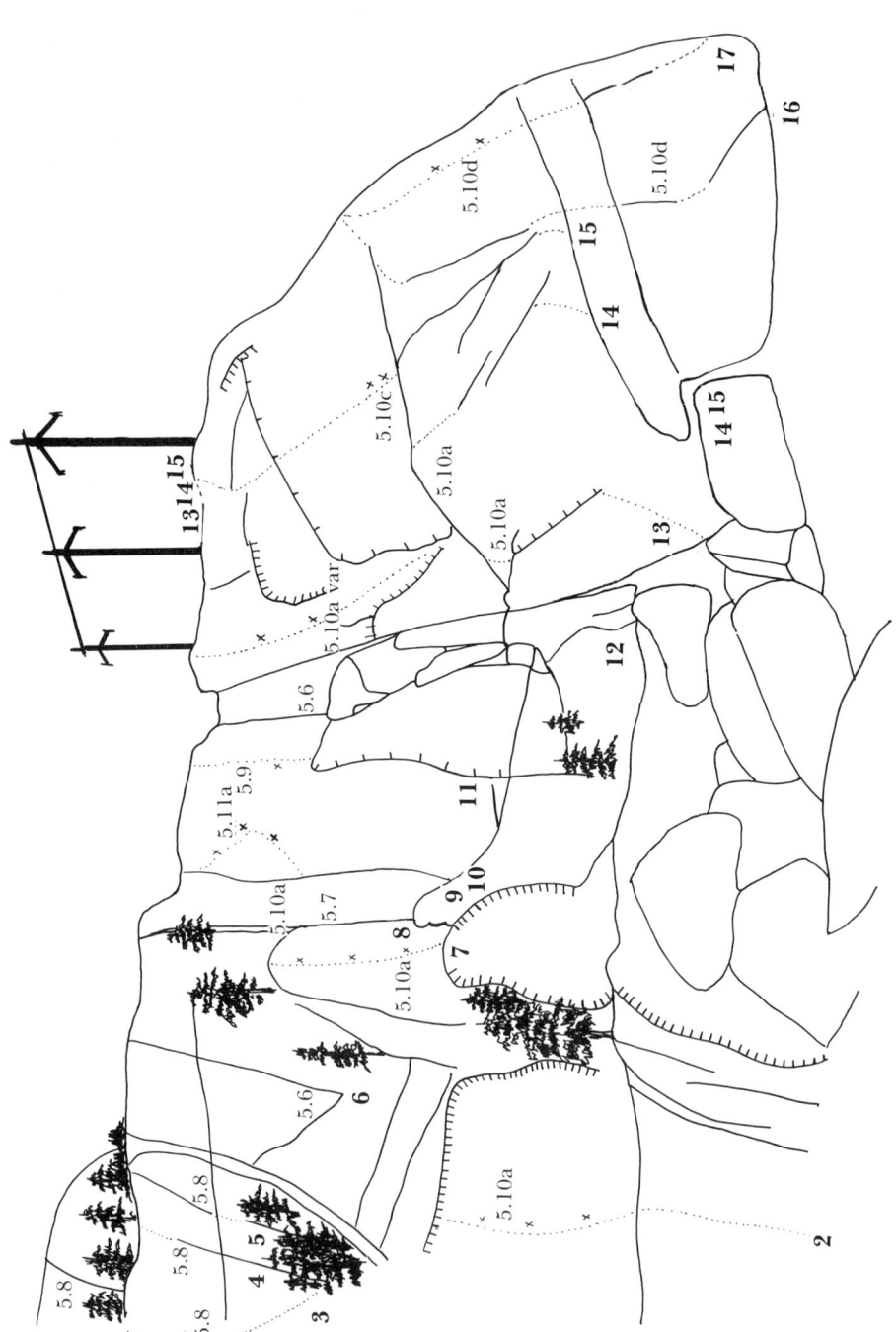

Little Smoke Bluffs

All routes established since 1977

1 The Smoke Bluff Connection III 5.10− Follow a trail several hundred feet past the Neat and Cool Cliff. Find the obvious parallel cracks. 1. Climb the right crack, 5.8. 2. Climb a long left-facing corner, 5.9. Walk left 200 feet to a long vertical crack. 3. Climb this to a ledge, 5.10−. 4. Go left around an arete and diagonal up and left across the wall, 5.9.

2 Pink Flamingo 5.10a
3 Wasted Days and Wasted Nights 5.8
4 Sally Five Fingers 5.8
5 Coffee Break 5.8
6 Cat Crack 5.6
7 The Edge 5.10a
8 Corner Crack 5.7
9 Flying Circus 5.10a
10 Fear of Flying 5.11a
11 Lieback Flake 5.9
12 Corn Flakes 5.6
13 Neat and Cool 5.10a
14 Gross Incompetence 5.10a
15 Geritol 5.10c
16 Where Ancients Fear to Tread 5.10d
17 Hans Groper 5.10d
18 Crime of the Century 5.11
19 Penny Lane 5.9

The Malamute
20 Clean Crack 5.11 R. Atkinson and J. Roshold, 1977.
21 Caboose 5.10b T. Cousins and J. Sinclair, 1963. FFA: W. Hack, J. Haeck and Eric Weinstein, 1975.

The Neat and Cool area on a busy day photo: Jim Campbell

Climbing on the Apron photo: Jim Campbell

The Apron
For all Apron routes, supplement bolt protection with a small rack of nuts to about 1½".
22 Snake II 5.9 P.Botta and R. Willmott, 1962
23 Unfinished Symphony III 5.10d A0 or 5.11 Fred Beckey and J. Sinclair, 1967. FFA: Peter Croft and Tammi Knight, 1979. Bring many small nuts for this difficult-to-protect route.

SQUAMISH CHIEF

The Apron

24 Dream On II 5.10+ first three pitches; Steve Flazelle and Dave Lane, 1976. pitches to top, Carl Austron, Richard Suddaby, Keith Flazelle, et al, 1981. Most parties only climb the first three pitches; the route goes free to Broadway, but is poorly protected and 5.11+, A0.

25 Bloodlust Direct III 5.11 Steve Flazelle and Dave Lane, 1976. Run outs.

26 Diedre II 5.8 Jim Baldwin and J. Sinclair, 1962. Pitches 1, 5 and 6 are poorly protected.

27 White Lightning II 5.10c Paul Piro, Gordon Smaill and Steve Sutton, 1973. Shown is the Sickle finish. The original finish between Sickle and Diedre is unprotected 5.9 and is rarely done. Traversing to Diedre is another possibility.

28 Sparrow II 5.9 G. Loset and T. Rollerson, 1970.

29 Banana Peel II 5.7 B. Hagen and D. Tate, 1965.

30 Broomstick Crack I 5.5 Jim Baldwin, P. Nielson and J. Sinclair, 1961. Rappel or downclimb from the end of the route.

31 Question of Balance II 5.9 Anders Ourom and Paul Peart, 1977. Just left of the prominent white streak. The last 40 feet of the first pitch is sustained 5.8 without protection.

SQUAMISH CHIEF

The Grand Wall

SQUAMISH CHIEF 331

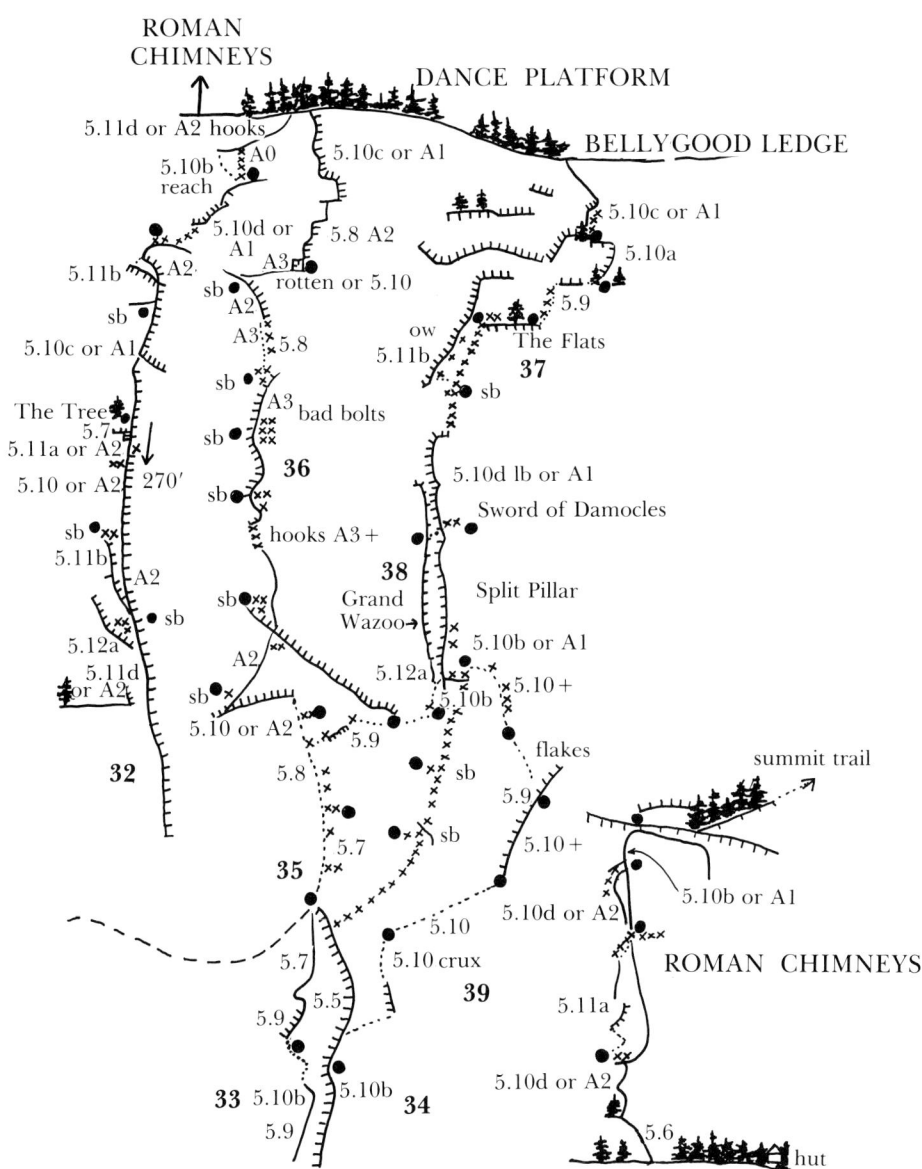

The Grand Wall

Further route information lies on the following page.

Peter Shackleton on Bellygood Ledge, Squamish Chief
photo: Bob Millard

The Grand Wall
32 University Wall V 5.12− or 5.7 A3 Tim Auger, Hamish Mutch, D. Tate and Gordon Woodsworth, 1966. FFA: Peter Croft and Hamish Fraser, 1982. One of the most difficult free climbs in North America, but also an excellent mixed route.
33 Apron Strings II 5.10a Tim Auger and M. Wisnicki, 1964. FFA: W. Burton and Steve Sutton, 1973.
34 Flake Route I 5.9 Jim Baldwin and Ed Cooper, 1961. FFA: unknown.
35 Mercy Me II 5.8 First ascent unknown. A delightful dike leading up an otherwise blank face. Bolt protection.
36 Uncle Ben's V 5.8 A4 Hugh Burton and Steve Sutton, 1970. Considerable skyhooking on the lower section. Pitons: 1 rurp, 5 KB, 10 LA, 6 Leeper, 6 ea. ½" and ⅝", 5 ea. ¾" to 1¼", 4 ea. 1½", 1 ea. 2" to 3½", copperheads and hooks.
37 Grand Wall V 5.11− A0 or 5.10 A2 Jim Baldwin and Ed Cooper, 1961. FFA: Peter Croft and Richard Suddaby, 1979. Include large nuts. This was the first major route at Squamish and is now one of the area's best free climbs.
38 Split Pillar, Left Side I 5.12− Tim Auger and Richard Culbert, 1972. FFA: P. Peart and Nic Taylor, 1975.
39 Phew!/Cruel Shoes III 5.10+ P. Beckham and Steve Flazelle, 1981.
40 Exasperator II 5.10c R, Crow and D. Tate, 1965. FFA: Dave Nicol and Eric Weinstein, 1975. Thin crack.

Rappelling back down Mercy Me photo: Doug Leen

Stoney Point

WEST COAST BOULDERING

Bouldering has been developed to an extremely high level in many areas of the West Coast. While all of the main climbing areas usually have good bouldering nearby, some of the best areas for unroped climbing are rather isolated from the big cliffs. Beyond simply after-work training, or as a weekend alternative to larger routes, some bouldering areas have achieved such renown that they attract climbers from long distances. The nature of the bouldering varies as much as the motives for climbing there. In most of these areas there are established routes with names and difficulty ratings, but rarely have these been collected into a guidebook form. Nevertheless, in a quick inspection of the area, one should be able to find the established problems by locating chalk marks. If anyone is around who knows the place, it should be no problem to discover some of the local classics.

MOUNT WOODSON

Mount Woodson is an exceptional area because of the large number of crack problems abounding on its smooth, unpolished granite boulders. Routes range up to forty feet in height and are often top-roped. A few easier problems exist, but most routes are 5.10 and above. Located in the hills behind San Diego, the weather is generally mild in the winter and

336 WEST COAST BOULDERING

hot in the summer. For route information, examine the guidebook on display at the Adventure 16 store in San Diego.

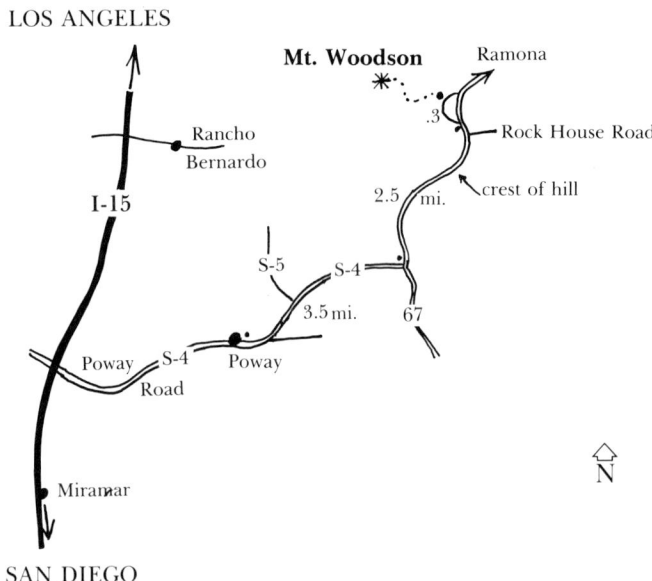

Mt. Woodson

Dick Shockley at Mt. Woodson

THE BEACH

A popular area on the beach at Pirate's Cove in Newport Beach, these sandstone cliffs offer many face climbing routes on vertical and overhanging rock. The bluffs range up to forty-five feet in height, and even some of the longer problems can be safely climbed without a top rope because of the soft, sandy landing. Unfortunately, litter and other signs of retrograde human activity mar the area. For route information, read *The Hunk Guide to Orange County,* by Randy Vogel, available in local stores.

STONEY POINT

Stoney Point's sandstone boulders played an important role in the development of California climbing. During the 1950's many of the emerging leaders in Tahquitz and Yosemite climbing trained at Stoney Point. The area is convenient (by car) to the University of California and the heart of Los Angeles, but is marred by graffiti and litter. For route information, read the *Stoney Point Guide,* by Hellweg and Fisher, available in local climbing shops.

Adele Hammond and Lupine at Stoney Point

WEST COAST BOULDERING

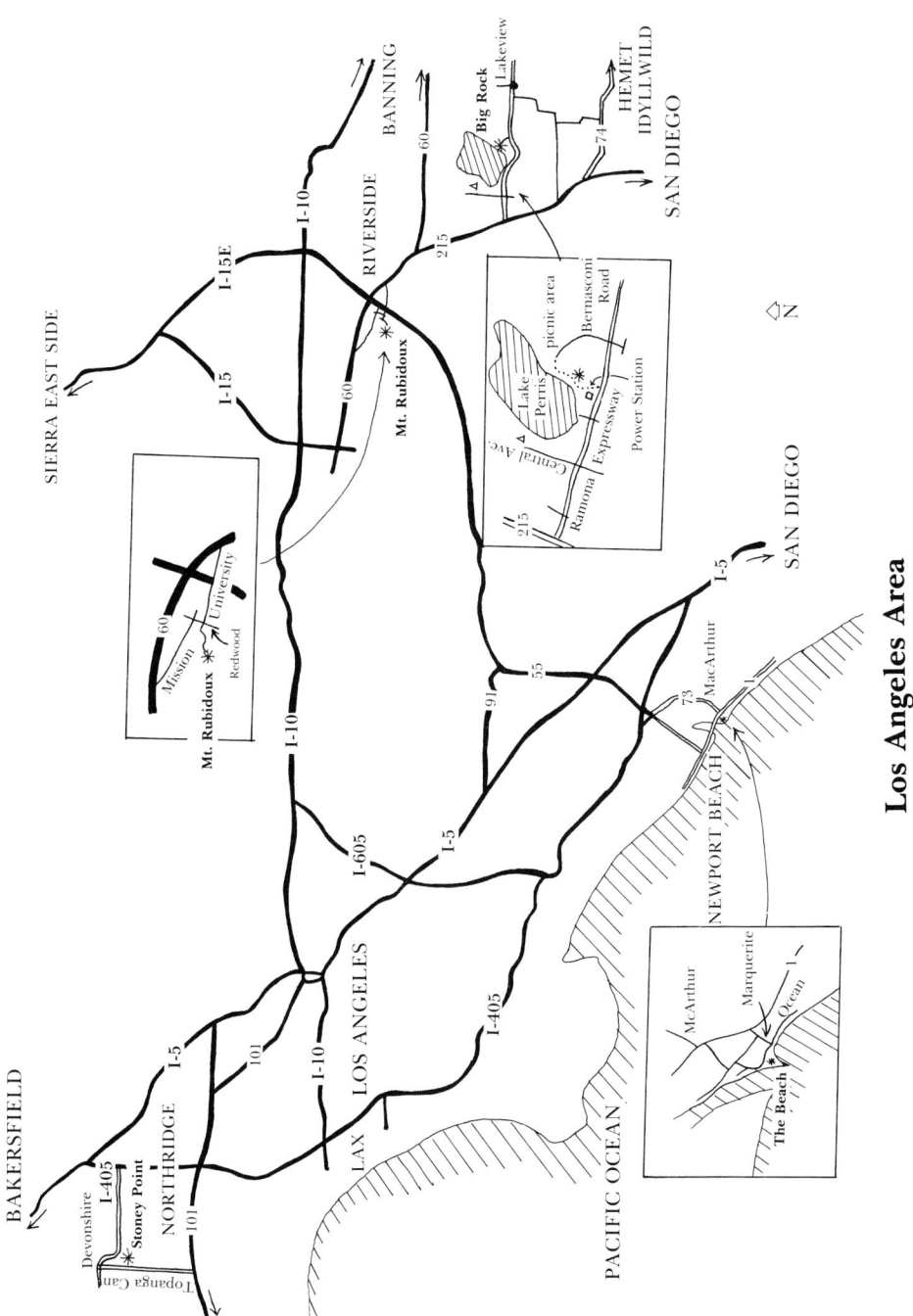

Los Angeles Area

WEST COAST BOULDERING

Mt. Rubidoux

Robs John Muir at Mt. Rubidoux

WEST COAST BOULDERING

MOUNT RUBIDOUX

Located atop a hill in Riverside, Mount Rubidoux commands an expansive view of the Los Angeles Basin. The sun setting into the western smog can be surprisingly beautiful. The granite outcroppings at Rubidoux offer many exceptionally good face and crack problems on boulders averaging twenty feet in height. In contrast to The Beach and Stoney Point, Rubidoux is clean and a pleasant place to hang out for the day.

BIG ROCK

Not strictly a bouldering area, Big Rock is a 200 foot low-angle granite dome that rises out of the coastline of a large reservoir in Lake Perris State Park. A warm place to escape winter or spring storms at Joshua Tree and Tahquitz, Big Rock offers camping and boulders in addition to the roped climbing on the dome itself. A small booth near the cliff's base displays route lines and difficulties.

Big Rock

WEST COAST BOULDERING

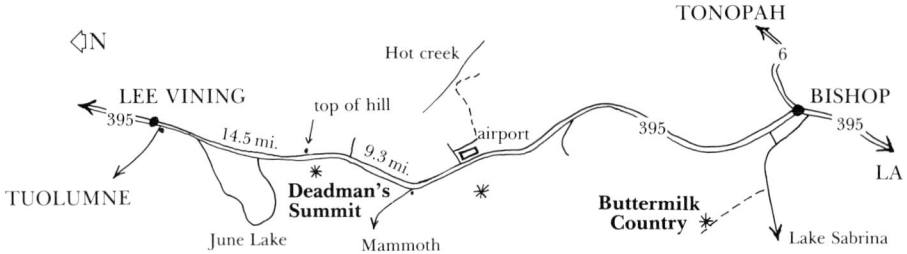

Deadman's Summit/Buttermilk Country

Buttermilk Country photo: Tim Forsell

DEADMAN'S SUMMIT

Located between Tuolumne and Mammoth Hot Creek—a popular spot in itself— this unheralded volcanic bouldering area offers fine face and crack problems on superb rock. Shaded by pine trees and set back from the road, Deadman's Summit has excellent bouldering on problems to thirty feet in height. The area holds snow in the winter.

photo: Adele Hammond

BUTTERMILK COUNTRY

The Buttermilk boulders offer some of the finest granite bouldering in America. Famed for their "jugs," many of the problems involve reaching between widely spaced, but incredibly good holds on vertical or overhanging rock. Because the boulders can range to fifty feet in height, top-roping may seem necessary—but often there is no easy way to set up a rope, nor anchors on the boulder's summit. Indeed, the local tradition is to climb boldly—both up and back down again. The views of the Eastern Sierra are truly outstanding and easily worth the drive along Highway 395. The band of cliffs seen near the Buttermilks are known as Little Egypt and are popular among the Bishop area climbers. See the Wheeler and Wilson Boot store in Bishop for route information.

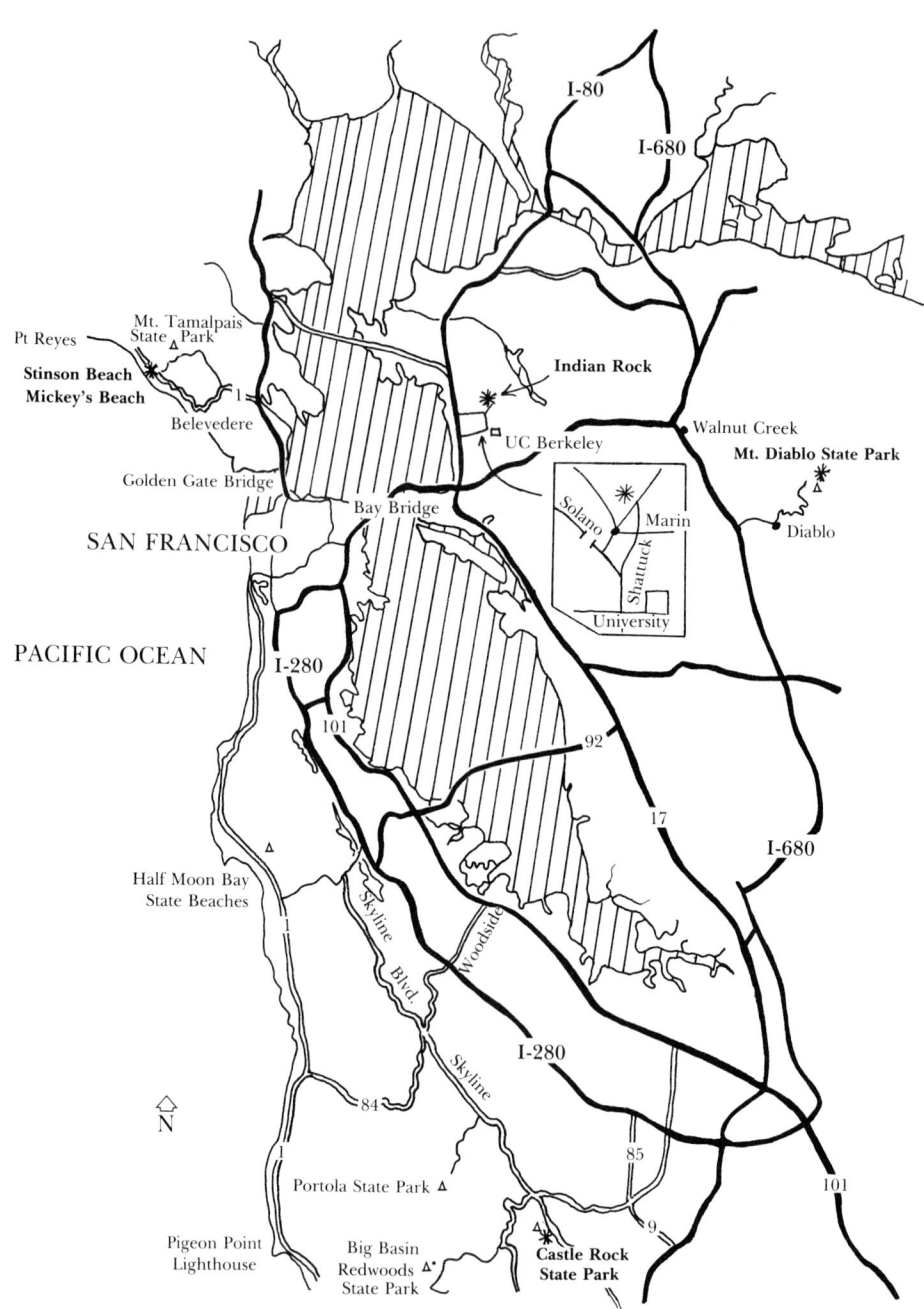

San Francisco Bay Area

CASTLE ROCK STATE PARK

High on a hillside, Castle Rock State Park features sandstone cliffs with many top-rope and bouldering problems of fifty or more feet in height. For route information, read *Bouldering, Buildering and Climbing in the South Bay,* by Marc Jensen, available in some local stores.

Indian Rock   photo: Adele Hammond

INDIAN ROCK

Near the Berkeley campus of the University of California, this volcanic plug, set in the heart of a residential area, helped launch California climbing. The Sierra Club Rock Climbing Chapter began meeting here in the 1930's to train and develop the rope techniques that enabled them to succeed in Yosemite. After school and on weekends, Indian Rock continues to receive considerable traffic. Some of the many face climbing routes here are extreme in nature and lend themselves well to local "sandbagging" of visiting climbers.

MOUNT DIABLO STATE PARK

Near the summit of a high hill, Mount Diablo State Park offers a wealth of top-rope sandstone climbs on cliffs almost 100 feet high. These bluffs are one-quarter mile downhill of the Rock City parking area and on the east side of the road. It costs two dollars to get into the Park, but on a clear day, the view from the summit is worth the price and the drive.

Stinson Beach

STINSON AND MICKEY'S BEACHES

Stinson is as wide open and sandy as everyone imagines California's beaches to be. Consequently, it is very popular with San Franciscans on sunny weekends. On the southern end of this beach are a number of fine conglomerate boulders ranging up to thirty feet in height and offering superb face climbing and soft sandy landings. A bit further south (within walking distance, or park high above on the road) is Mickey's Beach. Sporting a 5.12b thin crack on a sixty foot overhanging boulder, this area is popular for top-roping. Perhaps its popularity also stems from the fact that it is a nude beach.

SKINNER BUTTE COLUMNS

Located in downtown Eugene, Oregon, the Columns have a tremendous concentration of difficult top-rope finger crack and face climbs. For route information, read the reference guide on display at the River House, 301 North Adams Street and at the Outdoor Program, Eugene Parks and Recreation Department.

Skinner Butte Columns photo: Bob McGown

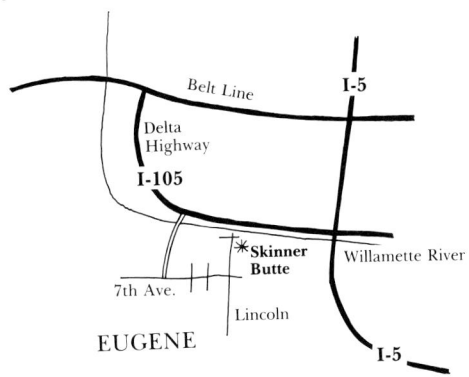

Skinner Butte Columns

UNIVERSITY OF WASHINGTON CLIMBING ROCK

Near the University of Washington Stadium, in Seattle, this climbable sculpture is almost unique in America. Designed to offer cracks, face and friction, the cement and stone monument is an excellent training center. But the designers did not learn enough from the equally rain-plagued British; located outdoors, the bouldering center is fully open to the weather. University of Washington rules state that you must be accompanied by a student or staff member to climb here.

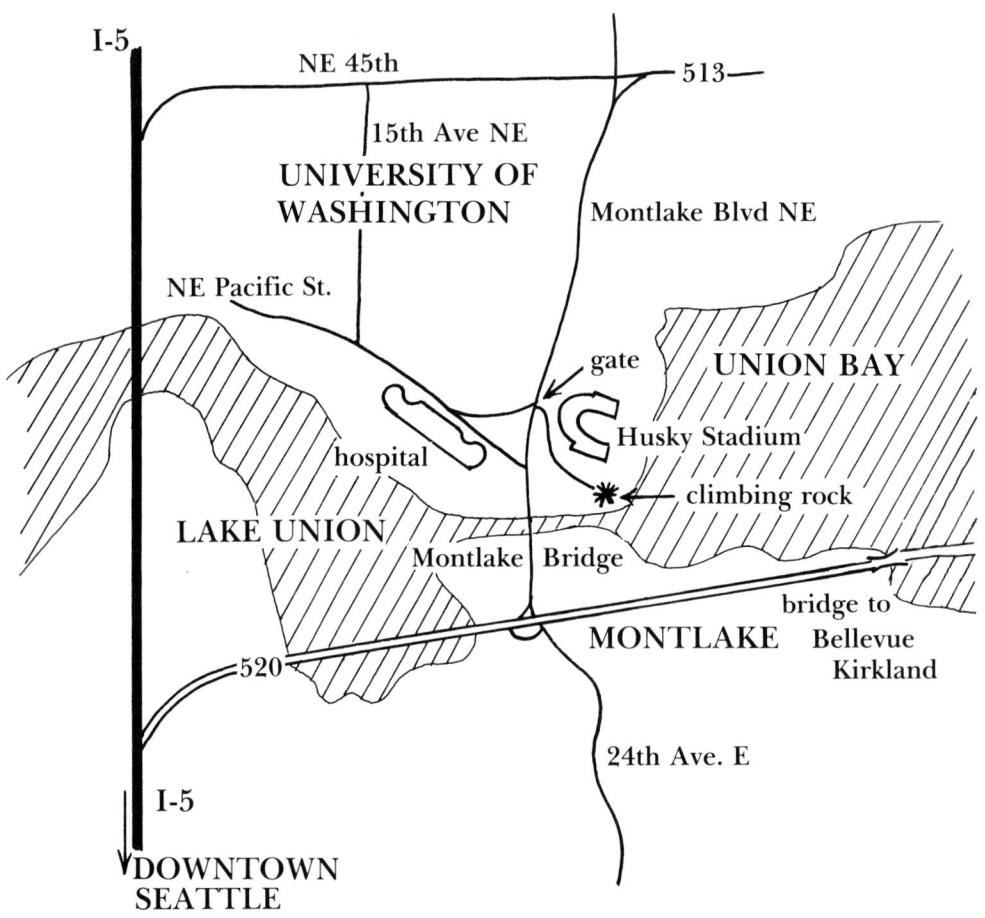

Seattle - University Climbing Rock

University Climbing Rock photo: Adele Hammond

INDEX
(route information)

After Six, 160
Agrarian, 128
Airy Interlude, 105
Anti-Jello Crack, 113
April Fools/ Dead Tree, 217
Apron Strings, 332
Apron, The, 328, 329
Arch Bitch-Up, The, 113
Archies, 308
Aries, 308
Astro Man, 167
Astro Monkey, 240
Atlantis, 104
Awl, The—Inside Corner, 245
Back of Hand, 132
Bad News, 203
Balconies Regular Route, 125
Balconies, The, 125
Ballet, 82
Banana Peel, 329
Barber Pole, 295
Beacon Rock, Southeast Face, 258
Beacons from Mars, 204
Bear's Reach, 214
Bearded Cabbage, 81
Bebop Tango, 75
Beckey Route, 297
Between Nothingness & Eternity, 113
Big Boys Don't Cry, 193
Billabong, 80
Bircheff-Williams Route, 158
Black Magic, 103
Black September, 230
Black Tide, 85
Black Tracks, 45
Black Wall, The, 229, 230
Blanketty-Blank, 63
Bliss, 229
Blob, The, 83
Bloodlust Direct, 329

Blownout, 258
Bluebird, 258
Bluebird Variation 3, 258
Bomb Shelter, 281
Bone, The, 270
Bookmark, 214
Bottomless-Topless, 231
Brass Balls, 270
Broomstick Crack, 329
Butterballs, 147
Butterfingers, 147
Caboose, 326
Calaveras Dome, 204
Calf, The, 164
Canary, 273
Cannibal Gully, 229
Castle Rock, 270-273
Cat Crack, 325
Catchy, 147
Catchy Corner, 147
Cathedral Peak, Southeast Buttress, 194
Central Pillar of Frenzy, 158
Chalk Up Another One, 82
Charlatan Needle, 104
Chimney De Chelly, 242
Chimney Rock, 82
Chouinard-Herbert Route, 162
Christian Brothers, 246
Ciebola, 187
Cinnamon Slab, 247
City Park, 309
Clean Crack, 326
Clean and Jerk, 78
Cleft, The, 147
Cochise, 45
Coffee Break, 325
Consolation, The, 60
Cookie Cliff, The, 147
Cookie Center, The, 147
Cookie Right, The, 147

INDEX

Corn Cob, 203
Corn Flakes, 325
Corner Crack, 325
Corrugation Corner, 217
Crack of Doom, 273
Crack of Infernity, 45
Crack-A-Go-Go, 147
Crime of the Century, 325
Crimson Chrysalis, 44
Cro Magnum, 281
Crucifix, 156
Cry in Time Again, 193
Daff Dome, 189
Damn Jam, 82
Damnation, 272
Damper, 82
Dancer, 246
Dandelion, 80
Davis-Holland (to Lovin' Arms), 313
Delila, 58
Desert Song, 77
Destiny, 122
Deviate, 81
Devil's Delight, 273
Devil's Fright, 273
Dick Enberg, 78
Diedre, 329
Dihedrals, The, 247
Dike Route, 184
Direct North Buttress, 158
Discovery Wall, 127
Dod's Jam, 256
Dogleg, 80
Dome Rock, 113
Don Juan Wall, 104
Double Cross, 80
Double Dip, 85
Down Syndrome, 242
Dr. Leakey, 281
Drain Pipe, 56
Dream On, 329
Dream of Wild Turkeys, 38
EBGB's, 86
Eagle Buttress Right Side, 216
Eagle Dance, 40
East Crack, 214
East Wall Route, 214
Echo Cove Formation, 84
Echo Rock, 85, 86

Edge, The, 325
Effigy Too, 84
El Capitan, 149-154
Empty Overgo, 229
Enigma, The, 147
Epinephrine, 38
Exasperator, 332
Explosive Energy Child, 244
Eyeore's Ecstacy, 216
Eyeore's Enigma, 216
Fascination, 229
Fairest of All, 190
Fairview Dome, 190
Fairview Dome, Regular Route, 190
Fantasia, 214
Fate in Place, 109
Fault-Catapult, 270
Fear No Evil, 214
Fear of Flying, 325
Fiend, The, 55
Figures on a Landscape, 93
Fingerlicker, 230
Fingertrip, 63
Firecracker, 229
First Sister, 131
Fisticuffs, 76
Flake Route, 332
Flake, The, 80
Flakes, The, 62
Flower of High Rank, 59
Fly-By, 127
Flying Circus, 325
Folly, Right Side, 160
Folly, The, 160
Foott Route, 184
Fort Knox, 184
Free For Some, 256
Free at Last, 309
Free Blast, 149
Free for All, 256
Frogland, 37
From Bad Traverse, 62
Full Moon, 229
Gemini Cracks, 203
Geritol, 325
Get Slick, 182
Glacier Point Apron, 164
Godzilla, 309
Golden Arch, The, 313

INDEX

Golden Bars, 184
Golgotha, 246
Good to the Last Drop, 82
Goodrich Pinnacle, Right, 164
Grack, Marginal, 164
Grack, Center, 164
Graduate, The, 45
Graham Crackers, 59
Grand Central Tower, West Face, 281
Grand Wall, 332
Grand Wall, The, 332
Gray Matter, 45
Great Northern Route, The, 308
Great White Book, 182
Gripping Gravity, 45
Gross Incompetence, 325
Guillotine, The, 59
Half Dome, 168-170
Half Dome, Direct, 168
Half Dome, Northwest Face, 168
Halfway to Paradise, 84
Hammer Dome, 203
Hand, The, 132
Hangdog, 273
Hans Groper, 325
Hard Case, 45
Hardd, 147
Harlequin Dome, 183
Hatchet, 131
Haystack, 214
Heart and Sole, 85
Heavenly Traverse, 273
Hesitation Blues, 246
Hex Marks the Root, 91
Higher Cathedral Rock, 156
Higher Cathedral Rock, Northeast Buttress, 156
Hobbit Book, 188
Hoodwink, 183
Hoppy's Favorite, 164
Horrorscope, 104
Hospital Corner, 217
Howling, The, 106
Human Fright, 63
Hyperspace, 277
Iconoclast, 277
Igor Unchained, 105
Illegitimate, The, 60

Illusion Dweller, 77
Imaginary Voyage, 229
In Harm's Way, 244
In The Pit, 75
Indirect Traverse, 129
Innersanctum, 105
Innnominate, The, 64
Inside Out, 230
Insomnia, 56
Intersection Rock, 80
Iron Cross, The, 56
Itsy Bitsy Variation, 203
Ixtlan, 37
J.J. Overhang, 270
Jam Crack, The, 62
Jensen's Jaunt, 63
Judas, 81
Karate Crack (to the Peapod), 247
Karot Tots, 247
Latin Swing, 75
Leave it to Beaver, 78
Left Gull, 258
Left Ski Track, 64
Left Ski Track Direct (J.T.), 80
Left Water Crack, 192
Lembert Dome, 192, 193
Lembert, Direct Northwest Face, 193
Levitation 29, 40
Lexington Tower, East Face, 292
Liberty Bell, 294-297
Liberty Crack, 294
Lieback Flake, 325
Lightning Bolt Roof, 230
Lightning Crack, 281
Line, The, 214
Lion's Chair, 248
Little Smoke Bluffs, 325
Long Climb, The, 60
Loose Lips, 82
Lucky Streaks, 190
Lunar Leap, 192
M.F. Overhang, 273
Machete Direct, 122
Machete Ridge, 122
Magician Needle, 103
Mainline, 217
Malamute, The, 326
Manic Depression, 231

INDEX

Manure Pile Buttress, 160
Mariuolumne Dome, 188
Mary Jane Dihedral, 276
Mary's Tears, 156
Meat Grinder, 147
Medlicott Dome, 187
Mercy Me, 332
Mesa Verde Wall, 242
Mescalito, 152
Mickey Mantle, 55
Middle Cathedral Rock, 158
Middle Cathedral Rock, East Buttress, 158
Midway, 273
Midway Direct, 273
Minas Morgul, 242
Misty Beethoven, 164
Misunderstanding, 37
Monkey Face, 240
Monkey Face, Southwest Corner, 240
Monkey Face, West Face Variant, 240
Monkey Paws, 231
Monkey Space, 240
Monolith, 129
Monolith Direct Route, 129
Monolith Regular Route, 129
Moonshine Dihedral, 247
More Monkey Than Funky, 90
More Raisins, 113
Morning Glory Wall, 248
Moscow, 249
Mr. Clean, 230
My Laundry, 92
Narrow Arrow Overhang, 309
Neat and Cool, 325
Necromancer Needle, 109
Needle and Spoon, 184
New Moon, 229
New Testament, 246
No Holds Barred, 127
No More Mr. Nice Guy, 109
No Smiles, 125
North Astro Dome, 93
North Early Winter Spire, Northwest Corner, 298
North Early Winter Spire, West Face, 298

North Overhang, 80
Nose Route, 152
Nutcracker, 160
O'Kelley's Crack, 88
Old Smokey, 204
Old Woman Rock, 80, 81
On Ramp, 229
One Hand Clapping, 229
One Toke Over the Line, 187
Open Book, 64
Orbit, 276
Ordeal, 127
Orphan, 80
Outer Limits, 147
Outer Space, 277
Overhang Bypass, 80
Pachyderm, The, 44
Paisano Overhang, 56
Panic in Detroit, 231
Papa Woolsey, 83
Pebbles, 281
Peking, 249
Penny Lane, 325
Peshastin Pinnacles, 279-281
Peter Principle, 231
Phew!/Cruel Shoes, 332
Piece de Resistance, 190
Piggle Pug, 92
Pinched Rib, 82
Pink Flamingo, 325
Pioneer Route, 240
Pisces, 308
Piton Pooper, 62
Piton Traverse, 129
Pope's Crack, 86
Portent, 127
Post Orgasmic Depression, 129
Potholes, 281
Primate, 281
Pywiack, 184
Question of Balance, 329
Ragged Edges, 45
Rainbow Buttress, 40
Rainbow Connection, 272
Rainy Day Dream Away, 76
Rated X, 230
Rawl Drive, 192
Rebolting Development, 58
Red Eye Express, 203

INDEX

Red Wall, 249
Regular Mouth, 164
Revelation, 58
Revelations, 246
Ride a Wild Bago, 78
Right Gull, 258
Right Ski Track, 64
Right Ski Track Direct (J.T.), 80
Right Water Crack, 192
Rixon's East Chimney, 160
Rixon's Pinnacle, 160
Rixon's West Face, 160
Rock Warrior, 38
Run For Your Life, 76
Rusty Wall, 88
Sabre, 273
Sahara Terror, 60
Saints, 272
Saints-Rainshadow, 272
Salathé, 132
Salathé Wall, 149
Sally Five Fingers, 325
Scimitar, 214
Scorpion, 187
Sea of Holes, 203
Second Wind, 258
Semi Tough, 75
Sentinel Rock, 162
Sentinel, The, 77
Serpentine, 58
Set the Controls for the Heart of the Sun, 203
Shake and Bake, 125
Sisters, The, 131
Skull, The, 110
Skywalker, 229
Slow Children, 309
Smiling Simian, 125
Smoke Bluff Connection, The, 325
Smoke Screen, 203
Snail, The, 132
Snake, 328
Snake Dike, 170
Snow Creek Wall, 276, 277
Snowshed Wall, 231
Sole Sacrifice, 204
Solid Gold, 92
Solo Formation, 75
Solosby, 75
Solosby Face, 75
Sorcerer Needle, 104
South Astro Dome, 91, 92
South Crack, 182
South Early Winter Spire, East Buttress Direct, 291
Sparrow, 329
Spectrum, The, 113
Spell, The, 109
Sphincter Quits, 78
Spider, 81
Spider Line, 81
Spiderman, 244
Spiderman Buttress, 244
Split Pillar, Left Side, 332
Spook Book, 105
Spooky, 104
Sports Challenge Rock, 78
Stage Fright, 203
Stately Pleasure Dome, 182
Steck-Salathé Route, 162
Steppenwolf, 256
Stick to What, 85
Sting, The, 183
Such a Savage, 92
Suicide Rock, 54-59
Sundance, 56
Sunset Slab, 279
Sunshine Dihedral, 247
Super Pooper, 62
Super Slab, 249
Superfluous Bolt, The, 59
Surprise, 58
Surrealistic Pillar, 83
Swallow Crack, 127
Swallow, The, 60
Sweet Jesus, 187
Sweet Nothings, 182
Swept Away, 86
T.S. Special, 86
Table of Contents, 182
Tahquitz Rock, 60-64
Tale of Two ..., 242
Taurus, 308
Temptation, 246
Ten Karat Gold, 58
Territorial Imperative, 45
The 'S' Crack, 109
Theme Book, 45

INDEX

Thin Fingers, 309
Thin Ice, 104
Thin Red Line, 295
Thunderbolt, 204
Tobin's Dihedral, 113
Toe Jam, 81
Too Bad, 203
Top Rope, 78
Touch and Go, 229
Touch and Go, (J.T.), 84
Town Crier, The, 313
Traitor Horn, 63
Traveler Buttress, 216
Tree Route, The, 113
Trezlar, 242
Triassic Sands, 37
Truck n' Drive, 192
Try Again, 85
Tsunami, 204
Tumbling Rainbow Formation, 76
Twinkle Toes Traverse, 122
Ultimatum, The, 55
Uncle Ben's, 332
Unfinished Symphony, 328
University Wall, 332
Unmentionable, The, 133
Upper Bandits Bench, 122
Upper Right Ski Track, 80
Valhalla, 56
Vampire, The, 62
Vendetta, 147
Vertigo, 281
Voodoo Dome, 110
Walk to School, 45
Wall, The, 82
Wangerbanger, 88
War of the Walls, 204
Warlock Needle, 106, 109
Warlock Needle, South Face, 109
Washboards, 281
Washington Column, 166, 167
Washington Column, South Face, 166
Wasted Days and Wasted Nights, 325
Waverly Wafer, 147
Werner's Wiggle, 192
West Crack, 189
West Face Overhang, 82
West Face, El Capitan, 149
West Face, Sentinel Rock, 162
Wheat Thin, 147
Where Ancients Fear to Tread, 325
White Lightning, 329
White Punks on Dope, 110
White Satin, 245
Wild Thing, 160
Willie's Hand Jive, 192
Windjammer, 113
Wings and Stings, 203
Witch Needle, 105
Witch Needle, North Face, 105
Yawn, The, 187
Zebra, 248
Zodiac, 154

THE AUTHOR:
Although born in California, John Harlin's early years were spent in the Alps—where his father climbed and his mother taught science. After his father's death on the Eiger in 1966, the family returned to America. During his teenage years, John spent as much time as possible in the wilderness, including several month long hiking and kayaking trips to the North Slope of Alaska. But climbing did not become a serious passion for him until his enrollment at the University of California, Santa Barbara, for a degree in Environmental Biology. Since then, he has climbed in numerous rock and mountain centers throughout North America and Europe. Besides writing, John shares his love of the mountain environment through guiding and lecturing.

THE ILLUSTRATOR:
A native of Colorado, Adele Hammond received her art training at the College of Creative Studies, University of California. She is a professional fine artist who makes colorful, interpretive paintings and pastels. Her art has little in common with the illustrations in this book, except that it shows a similar love of nature.

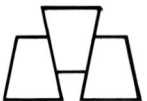

OTHER BOOKS FROM CHOCKSTONE PRESS

Yosemite Climbs George Meyers   16.95
Rock Climbs of Tuolumne Meadows Don Reid & Chris Falkenstein   13.95
Climber's Guide to North America John Harlin III
   Vol. 1 West Coast Rock Climbs   22.00
Breaking Point Glenn Randall   available Jan. 1985
Cross Country Ski Trails of Yosemite Tim Messick   available Jan. 1985
Climber's Guide to North America John Harlin III
   Vol. 2 Rocky Mountain Rock Climbs   available Spring 1985
Climber's Guide to North America John Harlin III
   Vol. 3 East Coast Rock Climbs   available Fall 1985

available from your local dealer, or postpaid with check or money order from:

Chockstone Press
526 Franklin Street
Denver, CO 80218